C000003930

KISS AND TELL

EVANGELISM AS A LIFESTYLE

KISS AND TELL

EVANGELISM AS A LIFESTYLE

PETE GILBERT

Copyright © Pete Gilbert 2003

Published by CWR, Waverley Abbey House, Waverley Lane, Farnham,
Surrey GU9 8EP

The right of Pete Gilbert to be identified as the author of this work has
been asserted by him in accordance with the Copyright, Designs and
Patents Act 1988.

All rights reserved. No part of this publication may be reproduced, stored
in a retrieval system, or transmitted, in any form or by any means,
electronic, mechanical, photocopying, recording or otherwise, without the
prior permission in writing of CWR.

See back of book for list of National Distributors.

Unless otherwise indicated, all Scripture references are from the Holy Bible:
New International Version (NIV), copyright © 1973, 1978, 1984 by the
International Bible Society. Used with permission.

Concept development, editing, design and production by CWR

Printed in Finland by WS Bookwell

ISBN 1-85345-285-8

CONTENTS

	Introduction	7
1	What is Church?	9
2	What is Evangelism?	25
3	Who Evangelises?	67
4	What is the Gospel?	95
5	Why Bother?	125
6	The Jesus Way	161
7	So How?	177
8	And There's More ...	209
9	Personal Witnessing, Jesus Style	229
10	Whose Turf?	251
11	Strategic Evangelism	271
	Resources	303

Dedication

This book is dedicated to the *first* church that Jesus will ever ask me about, namely my wife Nikki, children Freddi and Josh and my close friends, among whom I am privileged to number Richard and Linda Ward, Mark and Jane Hummerstone, Gavin and Julia Sell and Tim and Bec Raynes

INTRODUCTION

WHAT A FUNNY TITLE!

I don't know if the title of this book grabbed your attention. I really hope it did! But it may have needed the title and the by-line together to let you know what the book is about. This book is enthusiastically and unashamedly about evangelism. It is about mission. Witnessing. Call it what you will. But why is it called 'Kiss & Tell'?

The answer is simple. It is because evangelism is about passion. Passion for Jesus. Passion for the lost. In fact you can't have one without the other. And it is because evangelism is *not* methods and techniques. You've read enough books like that. You've been to enough seminars like that. Has it *really* made a difference? I suspect not. There is nothing wrong with tried and tested hot tips. Practical action points. Indeed, this book is full of them! But if that is all that a book on evangelism is about, then we have really lost the plot.

For intimacy with Christ precedes revelation from Him. The best witnesses to Jesus are those closest to Him. Nothing has changed since the observation in Acts 4:13 that the most effective witnesses were 'unschooled, ordinary men', but that 'these men had been with Jesus'.

So this book is a tangible expression of our intimacy with Jesus. It is an invitation to kiss Him, and then tell others all you know and have experienced of His wondrous love for you. After all, the Greek New Testament word *proskino*, translated 'worship', means 'to move towards, to embrace and to kiss'. In writing this book, it's my hope and prayer that you'll be encouraged, inspired, motivated and equipped to move closer to Jesus, in order to move others closer to Him.

The book covers a series of material, which I often deliver into the lives of local churches in monthly training sessions in order to 'prepare God's people for works of service' (Ephesians 4:12). The book is *not* meant to replace this approach in the life of your church, as your church will need to encounter real, live evangelists! Evangelism is as much about what is 'caught' as what is 'taught'. The book and its material is rather designed to complement such a teaching series. You can use it individually. But I would also urge you to use it corporately, in the context of small groups. At the end of each chapter you will find groupwork specifically designed to help you apply what you have been learning together.

The bottom line is this: if you *don't* want to witness to your faith in Christ, put the book down *now*! But if you do, then read on; I wrote this book for YOU ...

Chapter 1

WHAT IS CHURCH?

Isn't it funny how strongly we react to certain words? And how words and their impact change over the years? When I was a lad growing up in Lancashire we had dinner at midday and tea in the evening. Of course, now I am based on the south coast these are what I would call lunch and dinner! And as a carefree youngster to be gay meant you were happy. Some words can provoke a very negative response in us where once they didn't; how do you respond to the word 'mistress'? Some words we just use wrongly; because of a simple uncorrected mistake in early childhood my children have for years referred to their duvets as 'sofas'! And until the age of around seven it was not uncommon whenever they saw a large Victorian church building for them to refer to it as a 'castle'. Actually this was not a notion I was keen to disabuse them of as I have never been happy referring to buildings as 'churches'.

WHAT'S IN A NAME?

This brings me neatly to the subject of our first chapter. When we call the building on the corner of our road a church does it *really* matter? Is this chapter really just about 'political correctness'? Do we *need* the first chapter in a book on evangelism to pose the question, 'What is church?' Surely it's better just to get on with the job of sharing our faith and reaching the lost? I don't think so.

In the 2,000 or so years since Jesus established the church, we have lost track of some foundational questions. *Why* did Jesus found the church? *Where* did Jesus found the church? *How* did Jesus found the church? When it comes to evangelism, if we can only determine what the right questions are it is more likely that we will come out with the right answers, or at least reach towards them together.

As a starting place (and it seemed to me that Chapter 1 was a good place to start!) I'm going to make a statement for you to consider: Church is God's primary agent on earth of His kingdom. And in that statement we hit an immediate double problem. What do we mean by 'church' and what do we mean by 'kingdom'? The two words are often used as buzz words and interchangeably. But they're more important than mere sound bites and they aren't the same.

The kingdom of God is all about territory, but it is *not* geographical. We will come back to this in Chapter 10 when we look at spiritual warfare and evangelism. It isn't easy to define the kingdom of God. Even Jesus seems to have struggled as He reached for analogies to explain it to His disciples (Luke 13:18–20). With the coming of Christ to this fallen world, the kingdom of God was unleashed in the midst of humanity. However, although the kingdom of God *has* come, it is still coming. It has arrived, but it is still arriving. It is here, but not in fullness. At one and the same time it is both near (Matt. 3:2; 4:17) and come (Matt. 12:28). It is to be entered into (Matt. 19:23) and yet it is within you (Luke

17:21). Perhaps in the simplest of terms, wherever Jesus Christ is 'kinging it' in the hearts and lives, actions and reactions, voices and relationships of people, there you have the kingdom of God.

But then, of course, if we take this as a working definition of the kingdom, it becomes apparent that the kingdom of God is significantly wider than the church. This kingdom of God can infiltrate and include all elements of creation, culture, community and society. It can be found, demonstrated and expressed in the media, in politics, in education or in the health service. So the kingdom of God is wider than the church of God, yet the church remains the primary agent for the bringing in of the kingdom.

Perhaps you can begin to see the reason why I wanted to start here? It is because *biblical* evangelism is *kingdom* evangelism. Kingdom-based evangelism keeps us looking outward and seeking to express, explain and demonstrate the reign and rule of Jesus Christ in *every* sphere of creation, whereas church-based evangelism tends to focus on methods of 'outreach' in order to bring people 'in'. But the biblical mandate is for you and me to seek the *kingdom* (Matt. 6:33), while Jesus maintains that the job of expanding/strengthening the church is *His* (Matt. 16:18). We seek the kingdom, Jesus builds the church.

And so the link is complete; church is the primary agent of the kingdom of God, evangelism is to have a kingdom focus rather than a church focus; church is the primary agent of both evangelism and discipleship. In the New Testament there is no distinction made between evangelism and discipleship. Conversion in the New Testament, although it can happen at precise and dramatic moments, is epitomised as a process more than a crisis. We will come back to this in the next chapter. Enough now to note that the verb for salvation in the New Testament is often used in a present continuous tense: 'I *have* been saved, I *am* being saved, I *will* be saved'. The New Testament Christians (a name given to them by their *enemies* at Antioch, as noted in Acts 11:26) knew more about journeying than about arrival. More about process than about crisis. More about becoming than about being. Their own (preferred) name for themselves was 'follower of the Way', after Jesus' statement about Himself found in John 14:6. This is why the mandate for evangelism is actually a mandate to make disciples (Matt. 28:16–20) because evangelism, like discipleship, is a process.

So where have we got to? First statement: the church is the primary agent of the kingdom of God, but the kingdom of God is wider than the church. Second statement: the church is the primary agent of (and indeed the *result* of) evangelism/ discipleship. In evangelism as in discipleship our job is to seek the kingdom, and Jesus' job is to build the church. But all of this still begs the question: What do we mean by church?

THE IRREDUCIBLE MINIMUM

If you are really trying to get right to the heart of something, to understand its meaning and definition, it's a useful exercise to try to pare away everything that it *isn't* in order to reveal what it really *is*. Some of the world's greatest sculptors have maintained that their best work was as a result of chipping away at the stone simply to reveal the true form of what always lay within. At the end of this chapter I am going to suggest that you try this yourself with the concept of 'church'. There is a word in the New Testament, *kerygma*, which means 'the essence, heart, kernel' and is often applied to the gospel. But what happens in Scripture when you apply it to the church? What lies at the core of church?

THE HEART OF THE MATTER

When the word 'church' appears in Scripture, it is usually derived from the Greek word *ekklesia*. Obviously this word has given us the words 'ecclesiastic', 'ecclesiastical', 'ecclesiology' (the study and understanding of church), etc. The word 'church' now carries with it a whole host of nuances. For example, we think of elders, deacons, ministers, pastors, vicars, lay people, clergy, institutions, pews (or chairs!), organs (or soft rock!), buildings, etc. It's important then to strip it back. The word *ekklesia* itself comes from two Greek words – *ek* and *kaleo*, which together mean 'to call out from'. So originally the word *ekklesia* meant nothing more than a group of called-out people, where there was a sense of a common task or purpose. Certainly the word was not originally 'religious' in any way, shape or form. This can be demonstrated by the rather unexpected context in which you find the word being used in Acts 7. Here the group of people who gather together to accuse Stephen, the first Christian martyr, and who lay their coats at the feet of a certain Saul (later to become Paul) and stone Stephen to death, are referred to as an *ekklesia*! They were a group of called-out people with a particular purpose in mind! So the kind of church Jesus wants to build has three distinct elements.

1. It is animate, made up of people (please note, in the plural), not plant; beings, not buildings.
2. These people are 'called out' from who they were, what

they were doing, what they had become, to be 'set aside' by God Himself (1 Pet. 2:9–10).

3. They share a common destiny, destination, plan and purpose under the hand of God, which unites them in intent, attitude and action.

A LITTLE HISTORY

So the church is people, set aside by God, to effect the kingdom of God on the earth; their common purpose: to witness and disciple. But right from the birth of the church this simple definition with its inextricable emphasis on mission was under attack. Scripture encourages us to be mindful of the strategies and methods of the enemy (2 Cor. 2:11). I am in part indebted to Jim Thwaites' analysis (*Church beyond the Congregation*) for the following historical perspective on the enemy's attack on the church.

The seeds of this battle were sown in the fifth century BC. The context was the Spartan wars, which for more than 50 years so ravaged Greek culture and its capital Athens. Perhaps those most affected by the Spartan wars, those with the most to lose to the disorder and despair, the chaos and the conflict that war brings, were the noble, ruling classes. And so it was with the aristocratic, wealthy and influential Plato. So horrified was Plato by the ravages of war that he wrote a manifesto against anarchy and chaos, in which he made out a case for a ruling class of philosopher kings, who would establish and rule over Plato's greatest concept: the State. It was to and through the State that all things flowed. The State determined the greater good. The State demanded total allegiance. The State subsumed personal creativity and vision for the maintenance of the status quo and the corporate good. Ultimately the State became self-perpetuating; it existed in order that it might exist.

But for Plato this was not only a system of government. It was also a philosophy. Plato argued that the created order – that which could be seen, touched, heard, felt, tasted, in other words the material world – was actually utterly separate from and inferior to the spiritual dimension. For Plato, the spiritual dimension was the realm of the transcendent. This was where all truth, goodness, wisdom, spirituality, morality and so on were to be found. The material world was one of darkness and corruption, and was at best a poor reflection of reality, which could only be found in the spiritual dimension. Plato called this material world the realm of the imminent, or the land of shadows.

Imagine, if you will, two rooms next door to each other in a hotel. Completely separate and yet divided by a connecting door. One room is dingy, depressing and decrepit. It is one-star accommodation. The room next door, however, is full of light, life and loveliness and is definitely a five-star suite! This is how Plato viewed the realm of the imminent and the realm of the transcendent. And for Plato the dividing door was the State. The State alone could be the mediator between one realm and the other. The State became the arbiter of all decisions. The fount of all wisdom. The dispenser of all truth. The plumb line of all morality. The judge of all justice. And the access point to true spirituality. Everything went through the State. The State became the centre of everything.

With me so far? Stick with it. We now have the basic tenor of Plato's philosophy as outlined in *The Republic*. We also have an outline of what has come to be known as 'Platonic dualism', which views all matter as bad, and all spirituality as ethereal. These are the roots of the classic sacred/secular divide. In Greek thinking, the material is to be despised and is inferior and separate from the spiritual. Thus life divides neatly into compartments. Praying is spiritual. Eating a cheese sandwich is secular. Fasting is spiritual. Feasting is worldly. What a wonderful invitation for legalism and religion to sweep in; and so they did! The seeds of Platonic dualism and idealism sown in fifth-century Greece put out shoots into Western society and culture, which we are still living with. These tendrils infiltrated the Christian church at its earliest stages to produce Christians whose mind-set was more Hellenistic (Greek) than Hebraic.

Do you remember the date when I said all this was going on? The fifth century BC. It's not insignificant that this was the time period in which God was revealing Himself as Yahweh – the one true God – to the Hebrew nation. Could it be that Platonic dualism and its later effects upon the Christian church were a direct strategy from the enemy? I think so. The way that Yahweh revealed Himself to the Hebrew nation was completely different from this philosophical Greek concept. Hebraic thinking is far more holistic than this. There is no sacred/secular divide. To the Hebrew, God is both transcendent (removed from, greater than His creation) and yet also imminent (at work within and revealed through His creation). To the Hebrew there isn't spiritual and unspiritual. A cheese sandwich is as real and as spiritual as is fasting. For the Jew, *all* of life was about God. In fact he even had a prayer of thanks when he had his first bowel movement of the day!

But the seeds of this insidious Greek philosophy had been sown. By the first century AD the early church was already combating Greek ideas of Gnosticism, with its secret and higher truths revealed only to a select few. With its emphasis on the spiritual at the expense of the material. Its insistence that Christ would not have been materially and physically resurrected from the dead, but was only resurrected in ghost form. And its emphasis on ritual ceremony, high days and holy days. Whole books of the New Testament (Colossians is a good example) were written to try to combat this Greek heresy.

As Greek thinking massively influenced the Roman Empire, the effects upon the church became all the more pronounced when empire and church were joined in the fourth century. Plato's construct called the State became Christianised; the edifice of the State had a cross placed on its summit! As church and State became interwoven with the so-called conversion of Roman Emperor Constantine, so nominalism swept into the church. Where once it might cost you your family, your job, or even your life to proclaim Christ, now you stood a good chance of promotion by allegedly following Him – Christians in name only (nominalism)! Now the church became all that the State had been to Plato; it became the arbiter of right and wrong. The judge of justice (and injustice!), the wielder of power and of the sword, the accruer of wealth and of political influence, the dispenser of spirituality, the centre of all things.

Instead of existing for mission and to demonstrate that God is in all and through all, the church became a centre in its own right, existing in order that it might exist. Where nominalism reigns, mission becomes irrelevant. The church became at one and the same time the greatest patron (controller) of the arts and the greatest stifler (censor) of individual creativity and intellect. In the Dark Ages it dispensed indulgences. In the Renaissance it controlled creativity and suppressed invention. Even the Reformation did not challenge its constructs, instead placing only a (rightful) emphasis on an individual's access to

Scripture and to God. The much later Pentecostal movement restored spiritual gifts but didn't challenge the construct of the centrist approach to church and the dualistic approach to spirituality. The more recent Charismatic movement released team dynamic and a concept of the kingdom of God but didn't challenge the construct of the church. But regaining a sense of the Church's true mission has the potential to do just that!

THE LEGACY

So what have we been left with and what have we inherited? The sad reality is that many of us may have a theology and experience of God more derived from Greek Platonic thinking than it is from Hebraic biblical theology. Are you part of church because that is where you find your identity? That's Platonic. Is your time and energy consumed and subsumed by church meetings and activities in order to support the church, so that at all costs we might 'maintain the witness' and keep the church going? That's Platonic. Has our reliance on Scripture and the witness of the Holy Spirit been overtaken by church culture? That's Platonic. Does our time, energy, effort and money support the church and *its* vision? That's Platonic. If we dance before God in our worship, do we worry about whether we do it in the 'flesh' or in the 'spirit'? That's Platonic. Do we endure our workplace in order to earn money in order to free time in order to do the 'real' stuff at house group/cell midweek, and church meetings on a Sunday? That's Platonic. Do we serve our church leaders and their vision? That's Platonic. In our hearts do we believe that the really 'spiritual' people are the pastors/vicars/full-time workers in our churches? That's Platonic. Do we call the building on the street corner a 'church'? That's Platonic. Do we realise that actually church is about people and not buildings, but still talk about 'going' to church? That's Platonic.

Get the idea? A more Hebraic/holistic approach to church would recognise that church does not exist in order that it might exist. It exists with a purpose/mission. Church is not meant to be a 'centre' or a 'construct'. It isn't a building. You can't 'go' to church, because church is something that you do, something that you are. Church is not defined by rules, regulations or rituals, but by relationships. The ministries within church are not meant to serve church, but to serve the saints of God as they engage in the whole of creation. Church is meant to be the second body of Christ on earth and is meant to be growing corporately into maturity in all of the spheres of creation (Eph. 4:15), not just in individual personal holiness. There are no high days and holy days; every day is a holy day. There are no spiritual jobs and unspiritual jobs. We aren't called to serve our leaders' visions; we're called to serve one another, our leaders releasing and empowering us to the vision God has given to each of us.

The late Bishop Leslie Newbiggin made some incisive summaries of this legacy, maintaining that we are left with three main types of churches. The first is Sacramental church. The hallmarks of Sacramental church are that it places a great emphasis on its place in history, on its relationship to the state, on a separate priesthood/clergy, on the value of being institutional and with a weighting towards the offices of the sacraments. Even the physical layout of the church buildings, with the predominance of the altar, indicates these values (sacrifice, priesthood, sacrament). This is largely an Old Covenant model, and may be epitomised by denominations such as the Greek Orthodox and the Roman Catholic Church.

Second comes the Protestant church. Hallmarks of the Protestant church include an emphasis on the salvation of the individual (at the expense of corporate community /sin?), the unique mediation of Christ, the centrality of Scripture, the acquisition of Bible knowledge. Hence the physical layout of the church building places the pulpit (from which biblical truth is dispensed) as its central focus, six feet above contradiction!

Newbiggin's third category of church is Charismatic church, with its emphasis on experiencing God as well as knowing Him, on relationships, informality and cultural relevance, on the manifest power of God and on the essential presence (Shekinah) of God.

And so …?

If we don't understand what we mean by church and what church is for, if we can't agree that the church is the primary agent of the kingdom of God and the primary tool for evangelism and discipleship, then a book on evangelism at best is only going to give us a few individual and personalised 'hot tips'.

But, if you can agree with me that God hasn't changed the remit of the church or its nature, then we can really cover some ground. The Old Testament mandate was for the glory of God to cover the earth (Psa. 72:19) and the New Testament equivalent of this is that the glorious gospel of Jesus Christ should first be preached in all the nations before He returns (Matt. 24:14). The very *raison d'être* of church becomes clear. We have to decide whether we believe the Westminster Confession or Scripture! We are *not* here to worship God. We *are* here to make God known. If we were simply here in a fallen world in order to worship God then it's a capricious God indeed Who keeps everything going merely in order to accept our worship (as if He needed it) in a world where the majority of people don't know Him. No, the reality is simple. In a fallen world the best possible way to worship the God Who is unwilling for any to perish (2 Pet. 3:9) and Who paid such an enormous price for its salvation (John 3:16) is to bring others to a saving knowledge of Him! The church is here for mission.

FIRM FOUNDATIONS

We've taken time in this first chapter to unpick our understanding of church so that we can begin to understand what our instincts so often so clearly tell us. Namely, that many of our church structures actually are prohibitive and inhibitive to effective evangelism. Ephesians 4:11–13 shows us that the role of the evangelist is to work foundationally at the level of structure. Ephesians 4 lists the fivefold (apostle, prophet, evangelist, pastor, teacher) ministry gifts, which the Spirit of Jesus gives to His church as fundamental to the building of that church. It is the spirit of Jesus who gives these gifts because it's Jesus who builds His church and not us. Remember? We seek His kingdom. There are many other ministries (the word comes from the Greek *diaconos*, which means 'area of work or service'), but the Ephesians 4 list is foundational.

Now, most evangelists start off as driven and insecure people, activists by nature, filling their diaries with opportunities for proclaiming or preaching the gospel, building friendships with the lost, calling people to faith and so on. In other words, the 'doing' of evangelism. I know many who never progress beyond that. However, the Ephesians 4 biblical mandate doesn't involve only the doing of evangelism, but also the training/equipping of the saints for works of service; for example, in evangelism. So the biblical evangelist not only does evangelism but also *trains* others in evangelism.

However, it doesn't take long to work out that, if you train a whole bunch of God's people to do evangelism, they're going to end up extremely frustrated if they don't have a context and outlet for their training. It's immoral to train people without giving them opportunity for fruitfulness, and so the evangelist must be involved not only in *doing* and *training* but also in *strategising* with church leadership. This is so that the saints of God might work *together* and not just as a bunch of individuals doing their own thing. Only strategic evangelism can impact an area; more on this in Chapter 11.

The biblical Ephesians 4 evangelist must not only be involved in doing, training and strategising, but also be involved in church *structure*. Unless evangelists are allowed to work this way we're going to end up with a lot of evangelical churches that are defined by what they believe (evangelicalism) rather than by what they are and therefore do (evangelism). Or we're going to have evangelical churches that 'do' evangelism as a kind of 'bolt-on' extra, or even as a well-worked-out strategy, but still are not like the New Testament church, where the very *raison d'être* for church *is* evangelism/mission. This is the kind of church that lives, eats, breathes, sleeps mission. Cut it where you will, it bleeds evangelism. It's the very DNA of the church, its very heartbeat. This the heartbeat of God. It's the double heartbeat of 'the church ... the world. The church ... the world.' Is this your kind of church? If so, read on. If not, what can we do to serve the body to see our church become a mission church?

Effective evangelism demands effective church. You can

only change what you know, understand and love. Effective evangelism begins and ends with church. So before rushing on to explore what we mean by evangelism, start thinking/reading/talking/praying *now* about your church. The following questions may help you with this.

GROUPWORK

1. Discuss *together* what you think church is. What is its irreducible minimum (i.e. what needs to be present so as to constitute church so that if you took anything else away it wouldn't be church)?

2. Discuss as a group what you mean by 'spiritual' – are some of the following more spiritual than others? Why or why not?
   • Going to the cinema.
   • Fasting.
   • Praying.
   • A cheese sandwich.
   • Reading a thriller.
   • Reading the Bible.

3. Can you identify any evangelists in your church? If so, how are they equipping the saints? If they aren't, what could you do to encourage them?

4. Does the structure of your church serve you and your vision for evangelism? If so, how? Or do you serve your church's vision? If so, what could you do about this?

5. Is evangelism *the* agenda of your church? If so, how is this outworked? If not, what could you do about it?

Chapter 2

WHAT IS EVANGELISM?

A proper understanding of church can either help or hinder evangelism. So too can a proper understanding of evangelism!

PARADIGMS

Whether we know it or not, we all of us live our lives embracing paradigms. I recently worked with some churches together in Stratford, training on evangelism, at the end of which a wonderful older lady succinctly remarked, 'What's he want to call it a paradigm for? Why can't he just call it an attitude?' But the reality is that our paradigms go deeper than attitudes. A paradigm is really more to do with the way we think. It's a world-view or a mind-set. Attitudes, I would suggest, come subsequent to this.

So the challenge and purpose of this chapter is to achieve a change in our mind-set on evangelism because I believe that 'right thought' provokes 'right attitudes', which produce 'right choices', which then result in 'right actions'. If our world-view on evangelism provokes a right attitude toward it, we're more likely to make right choices about our active involvement in mission.

LET'S START AT THE VERY BEGINNING ...

It's really important we go in that direction (thoughts lead to attitudes lead to choices lead to actions) rather than the reverse. A book that simply aims at giving you hot tips to result in right actions will have a very limited effect. If our minds don't change then at best we'll go through the motions, at worst we'll think hot tips are mere gimmicks. But if our understanding is challenged and changed, so too will be our heart attitude and motivation. Before and behind every feeling and attitude there lies a thought. So our mind-set/paradigm on evangelism is crucial to our mission attitude, choices and actions.

THREE EXAMPLES

If I were to ask you which country you most associated with the production of expensive and quality wristwatches, you'd almost certainly say 'Switzerland'. This, of course, is helpful for the Swiss, because the other two things for which they are most famous (snow and chocolate) are somewhat temporary! But in the late 1960s, 80 per cent of world trade in *all* types of wristwatches belonged to the Swiss nation. They dominated the market. Their mass-machined system of production was second to none in the world. Individual watch parts would be made in factories dedicated just to the production of that item and sent to national assembly points called 'ebauche factories', then to be exported. At the end of the 1960s there was a world trade fair. The Swiss were there, demonstrating and marketing their quality, mass-produced watches. But so too were little-known companies, Casio and Texas Instruments from Japan and America.

A friendly rival advised the Swiss to look at the Japanese stand for there was to be found a revolutionary new type of watch. The Swiss technologist did exactly this, only to return a few moments later unperturbed by this potential new rival. The reason was simple. This 'so-called' new watch wasn't a proper watch at all! It had no moving hands. It didn't have a proper dial. There was no working button/winding stem. It didn't even have a mainspring! Instead, this rather odd-looking watch had a series of shimmering red numerals with which to tell the time, illuminated in a small black panel (a light-emitting diode, the precursor of the liquid crystal display). It had a button that you pressed to alter the time, but you never wound the watch up for the simple reason that it ran on a battery. The Swiss were confident; this was a gimmick, not a watch. It would never threaten their dominance of world trade in timepieces.

But threaten it it did. Within a decade, the focus for world trade in watches switched from Switzerland to Japan and also to America. Many of the ebauche factories were forced into closure. Redundancies were high. Export figures dropped. Chances are, if you now want to buy a cheap to medium-priced watch, it will have come from Japan. And why? Because the Swiss watch trade had a certain *paradigm* concerning what a watch is and what a watch does. Their paradigm was a filter or focus, through which they measured the things they could observe in the material world, and by means of which they could come to an analysis, an attitude, a decision and an action or non-action. Their paradigm told them that the digital watch wasn't a 'proper' watch at all and certainly had no future.

Another illustration. In 1965, when I was eight years old, my mother was diagnosed with cancer of the tongue. This was particularly distressing since cancer is virulent in soft tissue, and my mother was whisked away to the Christie Hospital in Manchester for what was then pioneering radium treatment. In effect, seven radioactive needles were placed into her tongue to burn the cancer away. On returning home and after a lengthy six-month recuperation, when she could neither speak nor eat solids and lived on Complan, my mother seemed to have made a good recovery.

However, two years later when I was ten, at a routine checkup (which my mother had to continue with for the rest of her life) her doctor spotted what he thought was a recurrence of the problem. But now the medical options had narrowed. She'd had a maximum dose of radium (itself a deadly poison) and it was unclear what could be done to help her. The urgency of the situation demanded her immediate admission back to the Christie Hospital. That night my grandfather (her father), a Methodist minister, rang around the Methodist churches in our local circuit and asked them to pray for my mother. The next day she was seen by the consultant. On examining her mouth, the consultant turned to his nurse in considerable irritation and said, 'You've brought me the wrong notes. The notes don't match the state of this woman's mouth. Get me the right notes!'

However, on closer examination it transpired that the notes *were* correct, but her mouth was completely clear of any recurrent problem. The doctor had no explanation; my mother, a committed Christian, had! On her notes the doctor wrote the simple word 'remission', but our testimony was that this was nothing short of a miracle. Yet that consultant could never have written 'miraculous intervention' across my mother's notes because in his *paradigm* of the world there was no God. So He couldn't intervene. Therefore there could be no miracles. The consultant's paradigm/mind-set/filter interpreted the circumstances as 'remission'. Ours interpreted it as a miracle.

My final example demonstrates the nature and power of paradigms and can be seen in Figure 2.1 overleaf. Before you turn to it, here's how to get the best effect. Flick the page over for a count of three seconds only. In that period of time immediately let your eyes register what is on the page, then after three seconds turn the page back. Try it now!

What did you see? Unless you've seen it before, chances are you saw the face of a native American Indian. Depending on your ability to scan detail you may have observed a feather in his headband, a large hooked nose, a rather thin-lipped open mouth. But if that's what you saw, turn the page again and this time have a look for as long as you like. See if you can see anything else, and then come back to me!

Could you see anything else? Hidden within the same picture is another figure. This is a very much smaller figure of an Eskimo going into the mouth of a dark cave. He has his back towards you. He is wearing a fur-trimmed coat, boots and mittens, right arm outstretched towards the cave entrance. Can you see him now?

Don't worry if you can't see both pictures, or if it takes you a little while! I've worked with some people who've never been able to see both pictures, but eventually most people do! The picture that you first see is your paradigm. It can take a little while for your paradigm to change. But once you *have* seen both pictures it's hard to 'unsee' them.

We're going to unpack an old and a new paradigm concerning the definition and practice of evangelism. Most of us are stuck with an old paradigm of evangelism, which is now outdated, irrelevant and increasingly unhelpful. But if we can see a new paradigm, then we'll find it hard to 'unsee' it.

FIGURE 2.1 – REVERSING IMAGES

The old and still-prevalent paradigm of evangelism has been born of a defensive view of mission. We've all too often felt under siege from the onslaught of Christian liberalism (select the bits you want to of the Christian faith/Bible and omit the rest!) Or from the onset of secularism (increasingly defunct in a postmodern world, but still to be found in the thinking of some who would deem the spiritual a complete irrelevance and unreality). Or perhaps our defensiveness has been provoked by syncretism (all the world religions and faiths eventually merging and blending into one great, spiritual smorgasbord where you can pick and choose a bit of this and a bit of that according to your preference). Maybe pluralism (not all faiths/world religions are the same, but they are all right, because after all, all roads lead to God, don't they?) has entrenched us in a defensive evangelistic position, which is such a hallmark of the old paradigm.

But if it is true that the old paradigm has been produced by liberalism, secularism, syncretism and pluralism, then I think it is also true that it has been perpetuated by a 'Christian ghetto' mentality. If we see ourselves as the last bastion of Christian truth, cowering behind the ramparts of absolute revelation, held together by the cement of dogmatic doctrine and eagerly awaiting the (unbiblical) rapture as our escape route to (unbiblical) heaven, then we are most likely to engage in what I call 'drawbridge evangelism'! From time to time we muster up enough strength, courage, finance, guilt, time and energy to lower the drawbridge of our fortress, sally forth, grab a few captive converts kicking and screaming, pull them back into the fortress, pull up the drawbridge and spend the rest of our time trying to stop them escaping over the battlements! This old paradigm of evangelism produces irrelevant and impersonal communication.

Yet thankfully there is an increasing shift in our postmodern world to find a 'new' paradigm of evangelism. Let me state it here and now. Actually, let's be clear. As the writer of Ecclesiastes would confirm, the new paradigm actually isn't new at all. It's simply a more biblical paradigm. It is only new because we moved away from it. If we can identify and abandon the old and embrace the new then we'll be on target for the two major goals of evangelism:

1. The motivating, mobilising, teaching, training and resourcing of the whole church to the task of mission (Eph. 4:11–13).
2. Fulfilling the purpose of the church in extending the kingdom of God, which is to reach the lost in order to make disciples (Matt. 28:16–20).

HALLMARKS OF THE OLD PARADIGM

Some while ago, for reasons best known to herself, my wife bought a huge, family medical dictionary! One day in a fit of idle fancy I took the book down from the shelf and foolishly began to browse through it. Up until that point I felt fit and well. I was content with the state of my health. I was blissfully unaware of the potential ailments from which I might be suffering! But I'd only been reading the medical dictionary for 20 minutes or so (yes, they really do make compulsive reading) before I began to think that I was afflicted with everything from Acne through to Zalinger-Ellison Syndrome!

There is a danger in introspectively picking through potential problems. Before you know it you end up thinking you have more than you really do! We're about to look at an outline of ten hallmarks of the old paradigm! *Don't* be like me and the family medical dictionary! If none of these hallmarks describes you, your way of thinking or your experience, then great! But, as you read through the descriptions, *do* carefully allow the Holy Spirit to search your mind and your heart, your attitudes and your actions, in order to 'see if there is any offensive way' in you (Psa. 139:24). Half the problem with a paradigm or mind-set is that it filters information automatically through familiarity. This means that we can develop blind spots or make assumptions. We need the help of Scripture, the Holy Spirit and the fellowship of the saints around us in order to break out and develop a new mind-set. What *are* the hallmarks of the old paradigm?

'Those who have …'

When I was growing up in Lancashire there was a common saying that described the difference between rich and poor: 'There's them as 'ave, and there's them as 'aven't!' The old paradigm of evangelism takes a very black-and-white, rather dogmatic view. It's the view that 'I have truth, and you don't!' The idea is that as a Christian, revelation has come to me, and as a non-Christian (horrible word, which is rather like calling someone 'non-person'), you have no revelation. It's a view that implies that it's we Christians who are made in the image of God. It ignores the biblical fact that *everybody* is made in the image of God, Christian and not-yet-Christian alike. I don't become made in the image of God when I become a Christian. Before I was a Christian I was already made in the image of God, but that image was terribly distorted. Now that I am a Christian that image is becoming less distorted. In God's heart and mind I am no longer to be conformed to the image of this world, but rather to be transformed by the renewing of my mind. God has now put Christ by His Spirit in me, and hidden me in Christ. This means that when God looks at me He sees His Son Jesus and when He looks at His Son Jesus He sees me! My righteousness is rubbish. Instead I have been clothed in His righteousness (Phil. 3:9).

What's more, the Bible is clear that *every* good gift comes from God (James 1:17). All truth comes from the Spirit of God (James 3:17). Wherever you find truth and goodness you have something of the revelation of God's character and purpose. And that *isn't* just restricted to Christians. Or even

Christianity. We *don't* have a monopoly on truth. We have a relationship with *the* Truth. If we embrace the mind-set of 'I have truth, and you don't', then there are likely to be at least two consequent attitudes. Neither of them are good.

The first attitude will be one of arrogance. Arrogant assertions about what the Bible does and doesn't say about creation, for example, sometimes flung in the face of people with greater scientific knowledge than we might have. Arrogant assumptions about another person's spiritual experiences when they don't match up to ours or to our understanding of the Bible. Or simply arrogance that in our 'enlightened state of revelation' we are inherently somehow 'better' than the person who doesn't know Jesus. Perhaps arrogance about our lifestyles or values, as though they were a result of *our* ability to recognise and respond to revelation instead of being a fringe benefit of the glorious goodness of the gospel of Jesus Christ! Arrogance is a very off-putting thing. It's very hard to receive something from someone who is arrogant. And arrogance, with its close links to pride, is anathema to the gospel.

The second attitude will be one of divisiveness. The very phrase 'I ... you ...' forces us immediately into a false dichotomy. It's 'us' and 'them'. It's dogmatically black or white, right or wrong. It's about exclusivity and exclusion. The gospel of Jesus Christ *does* divide. The word of God, which is 'sharper than any double-edged sword' (Heb. 4:12) really *does* divide. But that's a statement of ultimate fact. It's not an excuse for a bad attitude! In the parable of the wheat and tares (Matt. 13:24–30), while it's true that there is good cereal and bad weeds, the two co-exist together until the final, climactic harvest (a common Old and New Testament symbol for the final judgment). And so for every biblical reference like 'do not belong to this world' (John 15:19), 'do not love the world' (1 John 2:15), 'come out from them and be separate' (2 Cor. 6:17) and 'keep oneself from being polluted by the world' (James 1:27), there are vividly contrasting references like 'my prayer is not that you take them out of the world' (John 17:15), 'for God so loved the world' (John 3:16), 'go into all the world' (Mark 16:15) and 'everything God created is good' (1 Tim. 4:4). Check them out!

'The truth is out there ...'

The second hallmark. Since 'I have truth and you don't', truth must come to you from the outside through confrontation. Truth must impact you starkly, unarguably and unequivocally. But this mind-set of confrontation will again give birth to two unhelpful attitudes.

In the first place it is likely to lead us into aggressiveness, making statements, rather than asking questions. We can adopt a 'take it or leave it' mentality and approach, low on persuasion, high on confrontation. The second attitude is one of fear. This is precisely because most of the Christians I know are *not* inherently arrogant, exclusive or aggressive! Many of us aren't like that. Most of us don't want to be like that. But unless we change our understanding of evangelism, we end up pushed in both our attitudes and our actions towards an evangelistic approach and methodology that are inherently arrogant, exclusive and aggressive! And so our reaction is to fear this *and to avoid it*.

Most of us would rather run a million miles than be confrontational! So if we think that evangelism demands confrontation, then our natural response will be to flee from it! That's one reason why so many Christians think that their 'ministry' *isn't* witnessing and evangelism. They couldn't be more wrong from a biblical stance (see Chapter 3). But run from evangelism we do, because if truth comes through confrontation, and we are not confrontational, then it really 'isn't us'. Let the loud-mouthed, insecure evangelist get on with the street work on a Saturday morning, or the door-to-door visitation programme on a Sunday afternoon! If that kind of intrusive confrontation (which is how many of us view it) doesn't fit our personality types, then before you know it 90 per cent of the body of Christ have 'de-selected' themselves when it comes to witnessing.

We've all seen (and hated) the extremes of this kind of confrontational approach and attitude. I remember standing in a cinema queue in Leicester Square, London, on one rare day off when I was working for Youth for Christ in the East End of London. I'd already noticed the little man in the rather shabby raincoat with the satchel slung over his shoulder. It seems he had been busy thrusting tracts under the noses of unsuspecting passers-by. You could tell where he'd been as clearly as if he were on a GSM tracking programme. You could follow his trail by the litter of discarded tracts trampled under foot up and down the street! But now to my horror I saw him approaching the cinema queue with a fixed and rather fanatical gleam in his eyes.

He halted opposite the cinema queue some six feet away, then reached into his coat and from the dim recesses of his person he pulled out a tattered roll of wallpaper. Grasping one end of it firmly between his hands he stood with arms raised to the heavens, at which point the roll of wallpaper unfurled itself (and this was the best part), and hid the man from our view as it covered him from upraised finger tips to curling shoe leather. Facing us, scrawled in uneven characters in felt tip pen on the plain side of the roll of wallpaper, were all the most obscure texts and references from the minor prophets of the Old Testament that you could possibly imagine, where the only linking theme seemed to be one of sin and iniquity!

I didn't know what to do. It seemed that people around me, however, did. By turns they either stared stonily ahead and ignored him, or they grunted and grumbled. Some of them began to giggle. In my acute embarrassment as a 'fellow brother', I silently and fervently prayed that Jesus would just 'beam me up'! To make matters worse, in a muffled tone from a mouth covered by wallpaper the man began to berate us as a bunch of miserable sinners, hell-bent it seemed he was saying, because we might be found in a cinema queue when Jesus came back to judge us all!

Perhaps you've witnessed a similar scene? Perhaps you've seen something like a friend of mine, who while out shopping with his young son, suddenly discovered to his horror that he appeared to have mislaid his child! Running frantically up the street he espied his son standing entranced in the middle of the pedestrianised area, watching a group of local Christians in the process of 'witnessing'. This consisted of a line of sombre-looking men in dark suits each clutching a large, leather-bound Bible. In turns, one of them would step forward and begin reading out loud at the top of his voice some remarkably unsuitable portion of Scripture. After a short, pointed and somewhat accusatory explanation, the individual would then step back into line. Upon which the next would step forward and do exactly the same from a different portion of the Bible! This continued on down the line. As my friend reached his child, the boy slipped his hand into his dad's, looked up and said in a rather awestruck and bewildered voice, 'Daddy, what are they doing?' It is, I think, a rather perceptive question. Confrontation, aggression and fear – the second hallmark of an old paradigm.

'Who shall I say sent me …?'

The third hallmark is an assumed understanding of God. The assumption that when someone who is not yet a Christian uses the word 'God' they mean the same thing that we do. The reality is very different. Among Christians the word 'God' can be taken almost as a kind of shorthand to describe various attributes and concepts of the Supreme Being. Yet even among believers there would be disagreement and disparity. For example, does this God allow us free will and choice, or is the future fixed and predetermined? Does He still supply us with spiritual gifts, or has He ceased to do so, and so on? But if there is disagreement among the Christian family, you'd better believe that the word is used differently by those who are not yet Christians!

This assumed understanding comes in part from the fact that most people in this country do still believe in God. Statistics from varying sources (Christian surveys to Gallup polls) put it at worst from 40 per cent through to 80 per cent of people in the UK who believe in God. The 2001 Census indicate that 72 per cent of people reckon themselves to be Christians. Yet for 'belief in God' we cannot read 'understanding of God'. This is a flawed paradigm. We can no longer assume that people know the 'stories', or that there's still in existence a reservoir of common understanding when it comes to the nature of God, the Word of God or the workings of God.

I'll never forget nearly falling into this trap while taking a Year 11 RE lesson in an East End school in London. The whole lesson had focussed around the question, 'Who do you think Jesus is?' We'd had lots of fun and approached the question in a variety of ways, and then I asked the class to raise their hands and tell me their opinions. A lad at the back shot his hand straight up in the air.

'What do you think?' I said to him.

'Please sir, I think Jesus is a petrol pump attendant in Brick Lane!' he said, and put his hand down.

I don't know what it was that stopped me from telling the lad off, from taking him down a peg or two for his cheekiness. Actually, I think it might have been God! I suddenly realised that this lad wasn't being cheeky, trying to be funny or clever. He was deadly serious. It transpired that he had read in the newspapers an article by a guy (he's still around) called Benjamin Cream, the leader of an Eastern mystical cult, who claimed that Jesus Christ was about to be reincarnated as the seventh attava, and indeed was already present in the East End community working in Brick Lane. This lad really believed that this was Who Jesus Christ is.

It's not that people like this have rejected the gospel of Jesus Christ. It's that they have never really heard it. Any more than the two girls who went into a jeweller's shop and asked for a gold crucifix. On being shown an empty cross, one turned to her friend and said 'No, I want one with the little figure of the man on it. You know, Moses, isn't it?' We can no longer assume that even Christian young people, let alone those who are as yet unsaved, know and understand the stories of God's book, yet the old paradigm maintains this assumption concerning people's understanding of God.

'Get me to the church …'

The fourth hallmark of this old way of thinking about evangelism is an assumed understanding of church. Shortly after I first began to serve God in 'full-time' evangelism in the late 1970s, a European Systems Survey on values and beliefs was published, which indicated that around 11.5 per cent of the UK population were to be found on average at least once a month in a church service. Twenty-five years later that figure has declined to 7.5 per cent. So however enamoured we are of our churches (and I hope you are, or you probably should be serving elsewhere) we cannot assume that not-yet-Christians understand what church is, or what church does. However socially or culturally relevant you feel your church meetings to be, however much the Holy Spirit has impacted the life of your church with the 'Toronto blessing' or with revival fever, the reality is that the vast majority of the British nation know little, understand little and often care less! We dare not assume an understanding of church.

And yet there is an inherent desire for spiritual experience within the nation. Many more people claim to have had spiritual experiences than would claim to know God. Many more people pray (even regularly) than would claim to know the God they pray to and, in times of crisis and extreme emotion, there is still often an automatic turning to the church of Jesus Christ. But it would be a mistake to assume that in doing so people understand what church is about.

The old way of thinking about evangelism makes this assumption. It offers little explanation of what church is and what church does. By and large it asks people to make massive leaps in their thinking and their experience, to make major shifts in their cultural expectations and norms, in order to access church. That this is so can probably be demonstrated by statistical 'blips' that have occurred. In 1997, more people collectively said the Lord's Prayer together as it was transmitted from the funeral service for Diana, Princess of Wales, than at any other time in human history. Following that event, and more latterly, at the death and lying in state of the Queen Elizabeth the Queen Mother, church-going attendance rose (in Diana's case dramatically) in the few weeks and months following, but then slipped back into decline. We can no longer assume that the unsaved have an understanding of church, even if on occasion they register a need for it.

'And the score is …'

The fifth hallmark of the old paradigm places an inordinate emphasis on results. With this mind-set, the definition of evangelism almost equates to salvation. A focus on results means we become unhelpfully 'success-orientated'. The danger is of drivenness to achieve, as though our worth as individual Christians, or churches involved in mission, was directly proportional to our performance. And if 'success' *is* attained, then the danger is one of pride.

Alternatively, if 'success' is *not* achieved, we can become disappointed. In working with churches I've frequently asked the question, 'How many people have been directly involved in any form of evangelism?' Hands shoot up all around the training session. 'And how many of those people with hands raised were dissatisfied with that evangelism?' And the hands stay up!

If your understanding of effective and good evangelism is automatic salvation, then sooner or later you will be doomed to disappointment. And if your criteria for perseverance in evangelism place an emphasis on results, then probably sooner rather than later you will back off. It's a relatively short step from disappointment to disillusionment. Then from disillusionment to cynicism. There are large numbers of churches and individual Christians who have been disappointed, disillusioned and have become cynical when it comes to evangelism.

This was underlined for me by a church that had for several years run a well-received and highly acclaimed coffee shop in the centre of their market town. The shop was known far and wide in that rural area. It was known for its good value. For its friendly service. Its approachable staff. The excellent quality of the produce. It was known and favoured for its peaceful ambience. Everybody knew that it was run and staffed by the local church.

But what you didn't get at this coffee shop was any inappropriate evangelism, which would have violated the cultural context. You didn't find texts like 'You must be born again' printed across the bottom of the menu! Any more than you would find twee courses on the menu like 'Paschal Lamb' or the 'Five Loaves and Two Fishes Special'! Yes, there was high-quality literature available on a side table for people, should they wish to buy it, including some that was free. Yes, people had begun to realise that the establishment was sufficiently staffed for the employees always to have time to bend a listening and sympathetic ear, and even offer a word of advice or prayer if required.

Despite all this, that coffee shop is now an ironmongers! The reason? The perception/mind-set that evangelism is all about results. For no one had fallen to their knees in the midst of a cappuccino and cried out, 'What must I do to be saved?' As far as the elders of the church could tell, no one had been *directly* saved as a result of the coffee shop. But if you ask the wrong question, you get the wrong answer. If you apply the wrong criteria, you come up with the wrong judgment. The coffee bar wasn't just about results, any more than evangelism is. The quest for old paradigm results has nipped many a truly evangelistic opportunity firmly in the bud.

'Did he jump …?'

Our sixth hallmark of the old paradigm on evangelism sees

conversion largely as crisis. The clearest biblical analogy would be Saul and his encounter with the risen Christ in the form of a (literally) blinding light and a voice from heaven on the road to Damascus. And of course there are other examples to be found in Scripture. The jailer who encountered Paul and Silas springs to mind. As does the Ethiopian official. And indeed the 3,000 or so at the remarkable birth of the church in Acts 2.

But how many more do we read about in Scripture for whom there is no evidence of a sudden crisis conversion? What about the thousands who received Christ gladly and followed Him for days, weeks, months or even years on end before being clear about Who He really is? For every crisis conversion, like that of the woman at the well in John 4, how many are there back in the village who don't initially believe, but find faith only on persistently following Christ? Do we too easily skim over the many months and even years that Paul took to persuade some of the Greek thinkers and idol worshippers that he encountered and argued with endlessly as he church-planted from city to city?

And what of Jesus' own 12 disciples? You can't tell me at what point they hit a revelatory crisis that was their conversion in the three years that they followed Christ around Palestine! Even Peter's apparent moment of supreme crisis conversion as he declares, 'You are the Christ, the Son of the Living God' (Matt. 16:16) is quickly succeeded by Jesus' assertion that Peter hadn't realised that for himself but had had it supernaturally revealed to him, and then by Peter's obvious lack of understanding when he tries to prevent Jesus going to the cross! And later still by his thrice-repeated denial of Christ. So when *were* they (including Peter) saved?

If you tend to view conversion normally as crisis, then you may tend to dismiss people who can't tell you when they were converted. And in trying to find or even engineer such crises in the lives of individuals, you could be in danger of confrontation, aggression or your own fear reaction. Certainly it may skew your evangelistic methodology toward provoking crisis decisions/appeals.

Appeals were not the 'done thing' in the Lancashire Methodist church that I was brought up in, even though conversion *was* seen as a crisis. This was even worse because 'real' conversion was 'crisis' conversion but there was no opportunity for it! That's probably why I so vividly remember the visiting speaker who'd come from time to time and explain from the pulpit that 'everyone should have not one birthday but two'! Obviously he was referring to what it means to be 'born again', but as a 15-year-old I was more taken with the idea of getting as many birthdays (and therefore presumably presents) as possible! I think I'd have responded to any kind of appeal in order to accrue birthdays. And yet as I grew older my inability to identify my 'second' birthday (i.e. my date of conversion) came to plague and haunt me. It left me with a growing lack of assurance. I had been brought up to go to church. I couldn't remember a time I didn't believe in God. So when *was* I converted? And if I didn't know *when* I was converted, *was* I converted? If this emphasis of the old paradigm places confusion and concern in the minds of the believers, think what it does in the minds and experience of the searching unbeliever!

'Is it catching?'

The seventh hallmark is fear of contamination. In Chapter 1 we explored the statement that mission is the *raison d'être* for the existence of church in a fallen world. Yet the legacy of the church being linked to the state, and the nominalism that swept into the Christian faith when that first happened, is that instead of being centres for mission, many of our churches became havens of maintenance. Increasingly the fivefold ministry gifts have become internalised to maintain the saints as they in turn maintain the construct of church. And so, by and large, in the Western hemisphere, 'apostles' have gathered those who are already saved (reorganised and redistributed them), rather than planting vibrant church among those who are not yet saved. Prophets have, by and large, spoken the word of God to those who already know Him, whereas Scripture indicates that prophecy is primarily a tool for evangelism – 1 Corinthians 14:24–25.

Evangelists (that irritant gift to the body of Christ!) are either being thrust out from the mainstream of the body of Christ and having to outwork their gifting through ministry organisations or para-church setups, or have been increasingly unleashed to 'fish' in the shallow edges of the church family. (Statistics from most major crusades, certainly in the UK, indicate that the likes of Billy Graham and Luis Palau are largely seeing conversions from the margins of the Anglican and Baptist churches.) Pastors have made the mistake of imagining that they are called to pastor the congregation, as opposed to being called to pastor the flock, which includes the unsaved in the territory that God has given them. Consequently, much pastoral ministry has been about wiping spiritual noses as opposed to developing spiritual muscles. And the ministry of the teacher has tended to restrict Christ's eternal and globally practical values for living to the interpretations of the saints, rather than to the attention of the lost. Jesus taught a better way to live not just to the disciples, but to the lost.

I've had the enormous privilege of working around a large number of churches in the United Kingdom for the last 25 years, and have found that most of our churches are led by either individuals or at best team ministries, which in gifting and anointing are pastorally dominated. The voice of the evangelist is rarely to be heard on church leadership teams across the UK. All too often the next person to be released into 'full-time' ministry is another pastor/administrator/youth worker (all vital and honourable ministries in themselves) rather than evangelists who can equip the saints to fulfil the primary task of the church on earth – mission.

And so, with the best of hearts and intentions, our largely pastorally dominated church leadership, in a desire to maintain the safety, integrity and purity of the flock, can often demonstrate and teach levels of separation from the world because of fear of contamination. Young people are not taught how to witness at Halloween parties, but rather pulled out from them. For too long church members have been encouraged to keep away from pubs and clubs (and even cinema queues!), always supposing the pastoral maintenance of the church construct has left them with any social free time outside of going to 'spiritual' meetings! And lest we falsely point the finger at church leadership teams, the truth is that all too often church membership has itself become too cosy a club to put up with external additions (converts!). And so a fear that if somehow we get involved in society around us we will end up compromised by it, linked to the inertia of existing relationships, can keep us from effective mission at a cost to the lost.

'You can't do that!'

I began working full time as an evangelist in 1978. That December I had my first opportunity of attending an annual conference for evangelists in Derbyshire. With only three exceptions I have been back each year, although judging by the nature of those first few conferences, I do on occasions ask myself why. But the conference has moved a long way in terms of openness to God's Holy Spirit and charismatic gifts, and away from religiosity towards informality, embracing freer and more open styles of worship. Back in those early days it was more like stepping through a time warp! I really wondered what I'd come to. Everybody present was male. With few exceptions they were dressed in dark suits. Their links into the life of local church for fellowship and accountability seemed to be tenuous in the extreme.

At one point in the proceedings one year, a younger guy, with long hair, informally dressed in jeans and jumper, got up and made what proved to be the most controversial statement of the conference. He explained, with obvious enthusiasm and an air of excitement, how in his recent missions he had been using gifted dramatists to portray the power and the passion of the crucifixion of Christ. I can still hear the horrified gasps that went around the room! The slamming down of Bibles! In reply to this statement, evangelist after evangelist got up to maintain that when it came to the gospel there was only one God-ordained means of communication. And that was through 'the preaching of the Word!' So drama was out! The use of songs (as opposed to hymns) or of visual images was out! Even narrative preaching was out; it had to be expository teaching from the Scripture. The young guy who had spoken was shouted down and branded an 'angry young man'. My admiration went out to Eric Delve, who went on to become one of the UK's most gifted and creative evangelists and communicators.

Of course, things have moved on, and now very few of us would balk at the use of drama in an appropriate presentation of the gospel. Yet many of us will exhibit some of the symptoms of this seventh hallmark of the old paradigm, which is adherence to restricted practices. We change with time and with culture. It's certainly time for the church of Jesus Christ to stop thinking that changing with culture is a bad thing. Only the content of the gospel doesn't change, and even that is applied differently to different individuals. Even the briefest examination of how Jesus presents the gospel to people in the New Testament indicates this.

For some, the emphasis is on sacrifice (Mark 10:21). For others, it is on healing and forgiveness (Mark 2:5–12). Same gospel, different approach. So while the gospel remains constant, its application doesn't. Could it be that because on any given Sunday morning 7.5 per cent of the population of the UK is to be found in a church meeting that therefore 92.5 per cent of God's heart is to be found out in the world? Is it just possible that God is *at least* as involved in society, communities and culture in His desire to reach the lost as He is in the culture of the church? The gospel of Jesus Christ will happily accommodate and adapt itself to fit any culture unless the values of that culture cut across kingdom values, in which case the gospel of Jesus Christ will quite happily rupture that culture! In most of its *values* it is counter-cultural. But in many of its *expressions* it need not be. Why should we fear cultural adaptation? Why only embrace restrictive practices?

Some of the things that we might now hold to be acceptable practices were actually in their own day radical, unacceptable, unrestricted! Many churches will happily sing hymns to the accompaniment of an organ, forgetting that when the organ became prominent in church music in the seventeenth century, it was deemed to be the devil's own instrument! Perhaps in much the same way, but centuries later, the guitar and drums would still in some churches be denounced as heathen rhythms from pagan jungles!

In cathedrals across the land, clergy (now there's an unbiblical concept!) still chant out responses in a high-pitched monotone with a falling cadence at the end of each phrase. You've probably heard it done: 'a-a-men'. But the origin of this practice has become lost in the mist of antiquity, and what started as a creative practice has ended up as an irrelevant nonsense. Originally this sing-song means of response was adopted in order to find the sympathetic resonant pitch of the vast cathedral buildings, which in those days weren't equipped with public address systems. This made the voice carry better to the congregation so that they could join in with the responses. How ironic that this creative practice is now being done through a PA system!

And in evangelical churches and chapels up and down the country, we still have a 6.30pm gospel meeting, come heaven, hell or high water! Irrespective of whether there are any unbelievers present, the gospel must be proclaimed and the witness maintained! Why? Because the 6.30pm meeting is the gospel meeting. And evermore shall be! Again, something that originally had its source in great creativity has become a restricted practice. The 6.30 pm gospel meeting finds its origins largely in the rural Welsh chapels, when electricity was first being supplied to public buildings, including churches. By 6.30pm most of the farmers had finished their milking and feeding rounds, and were attracted by the cultural relevance of this new electric lighting, and therefore more likely to come to an evening meeting where they might then hear the gospel!

Even the way we use Scripture in evangelism is far less flexible and creative than the way the New Testament writers used it. Jesus, on the road to Emmaus, reinterpreted much of the Old Testament by making it apply to Himself. Paul frequently misquotes and takes out of context passages of the Old Testament in order to apply them to Christ and His gospel.

This may all be very obvious to you. Yet this I can guarantee; somewhere in your understanding and approach to the gospel of Jesus Christ you'll have accepted restricted practices on the understanding that they are biblical norms. Whereas the reality is that these restricted practices are more likely to be simply cultural expectations. So perhaps drama and the gospel *are* OK with you. But the gospel demonstrated and explained through friendship evangelism on the dance floor of a drug-infested rave might seem completely unacceptable to you. Or through Christians dancing their hearts out for Jesus in a nightclub. Yet that's what my church does. But, you see, my church would struggle with the concept of the gospel conveyed through, for example, opera (a subject close to my own heart!). We tend to think that we are radical in church life and evangelism if we're doing what *we* like to do. But actually, radical is about going back to the roots, and is much more likely to involve things that make us uncomfortable. Much of the old paradigm of evangelism never gets beyond restricted practice, safe within our comfort zones.

Expert: a drip under pressure!

I like the pun that forms the sub-heading to this paragraph (you have to say it to get it!). And I like the definition that an expert is someone who knows more and more about less and less until eventually he knows everything about nothing! And another (very challenging in church circles) is that an expert is anyone who is more than 25 miles away from home!

The ninth hallmark of the old paradigm involves experts, and a commitment to the expert or specialist approach. This mind-set sees the evangelist as the 'do-er' of evangelism. If your patch is particularly difficult evangelistically (most churches seem to think that theirs is) then the solution is to reel in the evangelist! This specialist approach often seems to centre around certain methods of evangelism; that is, it helps if the evangelist has a tent! The emphasis is often on 'preaching the Word'. Or on remarkable testimonies. Or on God's 'man (and it usually is a man!) of faith and power for the hour', exercising a remarkable anointing in preaching or healing. Please don't hear what I'm not saying! We need *all* these approaches ('by all means possible ... save some' – 1 Cor. 9:22). But is this approach normative? Does evangelism depend on experts? Or is there a better way, a newer paradigm? I think so.

Fringe benefits

The tenth and final hallmark of the old paradigm of evangelism is that of the self-centred gospel. For many years we have tended to demonstrate and proclaim a self-centred gospel, so much so that it's possible we've lost track of what the gospel actually is. It might be an interesting exercise for you to stop for a moment and jot down in the space below precisely what *you* think the gospel is. We'll come back to this in Chapter 4, but for now no cheating by looking ahead!

The gospel is _____

_____

_____

_____

_____

_____

Have a look at what you've written. Chances are you've jotted down things like good news, salvation, being saved from sin, friendship with God, destiny assured, etc. All these (and indeed many more) are wonderful things, but essentially they are the *consequences* of the gospel. They derive *from* the gospel. They aren't *the* gospel. They're the fringe benefits, and they tend to be individualistic; that is, they benefit us. Some might even say that essentially they're hedonistic. So that ultimately the gospel of Jesus Christ is persuasive because of what we get out of it. But this isn't the gospel itself. This self-centred gospel is one of the hallmarks of the old paradigm.

A BREATHER ...

I hope that's been a helpful trawl through ten of the most common hallmarks of an old way of thinking about evangelism. It would be unlikely that you could identify with all ten of those. However, it would also be unlikely that you don't find the Holy Spirit nudging you gently when it comes to one or more of them. Any of them have the potential of affecting our motivation, attitudes and actions when it comes to witnessing. So this is a good place to start. If we don't deal with the mind-set we will be unable to effectively and permanently adjust our responses and reactions when it comes to evangelism. Instead, the old mind-set will act like a default mechanism, constantly tugging us back to an old way of thinking, feeling and doing in mission. So it is worth taking a pause, a bit of a breather, and asking the Holy Spirit to help us own these symptoms in order that He might deal with the mind-set root.

I remain convinced that most spiritual strongholds are to be found in the mind, before they are found embodied in principalities or powers or in geographical regions. Hence the significance of Ephesians 6:17 talking about the 'helmet of salvation' for the protection of our thinking. Scripture clearly makes the connection between our paradigms and our identity; 'as a man thinks, so he is' (see Prov. 23:7, NIV footnote). Scripture highlights the need for the renewing of our mind in order to effect transformation and to avoid conformation (Rom. 12:1–2). The command and encouragement found in Philippians 2:5 is to have the same attitude of Christ Jesus. The word 'attitude' is translated from the Greek *phroneo*, which more literally means 'think – feel – do'. Right thoughts lead to right feelings lead to right actions.

HALLMARKS OF THE NEW PARADIGM

The best way of changing our paradigm is to get rid of all trace elements of the old way of thinking on evangelism that I've outlined above. We really don't want to be left with any ties to an unbiblical, historical, culturally irrelevant way of going about mission. So you may need to identify one or two of the hallmarks that you're stuck in, to own them so that you can disown them. But when it comes to the hallmarks of the new paradigm of evangelism, we don't want to be content with identifying just one or two to embrace, but rather to whole-mindedly and whole-heartedly opt for the whole paradigm! We don't want to be minimum Christians, adopting the least that we can possibly get away with, but rather maximum Christians going for broke! So as I outline ten hallmarks of the new paradigm, I encourage you to do just that.

Inclusive, not exclusive

If the first hallmark of the old paradigm is 'I have truth and you don't' then its opposite number in the new paradigm is inclusiveness and humility. The new paradigm recognises that *all* truth comes from God, wherever it may be found. The new paradigm genuinely respects people's belief systems, and gently explores the values that they derive from their beliefs. The new paradigm will make a bridge out of people's spiritual experiences (and about 80 per cent of the population have had spiritual experience) rather than form a chasm from them!

When my friendly neighbourhood Jehovah's Witness comes to call, it's the old paradigm that prompts me to argue with her. To concentrate on how wrong she is, and in how many areas. But it's the new paradigm that welcomes her in. That looks for mutual ground. That asks questions rather than making statements. That is keen to know what her experience of Jesus has been this week in order that I might share my experience of Him with her.

And of course this isn't new at all. It's simply biblical. It takes us right back to the apostle Paul in Acts 17 at Athens. Rather than berating the God-fearing Greeks for their superstition (they had even erected an altar to an 'unknown god', so scared were they that they might miss a god and by so doing offend him!), Paul is at pains to commend them for their spiritual sensitivity. In fact, so culturally relevant is Paul that in verse 28 he specifically quotes one of their own poets from a poem written in commemoration of Zeus! It is a wonderful phrase, and I can't tell you how many times I have prayed it: 'for in Him we live and move and have our being', but the bottom line is that it is pagan poetry in your Bible!

So the new paradigm recognises that we may all have glimmerings of truth, but that none of us has *the* truth. For *the* truth is to be found only in Jesus. We have received the revelation of this truth not by dint of our deserving it, but by dint of God's desiring it. And He desires the same for all people everywhere. It is the truth that is special, not us. No room here for exclusivity. No room for arrogance. The new paradigm engenders inclusiveness and humility.

Relational, not confrontational

This is fundamental to the new paradigm. Most people are not by nature confrontational. And most Christians in addition, are by the work of the Holy Spirit, growing in their love for God, for themselves and *for others*. So it's good news that a biblical ('new') paradigm of evangelism depends upon people who *aren't* confrontational, but who *are* relational. We're not all good at knocking on doors. Or standing on street corners doing Christian dramas. Or sharing our testimony in public. Or preaching the gospel from public platforms. But we *can* all love people. We *can* sweep our neighbour's path as well as ours. We *can* buy somebody a pint down the pub and extend the hand of friendship. We *can* be generous. The new paradigm doesn't look to confront. It looks to relate. It doesn't look to antagonise. It looks to build friendships. And this is massively and practically significant. You will see why, when, in later chapters, we investigate the power and the practice of friendship evangelism.

God is …

The new paradigm is peopled by theists and not by deists. Theists fully understand and have experienced that the God Who created everything is still very much involved in His creation. Even at the cost of the life of His own Son Jesus. And so God can be known. And God can be experienced. In the new paradigm the theist understands that most people who

55

believe in God do *not* believe that He can be known or experienced. The new paradigm acknowledges that for the deist God is remote. He is disconnected from the universe. He is more likely to be an impersonal force (perhaps the ying/yang of Eastern mysticism, or the life force of pantheism) rather than a personal God. He is a kind of super-extended cosmic rice-pudding! Or, to change the analogy, it's as though the God of the Bible had grown old and senile and forgotten where He popped the earth down somewhere in the cosmos! The majority of people in the UK who believe in God (and it is a majority) are therefore deists, and not theists. The new paradigm understands this and makes room for it.

Of course, it makes more sense for deists to believe that something created everything out of nothing, than that nothing created everything out of nothing! But the 'something' can't be known, according to the deist. That's quite handy, because if it can't be known, then it can't make moral demands of you! And so the deist believes in God, and then lives their life as though God wasn't around. It's not only crazy. It's tragic. The deist does, however, tend to shift position dramatically when they encounter personal tragedy or crisis. Then suddenly the God who was impersonal becomes the God at whom the question, 'Why me?' is directed. God is suddenly viewed with fear and distrust, as though He were a capricious being of great vindictiveness. Most deists are content for God to be impersonal until something goes wrong, at which point they conclude that God is a monster! And He is to be blamed. The new paradigm understands this and is prepared to grapple with it, rather than assuming that this viewpoint doesn't exist, or ignoring it.

Church is what?

Where the old paradigm also made an assumed understanding of church and its relevance, the new paradigm does no such thing. It can't afford to. For many church structures, let alone strategies, are inhibitive toward evangelism rather than facilitative of it. The new paradigm recognises that there is much ground to be taken in exploring the nature and form of church.

Rick Warren's concept of a 'purpose-driven church' takes steps concerning the *strategy* of church-based evangelism. In the UK, Nicky Gumbell's *Alpha* initiative is somewhat more flexible in that it can be bolted on as a strategy to outreach in the workplace, school, etc. The cell church initiative has pushed further into the *structure* of church and not just the strategy. But Jim Thwaites' work (already referred to in Chapter 1) goes the furthest, I think, in terms of deconstruction of the largely Greek church model, in order to find something that is much more fluid and flexible. This is a new-paradigm search for church, which releases the saints to fill out all the fullness of Christ in all the spheres of creation (outlined in Eph. 4–6 as personal mind-sets, workplace, marriage, family and spiritual warfare in the heavenlies).

Many people are currently asking questions about the nature and shape of church in postmodern society. It seems to me that no one has all the answers to these questions, but that they are healthy questions to be asking. Ask anything less and we are in danger of the equivalent of rearranging the deck chairs on the deck of the *Titanic*. It's the equivalent of the Russian clergy (as indeed they did) debating the colour of their vestments on the threshold of the Russian Revolution, which destroyed the Russian church! The new paradigm is prepared to grapple with these questions concerning a proper understanding of church and indeed of the church's image. For although the average person in the street is not asking these questions, they are voting with their feet concerning their view of the church's image. Most people in the UK (it is currently running at 92.5 per cent of the population) clearly think that church is irrelevant and boring, because they don't go.

In the new paradigm we need to be prepared to grapple with these last two points about God and church. Much previous evangelism has invited people who basically think that Christians are living proof that God is a monster and church is boring to 'Come and join us'! That isn't good news. In fact it is more devangelism that evangelism!

And the rest ...

If the old paradigm places a heavy emphasis on results, the new paradigm understands that evangelism is all of that, but very much more too. Once you change the definition of evangelism and widen it, you bring other criteria to bear on judging effective evangelism than merely 'hands in the air' or 'bums on seats'! In the new paradigm that coffee shop in the market town would never have been closed down, because evangelism is about *every* link in the chain, and not just the *last* link. Every meaningful positive contact that you can have with a not-yet-Christian is evangelism, not just leading someone to Christ, but the many steps that run up to that including helping people to realise that actually 'God is OK and you are normal'. Do we close the coffee shop because no one has been converted in it? Or do we keep it open because lots of people have a very positive encounter with Christians reflecting the values of their God, and consequently get moved on a stage in their process towards conversion?

You may be familiar with the Engel's Scale. Engel, a Christian sociologist, outlined the various stages toward conversion, and after conversion toward discipleship, along a kind of scale. The original Engel's Scale went from minus 8 to plus 8, which has always baffled me, so please forgive my simplified version in Figure 2.2.

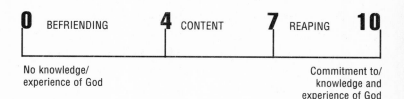

FIGURE 2.2 – ENGEL'S SCALE

The beauty of the Engel's Scale is that it depicts in visual form just how broad the definition of evangelism really is. Evangelism isn't just point 10 on the scale above, it's everything from zero to ten. You can see why this hallmark of the new paradigm of evangelism is inclusive of all the saints. For it means that potentially every good deed that you do, every good gift that you use, every good day you inhabit, every good conversation that you have, every opportunity recognised and taken is a part of effective evangelism. We can all be involved in this and let it build faith in us for our effectiveness and God's fruitfulness. One good gift used by you can lead to one good deed done for a not-yet-Christian, which can lead to one good conversation … and so it goes. Not only does this build faith in us, but it can also give us a sense of somewhere to go in our relationships, something to build upon, somewhere to take people to next in their quest for Jesus. Again, we will return to the Engel's Scale and process evangelism in Chapters 6, 7 and 8 when we major on friendship evangelism.

A time and place for everything?

Is there? For conversion? Or is there a better, more biblical, more realistic way of looking at conversion? The last ten years or so have seen a major debate in the UK on process evangelism. This is the idea that people come to faith in Christ more as a journey than through a crisis. That the journey is more relational/friendship-based than congregational; that often the not-yet-saved can feel they *belong* to a community of faith before they *believe*.This was, in part, sparked by research done by John Finney on behalf of the British and Foreign Bible Society, and published in a book *Finding Faith Today*. Over 500 UK Christians were asked to describe their journey to faith. Was their finding faith a crisis or a process? A total of 69 per cent described their journey as gradual, with only 31 per cent describing it as sudden. So shocked was Finney at these results that he assumed the statistics were skewed by a disproportionate number of 'liberal' Christians. He re-configured the statistics, this time looking specifically at evangelicals. These were people who would surely know what it meant to be 'born again', what it was to have a conversion experience? People who would recognise the crisis of the Damascus road!

But the statistics held true. There *was* a shift, but it was very slight. Even among specifically evangelicals, 63 per cent said that their journey to faith was gradual, with only 37 per cent describing it as sudden. What's more, the survey discovered that on average it took four years for a person to make their journey to faith. This begins to make sense of the fact that on average, in the Western hemisphere, people need to hear the gospel seven times to make an intelligent response to it, and that the most effective and biblical means of evangelism is friendship evangelism. Process evangelism makes the most sense. Again, more of this in Chapters 6, 7 and 8, where I'll reiterate Finney's analysis in more depth.

Breaking the ghetto …

For many years the old paradigm of evangelism has kept Christians cowering behind the walls of the church for fear of being contaminated by the values of 'the world'. A hallmark of the new paradigm is its potential for breaking new ground. Contagion without compromise is better than contamination. The church is not meant to be a hospital dealing in innocuous recuperation, but rather a medical SWAT team dealing in inoculation! We are to be not just antiseptics to clean existing wounds, but antibiotics that work preventatively against the disease of sin and selfishness. So new-paradigm evangelism engages with community, society and culture rather than disengages. And if it's fear of contamination that holds us back, then it is love that breaks the ghetto. For in the New Testament it's love that is the power or antidote to fear (1 John 4:18). The Bible is very clear: 'The one who is in you is greater than the one who is in the world' (1 John 4:4).

The unrestricted God

You have only to look around at the superabundant extravagance and ecstatic creativity of the cosmos, as Scripture exhorts us to, to gain a glimpse into the creativity of our God. In the Old Testament one of the primary functions of the Holy Spirit (Hebrew *ruach* – the breath or wind of God) was to come *upon* people to anoint them for *function*, in contradistinction to the New Testament where the Holy Spirit (Greek *pneuma* – meaning breath or wind of God) comes *within* people in order to affect their *character*. And one of the three prime functions that the Holy Spirit effected in the Old Testament was creativity (Exod. 31). The other two functions were leadership and prophecy (have a look at Num. 11 and Num. 24).

So we have a God who in His very nature is creative, and Who is generous in bestowing that gift upon His children. Why then should we imagine that it will be any different in His attempts to reach out to embrace people and to bring them into His family? Creative evangelism mirrors the creativity of God. Whatever creative opportunities *can* be taken for communicating the gospel *should* be taken. Whatever creative contexts *can* be experimented with in building friendships (the best vehicle for the gospel) *should* be explored. The only exception is where the gospel and its inherent relational moral demands upon people would be compromised. Please note that it's the gospel that must not be compromised, it's not about whether you or I are personally inconvenienced or compromised. Our unwillingness to compromise has usually got more to do with our insecurity or our pride, our fear or our temptation levels, rather than with our zealousness for the good reputation of the gospel. Obviously creative practices must be embarked upon with wisdom. With prayer support. In open fellowship. And rarely on our own. But embarked upon they must be!

The more the merrier

I don't know who it was who first said, 'If you ever find the perfect church don't join it, because you're sure to spoil it', thus highlighting the frailty of the individual members of the body of Christ. But I do know this; while it's true that if I was the only sinner on earth, Christ would still have come and died and rose again for me, the fact is that I wasn't the only sinner on earth, and that although Jesus died for me individually, He also died for church corporate. The church caught up with religion is one of the most potent forces for evil in the world. But the church filled with the Spirit of Christ is one of the supreme organisms in the created order. Please note that she is an organism, not an organisation! All of the pictures used in the New Testament for church speak of life and growth. She is most commonly alluded to as a bride (Rev. 21:2,9), a building of *living* stones (1 Pet. 2:4–12), a battalion of united soldiers (Eph. 6:10–18; 2 Timothy 2:3–4), but supremely as a body (1 Cor. 12:12–27; Rom. 12:4–5).

We've already seen that the biblical role of the evangelist is for the equipping of the saints for works of service – Ephesians 4:11–13. So rather than expect the evangelist with her expertise and specialist approach to do the evangelism, the new paradigm of evangelism looks to the evangelist to encourage, exhort, educate and empower the body to do the body's job. Evangelism *isn't* the domain of the evangelist. Or of the evangelism team. Or of the youth worker. Or of the schools outreach team. Rather, it's the function of the *whole* body of Christ working together. The new paradigm doesn't allow us to salve our consciences by passing off this task to the few. 'Never was so much owed by so many to so few' might have been a good sound bite for the Battle of Britain (Winston Churchill), but it *mustn't* be allowed to be the dictum of the church when it comes to mission. More of this in the next chapter.

Me, my, mine

With me so far? And so to the tenth and final hallmark of the new paradigm. As we've seen, the old approach was too often self-centred. A hallmark of the new mind-set on evangelism is that the gospel of Jesus Christ is a selfless gospel and not a selfish gospel. When it's demonstrated, explained and proclaimed it creates a gospel community and not just a bunch of hedonistic individuals. Forgiveness; freedom from sin; eternal destiny assured; healed bodies, minds, spirits, souls and relationships and so on are, as previously noted, fringe benefits of the gospel – they are not the gospel itself.

Preach a selfish gospel and you get selfish converts. Preach a selfless gospel and you're more likely to get followers after Jesus. That's because the gospel *is* Jesus Christ. We submit ourselves to a gospel of truth, because *He* is the Truth. Not because of what we get out of it. And we follow Him, not because of where we're going, but because of Whom we're going with. Because Jesus is the Way. For each occasion that Jesus is described as Saviour in the New Testament, He is described as Lord nine times more. And the word 'Lord' is often not a Messianic title (i.e. a description of status), but a description of function, and could be better translated as 'Boss'. This shift of paradigm, from a selfish to a selfless gospel, is more likely to create disciples without rights than create consumerist converts who have come to Christ on the 'it'll be all right on the night' ticket. These latter are what Christian author Dallas Willard has rightly called 'vampire Christians; they only want Jesus for His blood!' More of this in Chapter 4.

Phew! There you have it. Not an exhaustive (possibly an exhausting!) list of some of the hallmarks of the old and new paradigms on evangelism.

IF THE CAP FITS …

Which paradigm do you inhabit? The chances are you'll have a foot in both camps. If that's the case, then let me encourage you to be ruthless about rooting out any vestiges of the old paradigm, for they will hold you back. They will inhibit your witnessing. More importantly, they are harmful to the lost. As we finish this chapter let me summarise the old and new paradigms by placing the themes side by side so that you can see the direct contrast and the necessary shift from one to the other.

Old paradigm	New paradigm
I have truth, you don't	Humility
Truth comes through confrontation	The gospel is relational
Assumed understanding of God	Proper understanding of deism
Assumed understanding of church	Proper understanding of church's image
An emphasis on results	Evangelism is wider than results
Conversion as crisis	Conversion as a process
Fear of contamination	Love breaks the ghetto
Restricted practices	Creative practices
The specialist approach	Body of Christ
Self-centred gospel	Selfless gospel

GROUPWORK

1. Pray and fast, asking God the Holy Spirit to identify which elements of the old paradigm still hold you back.
2. Discuss and debate any of the paradigm shifts that you don't agree with.
3. Lay hands on one another and pray out the old, asking God to break the mind-set and pray in the new.

4. For each of the hallmarks of the new paradigm that you want to adopt, what would you have to do this coming week to demonstrate it?
5. Set a goal to do this with feedback to the group on how you got on.

Chapter 3

WHO EVANGELISES?

Evangelists are sometimes accused (sometimes rightly so) of being lightweight when it comes to biblical/theological content. It can be the case that because they're dealing time and again with the same content (the *Kerygma* or core of the gospel – see Chapter 4), they can become lazy in their grasp of it. Sometimes an attempt to make it accessible to the many will drive the evangelist into the use of superficial or inadequate illustrations. But I believe if we will truly root what we believe in Scripture, then we have a better chance of living it out. If we really believe it in our hearts *and* our heads then it must affect our lifestyles. Christian sociologist Jim Wallis said it: 'What you *do* on Monday morning is what you really believe, everything else is religion.' This is a kind of paraphrase of James 2:26: 'Faith without deeds is dead.'

So although I have alluded in Chapters 1 and 2 to mission as the *raison d'être* for the church, and evangelism as the job of the body of Christ, I think it is worthwhile to take a closer look from Scripture at the question, 'Who evangelises?' If you are already convinced that the answer to this question is 'I do!' then please feel free to skip to the next chapter. But if you've begrudgingly accepted that it's you but don't know why, and don't *want* the answer to be you, then this chapter *is* for you. Certainly if you've previously imagined that evangelism was for the evangelist, and just wasn't 'your ministry' then please read on with an open heart and mind. What I plan to do is take us through some key passages in Scripture, so that the Bible can inform your hearts and heads. And that while becoming convinced that the answer to the question 'Who evangelises?' is 'We do', we might pick up a few biblical hot tips. So here goes …

PASSAGE 1: MATTHEW 28:16–20

Then the eleven disciples went to Galilee, to the mountain where Jesus had told them to go. When they saw him, they worshipped him; but some doubted. Then Jesus came to them and said, 'All authority in heaven and on earth has been given to me. Therefore go and make disciples of all nations, baptising them in the name of the Father and of the Son and of the Holy Spirit, and teaching them to obey everything I have commanded you. And surely I am with you always, to the very end of the age.

This is one of the most famous passages in all of Scripture, and certainly one that you'll have heard expounded in the context of evangelism. Perhaps the first thing we should note about the Great Commission (it's almost sure to be called that in your version of the Bible) is that it has never been revoked. Jesus never said anything since to indicate that His master plan for His disciples has changed in any way, shape or form whatsoever. So first and foremost the Great Commission is still in force.

Second, not only is it unrevoked, but it is also unfulfilled. This is a job unfinished, a task uncompleted. In the context of an unrevoked and unfulfilled commission, verse 16 shows the importance of Jesus' disciples (any one of us) being in the right place at the right time. They *were* at the mount that Jesus had indicated. So who evangelises? His disciples, who are in the right place at the right time. This means being proactive in asking God for God appointment/opportunities to share our faith.

Being in the right place at the right time is about asking God for opportunities to demonstrate and then explain your faith. Only three days before writing this I had occasion to ask God for an opportunity to invite my neighbours to a birthday celebration as a part of our ongoing friendship evangelism. Ask I did. And provide it He certainly did! So for ten minutes over the garden hedge I got into a conversation not only about the party, but about the sad death of a relative, and the effectiveness of prayer. More than I asked for!

But I suggest that it is not only about geography and appointments. It is also about culture and context. Being in the right place at the right time is about recognising the life rhythms and culture that you embody. Because the truth is that homogeneous-unit evangelism is the most effective; we witness best to those who are most like us. You will evangelise best among your peers. The best youth evangelist would be a young person. The best evangelist to my neighbour is likely to be me! Of course, there are glorious exceptions, but there's enough truth in this for us to reflect on what it means for *us* to be in the right place at the right time, to identify *our* peers and those with communality or mutuality of interest, and to be active and effective in sharing our faith with *them*.

The third lesson from this passage is surely that the Great

Commission was given in the context of obedience. Who evangelises? Those who will be obedient to the commands of Christ. These disciples were in the right place at the right time, precisely because they were where Jesus had *told* them to go. This wasn't a request. It was a command. Later on in this book (in Chapter 5) we'll look in more detail at why we share our faith. But the bottom line has got to be this; if Jesus says do it, and He's the Boss, then we do it! Even if there were no other reasons given. Even if there was no explanation made. Whether we like it or not. Think we're good at it or not. It is the principle that Mary, the earthly mother of Jesus, seems to have learned very early on and have been keen to pass on to His disciples. Hence her urging of them at Jesus' first public miracle at the wedding at Cana (John 2:5): 'Do whatever he tells you.'

The fourth thing we can learn from this passage is found in verse 17. As a result of seeing Jesus (and if you *really* see Jesus this is *always* the result) His disciples worshipped Him. So not only was the context of the Great Commission one of right place right time, and of obedience, but also of worship. Who evangelises? Those who would worship Jesus. This isn't just about what has come to be known as celebration evangelism, although it is about that too. If we can find valid and relational means of getting the unsaved into the presence of God in the context of praise and worship, then some of them will respond to that.

This is certainly true. The impact of non-religious and culturally relevant praise and worship in a corporate setting had a major effect on the lives of some of my wife's family at our wedding. I'll refer to this later when we look at friendship evangelism; enough to say that we had prayed consistently for months before that God would use our wedding to reach the unsaved, and reach them He did! The presence of God, the reality of contemporary music and words, and the evidence of God's love for one another among His people all proved to be powerful evangelistic tools.

But we all know that worship is much more than the songs that we sing, the hands that we raise (or not!), the celebration events that we go to. According to Scripture, worship is our lifestyle. The word most commonly translated worship in the New Testament is the Greek word *proskino* – which as I have said literally means 'to move towards, to embrace and to kiss'. Worship is to do with relationship. It's to do with intimacy. It's to do with lifestyle choices. With finding out what pleases the one we love and doing that. Finding out what doesn't please them and not doing that!

Probably the pithiest definition of worship that you will find in the New Testament occurs in Romans 12:1: 'Therefore, I urge you, brothers, in view of God's mercy, to offer your bodies as living sacrifices, holy and pleasing to God – this *is* your spiritual act of worship' (my italics). In the Old Testament there were plenty of dead sacrifices, but in the New Testament we're *called* to lay our lives down as a 'living' sacrifice. And the problem with living sacrifices, of course, is that they keep getting up off the altar! So every time my will cuts across the revealed will of God I have a choice to make. I stand at a crossroads. Will I go *my* way? Or will I go *God's* way? Every time I choose God's way, *this* is worship. So the context of the Great Commission provokes questions about our lifestyles and our choices.

Two other interesting features on worship before we move on to the second half of verse 17! Scripture makes a clear connection between worship and authority. Whatever we worship, ultimately we give authority to. If I worship money, it will come to rule over me. If on a Sunday morning I bow down at the altar of my car and clean it, it will come to have authority over me. Even good things inappropriately worshipped will come to have authority over us. I can make a 'god' of relationships, and I will ultimately come to live for them. They will hold an unnecessary and unhelpful sway in my life if I live for/worship them, as opposed to Jesus. Biblical teaching is clear; we worship Jesus and Him alone. And then He alone commands us to do relationships properly. That's the correct order. This is well demonstrated in the temptations of Christ in Luke 4. There in verses 6 and 7 Satan promises if Jesus will but worship him, then Satan will give Him authority over all the kingdoms of the earth.

And finally, doesn't it strike you as interesting that the only time in the New Testament that Jesus mentions worship is in the context of personal witnessing and evangelism? We have tended to make worship an 'in-house' thing, sometimes a thing of great beauty and creativity, and sometimes a thing of great religiosity and irrelevance, but in either case potentially introverted and incestuous! And yet when Jesus mentions worship, it's directly in the context of speaking to an unbeliever about the true nature of God. Check it out for yourself in John 4:21–26.

So, people who out of obedience are in the right place at the right time, who in their lifestyles are seeking (nobody gets it perfect) to worship Jesus are those to whom the Great Commission is given. The second half of verse 17 adds another category of people to that list. Who evangelises? Those who doubt!

If you're reading this book because you're committed to evangelism and just want some help with changing mind-set, changing heart, changing motivation, changing practice to make you more fruitful in that, then this will come as good news to you. Because it is highly unlikely that you've never doubted God, His plan, His purpose or His Word! And a careful look at the end of verse 17 and into verse 18 clearly indicates that you're included!

On the other hand, if you're reading this book because you *don't* like the idea of evangelism/mission, because you *can't* stomach the thought of having to be involved in it, much less getting to enjoy it and be fruitful (!) then Matthew 28:17–18 is really *bad* news for you! Because you're also included! Jesus has never commissioned just those who do not doubt. All the way through His earthly ministry you can see the doubts demonstrated and voiced by His disciples. And not just Thomas who, because of one incident post-resurrection (John 20:24), put himself in the wrong place at the wrong time, doubted Jesus, and has forever after earned himself the epithet 'Doubting Thomas'.

Who never doubted Christ? Were they disqualified? No. And Matthew 28:17–18, part of the Great Commission, indicates the same again. Doubt your ability as a witness? Doubt your past track record? Doubt your inner motivation? Well, you qualify! The very beginning of verse 18, *at the very least* means that Jesus came to *all* of the disciples, but is as likely to mean that He came *specifically* to those who doubted. So doubt doesn't disqualify you when it comes to evangelism, it just means that you have to let Jesus come to you all the more.

For there was nothing special about the early disciples either. From a bunch of scared 'no-hopers' cowering away in an upper room in antagonistic Jerusalem, they became people who turned the world right-side up! But they were still ordinary. They still got confused. I expect they still doubted. Certainly they made mistakes. All of these things can be found in the remarkable honesty of the New Testament, particularly as evidenced in the Acts of the Apostles and the Epistles. It's made clear by verses like Acts 4:13, where Peter and John are hauled before the religious leaders (it's always the religious people who hinder the work of evangelism!). The text says that they realised Peter and John were 'unschooled, ordinary men'. The original Greek is *ungrammatoie idiotae*, which you can see could literally be translated as 'ungrammatical idiots'! That certainly includes me in. How about you? But the big difference with Peter and John was simply this: 'they had been with Jesus'. They had let Jesus come to them in their humanity, their weakness and their doubting. How about you?

What's the fifth thing Matthew 28:16–20 teaches us? It teaches us in verse 19 that those who evangelise are an invasion force, not a retreating army. For this glorious gospel of Jesus Christ is a 'going' gospel, *not* a 'come to me' gospel. Its mission and its missionaries are expansionist and not retractionist. They take initiative; they are active and not passive. These are those who evangelise.

What else can we learn from verse 19? What do they do when they go? They *disciple*. In the English text we have a verb ('make') and a noun ('disciples'), whereas in the original Greek text it better reads 'go and disciple all nations'. It's about process again. It's about helping people to belong before they necessarily believe. It's worth noting that in this the most famous of all passages on mission in the New Testament, the command and the emphasis is not on doing evangelism, but on discipling. You can't disconnect the two. The New Testament doesn't. The evangelist must be about the business of equipping the saints to disciple. You might find it helpful to look at other books on the purpose and nature of discipleship. You could even try mine, *Inside Out*.

So those who disciple and are being discipled are those

who evangelise. But there is another lesson lurking there for us in verse 19! *Whom* do they disciple? They disciple the nations. Part of the problem with that statement is that historically we've interpreted it to mean that because the gospel of Jesus Christ is a 'going' gospel then those who are *truly* involved in evangelism are *probably* missionaries. They have already 'gone' to the nations. This was one of the great divides between the church and the missionary societies of the nineteenth and twentieth centuries. It's probably put more people off evangelism and mission in their true sense than it's put them on. It has certainly been used as a 'cop out' by means of which many of us have let ourselves off the hook when it comes to evangelism. If I'm not called to the nations, am I called to evangelism? If the UK is a Christian nation (surely no one can believe that any more, if it were *ever* true?) then is there a need for me to be involved in evangelism here? The answers, of course, are YES and YES!

The confusion and the excuses are based at least in part on a misunderstanding of the phrase 'all nations' found in verse 19. Yes, it is valid to interpret that as a commission to other countries. But the Greek phrase translated 'all nations' is the phrase *te ethne*, which more properly and more inclusively means 'all people groups'. It's the same root word that gives us 'ethnic/ethnicity'. So the command of the Great Commission is more properly to go to every people group. The UK is heaving with different people groups! And you fit some of them! This verse is not a reason to avoid evangelism in the UK, any more than it's a reason not to go to the nations. It's not either/or, it's both/and. We are going to do some work on this in Chapters 6, 7 and 8, where we will identify what our people groups /networks actually are and how best we reach them.

This passage also teaches us that (as with all of the teaching of Christ) it was never meant to be delivered to and obeyed by a small, historical and select band of specific followers of Christ. For buried there right in the midst of verse 20 are the seeds of multiplication! Jesus' command as part of the process of discipleship was to teach those that His original disciples reached with the gospel *everything* that he had taught the Twelve. So everyone who follows Jesus gets taught to teach everyone else to go and make other disciples. Simply reach others and tell them to reach others! By a process of multiplication the Great Commission of Christ echoes down across the millennia and ripples out across the world, stretching out over 2,000 years and more than 2,000 miles to impact the heart, mind, life and moral choices of you and me!

My last comment on this passage is that, according to Jesus, it's when *this* is going on that *then* He'll be with us. How very significant that the very end of Matthew's good news about Jesus Christ echoes the very end of what is in effect the Jewish Bible with the same promise (have a look for yourself at 2 Chron. 36:23).

PASSAGE 2: ACTS 1:8

You will receive power when the Holy Spirit comes on you; and you will be my witnesses in Jerusalem, and in all Judea and Samaria, and to the ends of the earth.

What can this passage teach us in answer to the question 'Who evangelises?' First, the interconnection between the *power* of the Holy Spirit and the *purpose* of witnessing. In this verse there is a direct correlation; the purpose of power is proselytisation. The word translated 'power' is the Greek word *dunamis*, which is the same root word that gives us the word 'dynamite'. This is real, explosive power! But in the New Testament the power of God is never disconnected from the *person* of God and the *purpose* of God. We're not just talking about some kind of supernatural 'power encounter' here. When I pray for people to be filled with the Holy Spirit, or to be physically or emotionally healed, or to be delivered from demonic influence, I don't just want them to fall over, or shake like a leaf, or laugh like a hyena, or even bark like a dog! I don't want them opening their eyes and saying, 'Wow, that was powerful!' What I want more than anything is for people to open their eyes and say, 'Wow, I really met Jesus!'

Since Jesus has ascended back to His Father, the contact person for us now on the earth is the Holy Spirit. It is the Holy Spirit who is the conveyor of God's power to us and through us. Indeed in the whole of the New Testament there are only three things that are directly defined as the 'power of God'. Each of the three directly refers to the gospel. In Romans 1:16 the apostle Paul describes and equates the gospel as the power of God to an end purpose; namely salvation: 'I am not ashamed of the gospel, because it is the power of God for the salvation of everyone who believes.' The second definition of the power of God is found in 1 Corinthians 1:18, where Paul maintains that 'the message of the cross ... is the power of God'. And then in verse 24 Paul uses the phrase, 'Christ the power of God'. So if you really want to know and experience the power of God as conveyed to you by the Holy Spirit you must be involved in witnessing, for it is there that the power of God is made manifest; the gospel, the cross, Jesus Christ.

The second thing that Acts 1:8 can teach us is that witnessing is more about identity than it is about function. It has more to do with who you *are*, than what you *do*. This is a hard lesson for many of us, and especially for most evangelists to learn, as most of us tend to start out as rampantly insecure, driven activists (I speak from personal experience!). But this truth is fundamental to our walk with God. It applies at a very much wider level than simply witnessing. If we don't bottom this one out then most of our Christian life, many of our relationships with other people, and the extent to which we grow to understand and love ourselves, will all be driven by a kind of 'performance equals worth' mentality. Put another way, I'll end up believing that as the evangelist I will only be as good as my last talk. My security, self-image and self-worth will be determined by how many people got saved last month.

This is to fundamentally misunderstand two essential facts about the gospel of Jesus Christ. First, that it is a gospel of grace and not of works. And second, that in nine separate places the Old and New Testaments exhort us to learn 'to love our neighbour *as we love ourselves*'. This is a double command. We aren't allowed to love our neighbour and hate ourselves! Indeed, if we do hate ourselves then we'll find it very difficult to love other people. This is because we will not believe that we have anything to give away, and also because we're in fundamental disagreement with God Himself, Who has valued our life at the price of His Son Jesus Christ. But if our identity in Christ is more important than our function for Him (and it *is*) then we'll be better able to love God and love our neighbours as we love ourselves.

This is an inherent part of evangelism. The way that we believe that God sees us will radically affect the way that we believe God sees others, as well as the way that we see others. Ultimately evangelism is about loving the lost. Christ Himself demonstrated this; before He ever did a single miracle, raised anyone from the dead, cast out any demons, healed the sick, or forgave any sins, God looked out of heaven and declared to a watching world, 'You are my Son, whom I love; with you I am well pleased' (Mark 1:11). God's pleasure in His Son was based on relationship, not on performance.

So who evangelises? Those who are full of Holy Spirit dynamite power (the gospel, the cross, Jesus Christ) and who are learning that witnessing is more about who we are than about what we do. It's amazing how many times I have deliberately misquoted Acts 1:8 and never been corrected by Christians in the process. Most of us automatically and subconsciously read it as, 'You will *do* witnessing in Jerusalem', rather than, 'You will *be* witnesses'. The first is an action; the second is a state of being. After all, God never called us to be 'human doings' but to be human beings!

There's one other lesson that we could validly squeeze out of Acts 1:8. The verse ends with what seems to be a deliberate geographical progression. *Where* are we to be witnesses? According to Jesus, first in Jerusalem and then onto Judea, Samaria and finally to the ends of the earth. If you were to look at this sequence on a map, the lesson would become more obvious. Jerusalem was where the disciples were actually at. So witnessing starts where we are at, to inhabit the territory/geography where God has placed us. But surely it isn't just about geography? Jerusalem was also about a cultural context. The disciples were to witness to those with whom they had much in common – fellow Jews. This is where we start, with those around us, nearest to us, most like us, those with whom we have some degree of communality/mutuality.

The command then moves on to Judea. To the Jew this was the second kingdom. There was still much in common, but Judea was a little further afield, not only geographically, but also culturally. In our desire to be witnesses we shouldn't only be looking for those who are the same as us to be impacted by the power of God, but also for those who are *similar* to us. Here our similarities help us to reach across and to bridge the gaps formed by our differences.

And after Judea? The command progresses to Samaria. This is more challenging! For the Samaritans were sworn enemies of the Jews, and would have nothing to do with them. They were more marked by their differences than their similarities. There was active enmity involved. To witness to a Samaritan would be to place a Jew way beyond their comfort zone. We'll come back to this in Chapter 9 when we look at the story of the woman at the well. And after Samaria? Well, then it's to the ends of the earth, which for me includes Portsmouth and for you includes wherever you live!

So, who is it who evangelises? Those who seize the opportunities that geography and friendships afford them, but are not restricted by these. Instead they look around for initial points of contact with those who are only similar to rather than the same as themselves. And to widen the gospel net still further, they are prepared to embrace those who are utterly dissimilar, even their enemies. Am I describing you? And if I'm not, could I be describing the person you are determined you should become?

One last point on this. Please note, witnessing across this sequence is like throwing a rock into a pool; the ripples move outward from the centre concentrically at one and the same time. You don't get one ripple from the centre that breaks on the shore before the next ripple begins! And so it is with this sequence of witnessing. We don't wait until we have thoroughly covered Jerusalem before we moved on to our Judea, Samaria and so on. No, we look for God to use us in all of these areas at once. Being aware of the different circles will help us devise different strategies to reach different people groups. For no one approach in witnessing will meet every situation or fit every person. Worth remembering? I think so.

PASSAGE 3: ACTS 2:14

Then Peter stood up with the Eleven, raised his voice and addressed the crowd ...

It's not unusual for this verse to throw up some very strange reactions in training sessions. It can seem a little out of context. Because it's so short it doesn't seem to say very much. It has even prompted as the answer to the question 'Who evangelises?' – 'Peter'! But the context of this verse is great.

First off, of course, it's about the birthing of the church at Pentecost. Please note that the church wasn't birthed in the upper room, as many assume. The church was birthed in the marketplace, when the disciples left the upper room and began to demonstrate the power of God with supernatural signs and wonders (gifts of the Holy Spirit still available today) to the people round about them. This may seem a small point, but if you believe the church was birthed behind closed doors in the privacy of existing followers of Christ, the danger is you will perpetuate that model. Church will be something for the select few, indulged in behind closed doors! But if you see church as something to be demonstrated and given away in the cut and thrust of the marketplace, then that approach can have a striking (and healthy) effect on your spirituality and witnessing.

It's true that in the passage that succeeds this verse Peter adopts the role of spokesperson. It's he who explains the supernatural outpouring of God's Holy Spirit. It's he who, for the Jews present, relates to the context of the Old Testament. He then makes the connection to Christ, describing His death and resurrection, and it's Peter who explains what his listeners must do to be saved. This looks like classic 'old-paradigm' evangelism! It's the specialist approach. It's the preached word. It's the appeal with a response. As an evangelist I'd certainly settle for the 3,000 or so who were added to the number of the disciples that day (Acts 2:41)! But is it really old paradigm, or does it show us something different?

We shouldn't be surprised that it was Peter who was the mouthpiece that day. After all, he was one of the 'triumvirate'; the three disciples (Peter, James and John) who came in for particular mention out of the Twelve and to whom Jesus took special pains to give added moments of experience and revelation. (If you haven't picked that up before, have a look through one of the Gospels – Mark would be a good place to start.) Peter often comes across in the Gospels as a rather hot-headed, impulsive, insecure individual with a tendency to shoot his mouth off before engaging his brain. You've only to think of his attempt to walk on the water (at least he was the only one to get out of the boat!); his promise to build three altars (two of them highly inappropriate!) on the Mount of Transfiguration; his rash promise never to deny Christ and even to die for him (cock-a-doodle-doo!); and, after refusing to let Jesus wash his feet prompted Christ to explain that He must, Peter has the over-the-top reaction of 'Wash me all over!' Certainly I can relate to this larger-than-life, insecure, bold but impetuous big mouth! But how does all this help us answer the question, 'Who evangelises?'

I need to take you back to the text. It *does* show us something different from the specialist approach of the old paradigm. The focus may be on Peter. But look what the verse actually says. Peter *wasn't* on his own. This *isn't* a solo effort. This is not the specialist approach, not about 'God's man of faith and power for the hour'. What the text actually says is that Peter '*stood up with the Eleven*'. This is about *team*. Who evangelises? *We* do, together. You're not in it on your own. It doesn't all depend on you. A keen sportsman friend of mine used to say, 'To achieve a dream, be part of a team.' This is never truer than in the realm of personal witnessing. Even friendship evangelism. It's not just about you and your friends. Their salvation doesn't just depend on you, simply because you are their friend. Personal witnessing, friendship evangelism; who evangelises? We all do, but we don't do it alone.

PASSAGE 4: 1 PETER 3:13–16

Who is going to harm you if you are eager to do good? But even if you should suffer for what is right, you are blessed. 'Do not fear what they fear; do not be frightened.' But in your hearts set apart Christ as Lord. Always be prepared to give an answer to everyone who asks you to give the reason for the hope that you have. But do this with gentleness and respect, keeping a clear conscience, so that those who speak maliciously against your good behaviour in Christ may be ashamed of their slander.

We have a remarkable aptitude, with our Western mind-sets, to individualise and personalise everything. Oftentimes I read Scripture looking for what God will say to *me*, rather than what He would say to *us*. It's a bit like the words of the old Sunday-school hymn: 'You in your small corner, and I in mine'. We can make the mistake of thinking that because our walk with Jesus is a *personal* one, it's also an individual one. But the Bible is clear. I'm part of a body. My sin is both personal and collective. My forgiveness is likewise. And my outworking should be the same. If I don't have a personal relationship with Jesus, then I'm nothing, but if I don't also have a corporate expression of that, then likewise I'm nothing (1 John 3:14–18; 4:19–21). Yet still I can use the same highly individualised filter to interpret Scripture. But with very few exceptions, this is not acceptable. The Bible was written to collections of people, rather than to individuals. Similarly it was preserved for us at enormous cost (often the lives of the martyrs), not merely in order that we might be afforded some historical glimpse into the life of the individual – Paul, Peter or Mark or someone. Rather we have the Bible so that eternal truths and values might be eternally applied to 'us plural'. In the vast majority of cases, whenever we read the word 'you' in the Bible it's not just addressing me, but us. It's 'you plural', not 'you singular'.

So the 'you' of the passage from 1 Peter 4 cannot be evaded as though applying to someone else. It's written to the church. It's almost certainly a circular letter meant to be read aloud to the many. It's written to you and me. The directives contained in this passage on to whom and how to witness apply to us. That's the first point. But what else can we learn from this passage?

This is the classic passage that tackles the Christian discipline of apologetics, the practice of dealing with or answering difficult questions concerning the faith. The word 'apologetics' has a different meaning from the word *apology*. Apologetics is not about learning to say to your not-yet-Christian friend 'I'm really sorry, I'm so sorry. I'm really, really sorry but I'm a Christian!' Rather, the word 'apologetics' comes from the Greek word *apologia*, which occurs in this passage at verse 15. It simply means 'to give the reason for the hope that you have'. So who evangelises? Those who have reasons, which they can explain. This demands you and I do our 'homework' when it comes to those reasons. It's not enough to know what we believe. We must also know why we believe. If we're to take these verses seriously then we must be prepared. We must have done the work in advance. This is not difficult to do. You don't have to be an academic. Nor must you have a blind faith. Faith is not blind. It's not a leap in the dark. It's a step into the light. More of this at the end of this chapter, because first there's something more important than our answers to difficult questions.

The overriding thing that we can learn from this passage is not to do with giving right answers. It's to do with having a right attitude. In this passage there's a huge preponderance of words that deal with attitudes: 'eager/not frightened/hope/ gentleness' and 'respect/clear conscience'. These attitudes derive from the command in verse 15 to 'set apart Christ as Lord' in our hearts. In Jewish thinking the heart was not the centre of emotions and affections. For the Jew the emotions and affections were symbolically centred in the bowels! That would certainly lend a whole new dimension to today's Valentine cards, wouldn't it?! No, for the Jew the heart was the centre of your personality, character, choices. This is where you set apart Christ as Lord. The emphasis of this passage is not on having the right answer, but having the right attitude. It's not about winning an argument and losing a friend. Or even worse, losing a convert. This is more about winning and wooing.

So who evangelises? Those who count themselves in. Those who put Christ at the centre of their beings. Those who let

Him adjust their attitudes, who do not fear, do not get arrogant and defensive, but who are gently humble and who respect their questioner. We can't do less than give people our respect, because that is precisely what the gospel does. The gospel of Jesus Christ restores human value and dignity and bestows respect again on those who inherently don't deserve it. If that's what the gospel does for you and me, we dare not treat others differently.

PASSAGE 5: EPHESIANS 4:11–13

It was he who gave some to be apostles, some to be prophets, some to be evangelists, and some to be pastors and teachers, to prepare God's people for works of service, so that the body of Christ may be built up until we all reach unity in the faith and in the knowledge of the Son of God and become mature, attaining to the whole measure of the fulness of Christ.

Can we agree that so far Scripture teaches that the answer to the question, 'Who evangelises?' can be summed up in two succinct words: 'We do'? But this passage seems to put something of a spanner in the works. We've had some lively debates in training sessions provoked by this reference. Surely we are back to the specialist again? It's a small step from there to 'leave it to the evangelists!' After all, if God only called 'some' to be evangelists, and if I'm not one of them, then surely I can count myself out of evangelism?

Not so. That's because this passage makes it very clear indeed that the role of the evangelist, as noted in Chapter 2, is for the equipping of the saints. And what possible kinds of 'works of service' could an evangelist equip the saints for? For evangelism! The evangelist isn't there merely to do evangelism. The evangelist is there to train others to do evangelism. Of course, you can't really train someone to do what you are not doing yourself; this is called hypocrisy! As Christian missionary Albert Schweitzer noted, 'Example is not the best form of leadership, it's the *only* form.' So the evangelist does evangelism, first because we are *all* called to do it; second because that's how we grow in Christ (Philem. 6); and third because she loves doing it, can't help herself and is good at it! (1 Cor. 9:16). But perhaps the most important reason why the evangelist does evangelism is, fourth, because it qualifies her to teach others and so multiply the effectiveness of the spread of the gospel through the lives of all the saints.

Ephesians 4:11–13 places more emphasis on the works of the saints than on the work of the evangelist. And that emphasis is born out statistically throughout the New Testament. Let me show you what I mean. When God first called me to be an evangelist I struggled against the idea for several years, because I had a very limited, negative understanding of what an evangelist was. Eventually I gave in to God, which is always good to do sooner rather than later. Ultimately He gets His way anyway, so you might as well surrender quickly, particularly since His will will be for the best anyway. So rather grudgingly I decided to make myself feel better by proving from the Bible just how important evangelists were! I was utterly convinced that I served a God who was 'not wanting anyone to perish' (2 Pet. 3:9). A God who wanted '[people] everywhere to lift up holy hands in prayer' (1 Tim. 2:8). It only stood to reason that this God who was into evangelism must have crammed His Bible full of references to evangelists. I embarked on a word search, determined to make myself feel important and to boost my ego. You can imagine, then, my consternation when this revealed that the word 'evangelist' appears in the New Testament a grand total of only three times! I couldn't believe it!

A text without a context is a pretext!

But what I did learn from this was that the context in which a word appears was very important. I guess you might expect this, if God in His economy was only going to use the word 'evangelist' three times. The first place it appears is in Acts 21:8. Here the word appears uniquely as a description of an individual: 'Philip the evangelist'. But it's a bit of a passing reference. In fact, if I'd been God, I wouldn't have called Philip 'the evangelist' here at all! I'd have called Philip 'the evangelist' back in Acts 8, some seventeen years previously.

This is the famous occasion where Philip is supernaturally removed from a revival going on in Samaria, out into the desert on the Gaza strip. A lesson there, perhaps? That evangelists should never be content to remain where the blessing of God is being poured out, but should also look for where it isn't, in order to see where it could spread? Anyway, it's at this point that Philip has his God-ordained appointment with the Ethiopian official. The official gets converted and returns to Old Testament Cush (modern-day Ethiopia). And as far as we can trace through church history, this is how the gospel of Jesus Christ got into Africa. You're probably aware of the remarkable revival that continues to sweep that continent. Surely *that's* the context in which to call Philip 'the evangelist'? And yet it isn't until 13 chapters and 17 years later that God bestows that description upon Philip. Why? The context is clear. Because by then Philip is rooted, known and accountable in the life of church at Caesarea. Not only that, but his family is in order; his daughters are prophesying. I don't think that's a wasted description. In the economy of God we're getting a glimpse into the role of the evangelist; that he and his family are to be rooted into the life of church, and not separate from it.

The second place in the New Testament where the word 'evangelist' is used can be found in the passage we're currently looking at, Ephesians 4:11–13. Again the lesson is the same. Paul is writing to a city church, and he is writing about the establishing of church. Once again the context of the evangelist is the context of church.

The third and final place where the word 'evangelist' occurs is 2 Timothy 4:5. And again the lesson is the same. As Paul writes to his young protégé (some commentators give us to understand that Timothy may have been as young as 17) he's at pains to stress that even if he's not an evangelist, Timothy should do the *work* of an evangelist. And what was Timothy's context? Church. Indeed, not only church, but a resource church of some 25,000-strong, which as a teenager Timothy was leading!

Incarnational communication

We begin to see something of the context of the evangelist, and that context is the church. Why is it so important that evangelists are rooted into church life, and not simply sent out from it? Because church is about incarnational communication. It's the way that God has always communicated. God is love, but He demonstrated that by pouring His love into creation, and making people in His image. When people blew it, God communicated through His prophets, but they didn't simply use words, they incarnated their message. Fleshed it out. Some of them ran naked through the streets, or lay on their sides staring at piles of dung or married a prostitute. And although God incarnated His communication in all these ways previously, now supremely (Heb. 1:1) He has incarnated His message in His Son Jesus Christ, Who is the Word made flesh. Now the second body of Jesus Christ on earth is, of course, His church.

So church is about incarnational communication, which is the best possible kind of communication. Don't *have* a message. *Be* a message. This is why the evangelist must be found in the context of church. For church is about community, it's localised, it's the family of God demonstrated. It's a gospel people, where once there wasn't a people (1 Pet. 2:9–10).

Consequently church is able to profile the people of God. It is the proper demonstration of the supernatural unity that the love of God can create among disparity. This is the unity that is written of in 1 Corinthians 13 and Ephesians 4:3 and that Christ prayed for in John 17. Do have a look at these references. Church is the proper corporate context for praise and warfare and the taking of territory and turf. Church is the depository of the resources of God (particularly people). And so, for all of these reasons, church is where the evangelist must be found. Church carries with it the potential for accountability, mitigating against the unhelpful distraction of the 'lone wolf' or utter crank! In church is to be found the potential of safety, team and of Christ's authority delegated along with all the saints to the evangelist, because in church life the evangelist is in turn under authority (Matt. 8:9). If you would exercise authority you must be under authority, even as the centurion recognised that Christ was under the authority of His Father (John 5:19). These are some of the reasons why we are commanded not to neglect meeting together (Heb. 10:25).

There is a consistency about church. It's not about 'hit and run' evangelism, or 'fly by night' spirituality. Rather, it becomes a model to bridge the credibility gap, which can all too often exist in the life of individualistic Christians who live by the dictum, 'Do as I say, don't do as I do.' When I am witnessing to my neighbours I need to be able to point to a community of God's people who are reaching out for their own transformation and that of the society around them. Church becomes a prophetic model to all the nations (Gal. 3:28). The lone evangelist may be able to use words to proclaim the gospel. She may be able to seek God for wonders and warnings to confirm the gospel. But on her own she cannot fill the gospel out with works; for that, church is necessary. And since the gospel is words, wonders, warnings and works, the church is necessary.

Indeed, the keys to the kingdom of God are given to the church (Matt. 16:19). The Old Testament is the prophetic backdrop to this same emphasis on the body of Christ. In Isaiah 9:8, the government of God's kingdom rests on the shoulders of the Messiah; that is, on the body. Now, since the New Covenant, we are the second body of Christ on earth. Christ is the head of His church, and the government of His kingdom rests on his body, the church.

Why so few?

So the three occasions where the word 'evangelist' occurs in the New Testament are all in the context of church, and the gift of the evangelist is given to the church by Christ Himself (Eph. 4:11). This makes perfect sense because (as we have seen in Chapter 1) it is Christ who builds His church and not us (Matt. 16:18)! But at the end of the day, the word 'evangelist' is still mentioned only three times! Why, if God is so into evangelism? The answer is simple. When it comes to evangelism, the *least* important person is the evangelist. The *most* important person is the witness. In the New Testament the word 'witness' (in Greek *martus*, which gives us the word 'martyr' – isn't that encouraging?) occurs 66 times more than the word 'evangelist'! This is the correct emphasis of Scripture. The main weight of evangelism lies with the witness. The reason why the Greek word for witness gives us the word 'martyr' is because many of the early Christian witnesses were martyred for their faith. Isn't it strange how although martyrdom is listed as one of the spiritual gifts, it's one that we don't often ask for? Perhaps that's because it's the one that we get to use only once! In a Jewish court of law the concept of a witness was a familiar one. As in an English court of law, a witness could testify only to what they personally knew first-hand. They were never allowed to use hearsay evidence. So it is with you and me in our witnessing to Christ. It must be first-hand testimony of our personal knowledge and experience of Jesus. Not second-hand or inherited hearsay. We get nothing of God second-hand. God has no grandchildren; only children.

Vive la différence!

Since Scripture uses two words, there is a difference between the evangelist and the witness. What is that difference? Perhaps it can best be summarised as follows. Everybody is a witness. If you profess the name of Christ then you are a witness to Him. You're either a good witness or a bad witness, but a witness you are. So all of us are witnesses if we are disciples of Christ. And the role of the witness is from first-hand knowledge and experience to point the way on to Christ. A witness does that in all the ways discussed in all the passages outlined above.

But *some* witnesses are *also* evangelists. The evangelist will have a particular propensity for witnessing. They'll have a proclivity for proselytising. They'll tend to find and make opportunities where others won't. There will be a greater consistency toward reaping and not just sowing. Evangelists are more likely to see people become Christians and with greater regularity than will the witness. This isn't to say that the witness won't see people saved. They can and they must. But the evangelist will see it more often. And more importantly, the evangelist will also be used by God as an *agent provocateur*. They'll be an encouragement, an exhortation, an equipper, an edifier, an example and an irritant in the life of the saints, individually and corporately (church), towards effective mission. They will view everything in the life of the Christian and the church through the focus of evangelism.

The evangelist will push against the great enemies of mission in church life, namely introversion, comfort and settling, religion and tradition. The evangelist, at least initially, is often something of a rough diamond in terms of their character, not least because of their ability to reach out to the lost. They will need and should increasingly want to be held into church life with the firm hand of friendship and fellowship as they with the other hand reach out. Otherwise the danger is that the evangelist will spin off out of corporate church life into evangelistic activism. The evangelist does tend to be a doer, a breakthrough person, someone who God will often use for pioneering evangelism and to break up tough territory, but they should also be a trainer, a developer, a releaser of people, and increasingly able to work in consultation with leadership teams, to which the evangelist must have access (see Chapter 1).

I really hope this chapter has served to convince you in your head and your heart of the answer to the question, 'Who evangelises?' Like it or not, do it or not, the answer is still you and me. But I would also like to think that there's been enough provocation and a few handy hints along the way so far to actually get you excited about the prospect of witnessing. As we go on in this book we're going to get increasingly practical, with hot tips and tools to aid us in our fruitfulness. But before we get there, there are a couple of important topics we must tackle. The next one is crucial. If we are to develop lifestyles that necessitate our gossiping the gospel, then it's probably important that we know what that gospel is.

GROUPWORK

1. See if together you can find additional scriptures in answer to the question 'Who evangelises?'
2. Reflect further on the scripture passages used in this chapter, and discuss them together.
3. Hear one another's stories of how God has used/is using you as a witness.
4. Pray for one another in your commission to be a witness.
5. Prepare yourself (1 Pet. 3:15) by reading and discussing together one or more of the following books:
   Questions for Life' – Nicky Gumbell
   It Makes Sense – Stephen Gaukroger
   More than a Carpenter – Josh McDowell
   Evidence that Demands a Verdict – Josh McDowell
   More Evidence that Demands a Verdict – Josh McDowell

Chapter 4

WHAT IS THE GOSPEL?

I was brought up in the kind of church (the denomination isn't important, but they were very Methodical!), which was quite good at telling you *what* you should believe. By and large the church and its teaching was well founded on the Bible, and I'm very grateful for my roots. However, they were less good at telling you *why* you should believe it, and even weaker at the application; *how* you should live it.

That scenario is not particularly uncommon. But if it's not uncommon, it is frustrating. You'll have discovered that the more and more information you accrue, the more and more frustration you experience. This is because you know what you should believe, but you don't know why and you don't know how to live it. And so the cycle is complete; information alone leads to frustration.

But clearly information isn't a bad thing. When God saves us, He saves the whole person, which includes our minds. We have already seen how important it is to have our mind/paradigms redeemed. God makes this clear in Scripture, for example in Hosea 4:6, where He tells us that 'my people are destroyed from lack of knowledge'. So what is it that prevents information from leading us down the path of frustration? The answer lies in revelation. Information plus revelation leads to transformation. Revelation is the God-breathed dynamic that releases life, a sense of purpose and a sense of destiny. The Bible alludes to this need for vision/revelation in Proverbs 29:18, 'Where there is no revelation, the people cast off restraint.'

So there I was, around the tender age of 15, brought up in a church that was higher on information than it was on revelation. Lack of how and why meant a lack of application, which meant an increase of frustration. And that was my position when it came to witnessing. My church had told me very clearly that I was right to believe in evangelism. Indeed, if I believed in Jesus, then I ought to be witnessing. But they were less adept at telling me why, or how. So, out of a sense of growing frustration and not a little guilt-induced duty, I embarked on my own methods of witnessing. I share them here with you as an example of 'how not to ...', so please don't emulate my early attempts at evangelism! They are in direct contrast to the notion of friendship evangelism, which we will look at in Chapters 6, 7 and 8.

GANGSTER EVANGELISM!

I used to set out on my own on witnessing forays at lunchtime on the school playing fields. My method was simple; first I would find a suitable 'victim' who was known to me (at least I got that bit right!), smaller than me, and on his own. Then I would confront him face to face and ask the question, 'Do you believe in God?' When, as it usually did, the answer came back 'No', I would then punch him on the nose! 'Do you believe in God *now*?' Ruefully rubbing his nose, and by now in a rather nasal voice, the answer was usually again (although rather less assured), 'No'. Then I would punch him again! So it went on, with varying degrees of resistance, until finally my hapless victim would say 'All right, all right, I believe in God.' At which point I would throw up my arms, with an inward response of, 'Hallelujah! Another convert!'

It's an amusing scenario – isn't it? Although not, I guess, if you were on the receiving end of the punches! And it is, of course, somewhat exaggerated. But only somewhat. I really would seek out an individual I knew, who was on his own. I would confront him face to face. I would badger him and argue him into acquiescence, if at all possible. I did it because I knew I had to. I did it because if he ultimately agreed with me (however much in word only) it made *me* feel better. I did it this way because I didn't know why I had to, or how to do it differently.

Imagine then, my surprise, when one day a friend of mine approached me and said, 'You believe in God, don't you, Pete?' I was so surprised that I'd said the word 'yes' before I knew whether I ought to have done or not! 'So what *is* a Christian and *how* do I become one?' my friend rejoined.

I could have fallen over backwards. I very nearly did. I never expected someone to *ask* me. I'd never expected someone to *want* to become a Christian. And now I was faced with a terrible dilemma. It was almost like a biblical scenario: 'What must I do to be saved?' Only I couldn't remember the answer from Scripture! And moreover, (and here's the point of this chapter), I didn't know what the gospel was! A series of jumbled thoughts flashed through my mind. What do I need to tell him to do? What is it he has to believe? Suppose he asks me why! How do I lead him to Christ? What *is* the gospel? Suppose I try to explain the gospel to him and only included half of it. Would he only be 'half born again?' All these years later I am reminded of the birth of our first child, our daughter Freddi, whose head emerged into the world with one contraction, while the rest of her seemed perfectly happy to stay where it was! So there she was, half in and half out, which was neither helpful nor comfortable for either daughter or mother! Would it be any better to be 'half born again'?

The story does have an ending. It really did happen. By the grace of God I stumbled on the idea of taking this guy Nick through the Catholic catechism, which as a practising Catholic he had on him. I remember going through it with him phrase by phrase, pointing out the bits I agreed with, and that I thought were from Scripture, and the bits I didn't and thought weren't. At the end of it he expressed interest, but I don't think it went any further than that. Many years later I met his step-sister at an evangelistic event I was doing in London. She herself had recently come to faith in Christ and told me that Nick still remembered our friendship (and his catechism) from all those years earlier.

If only I'd had a ready grasp of what the gospel is, what the gospel does and how we can encounter it. If only I had been ready. Now, my question is, are you? If not, then I really hope this chapter will be of some help to you.

WORDS, WORDS, WORDS ...

It might help if we start off with a clearer understanding of the words that the New Testament uses in connection with the gospel. The word 'gospel' comes from an Old English word 'godspell', which meant then what its modern counterpart means now: 'good news'. And so we have the first four books of the New Testament (Matthew, Mark, Luke and John) referred to as the 'Gospel according to' its author. Or in other words, the 'Good News according to Matthew, Mark, Luke or John'.

We know a little bit about these four writers. Matthew, whose family name seems to have been Levi, was one of the original 12 disciples. He was unusually selected by Jesus as he was a tax collector, part of a feared and despised element of the Jewish community. Mark, on the other hand, wasn't one of the original 12, but does seem to have tagged around the disciples on a number of occasions. It's quite likely he makes a fleeting appearance in his own Gospel, described as the young man who fled from the scene of Jesus' arrest, leaving behind his clothes in the process (Mark 14:51–52)! At the time of the events Mark writes about he was probably around 15 years old. Mark's Gospel was written in Rome and its eyewitness source was Peter, and the Gospel has the distinction of being both the shortest of the four and also the earliest, being the source for much of the material found in Matthew and in Luke. For this reason those three Gospels are usually referred to as the Synoptic Gospels, those that see things together from the same perspective.

Luke was not one of the 12 disciples either, but was clearly an earlier follower of Jesus and a doctor by profession. He was also the author of the Acts of the Apostles, both books being written for his friend Theophilus. The fourth and final book of 'good news' was written by John, who was one of the original 12, and refers to himself (modestly not by name) in his own Gospel as the disciple 'whom Jesus loved'. At the time of the events of his Gospel, John was probably in his late teens.

BACK TO BASICS

So 'gospel' simply means 'good news'. But if we press further back into the Greek words used in the New Testament, we learn even more. In Greek, the word 'gospel' is *euangelion*. And while this word does mean 'good news', it actually means much more, which will help us in our understanding of what constitutes the gospel. The New Testament writers were masters of communication. They knew that the gospel of Jesus Christ was so radical that on occasions it would demand entirely new words to be coined, in order to convey entirely new concepts. But they also knew, as a basis for good and ready communication, that wherever possible it would be better to adopt words in common current usage and adapt them as necessary to explain the good news about Jesus. This way more people would more easily understand and potentially experience the realities of the gospel.

Euangelion is one such word. The Gospel writers were familiar with the word. And so too would their hearers and readers have been. Certainly the word wasn't a religious one. It derives from military life. To understand it fully, I want you to imagine the following scene.

Imagine that you are an inhabitant of a fortified city, such as Samaria, round about the time of Christ. There are many examples in the Old Testament; see 2 Kings 6 and 7. One day bad news is brought to the elders of the city. Originally elders were guardians of geographical territories covering groupings of people, and in the New Testament church elders also exercised the same geographical and outward-looking focus, never being content to merely 'pastor the flock'. This bad news is of an imminent attack by your enemies. Attack on a fortified city usually took the guise of a siege. This was a terrible and protracted way of losing to your enemy involving, as it did, long, slow starvation, deprivation, disease and even cannibalism (2 Kings 6). A siege was to be avoided at all costs. So the elders of your city would order the city army to engage with the enemy across the plains, before they could reach the city walls, encamp around them, refuse egress or exit, block all trade and food routes, and poison any external water source.

And so your city's army begins its march across the plains towards its enemy. By day the cloud of dust can be seen at their feet. And by night the campfires can be seen burning in the distance. Comes the day when the two armies clash, and the sound of the ensuing battle echoes across the plains. The elders gather by the gates of the city. City (and church) gateways – points of egress and exit – have always been important in both the Old and New Testament, and were the place where strategies were devised. Hence Christ's declaration that 'the gates of Hades will not overcome' the church (Matt. 16:18). Above the elders on the battlements the watchkeepers scan the horizon with diligence, looking for evidence of either defeat or victory. At this point a lone rider is seen charging across the dusty plain towards the city walls. As he gets closer the watchmen strain their eyes to make out who it is. Is he all that is left of your army? As the lone messenger draws up to the city walls a sigh of relief goes around. At least it's one of your men. Then, with bated breath, the watchkeepers, the elders and the people of the city listen to catch his words as the messenger shouts them up to the gatekeepers. 'We've won!' The city is in uproar with riotous rejoicing! The battle has gone against the enemy! The victory is yours!

Forgive the narrative approach, but it's the best way I can think of to depict the real meaning of the work *euangelion*. The fact is that in Old and New Testament culture the message that is proclaimed to the city is the *euangelion*. It is ultimate good news. Like many Greek words, it has a number of meanings packed into the one word. It carries with it the concept of victory. Of freedom from fear and oppression. Of salvation from injustice and destruction. Of the defeat of an enemy. *Euangelion* literally means 'life-changing victory news of a military defeat'. And what of the herald on horseback? The one who proclaims the good news? He is known as the *euangelistes*, a word we've seen before in Chapter 3, used only three times in the New Testament, and which we translate as 'evangelist'.

There are a couple of other words worth looking at to aid our understanding of the gospel. The first is the Hebrew word *malkuth*, which in the Old Testament is translated as 'kingdom', and its Greek equivalent in the New Testament *basileia*, which is used 102 times in the Gospels alone! This word is made important by its common linkage to the gospel. So this glorious gospel of wonderful good news is the gospel of the kingdom. This army has a Captain. This kingdom has a King. This gospel establishes a territory. It's the gospel of the kingdom. All of the Gospel writers refer to this. Most do so interchangeably, so the gospel of the kingdom is the kingdom of God. The exception is Matthew, who calls the kingdom of God 'the kingdom of heaven'. This is because he was writing predominantly for Jews and didn't want to offend them by using God's name, Yahweh.

And the other word worth noting? This is the Greek word *scandalon*, which also on occasions gets translated 'gospel' in the New Testament. As may be obvious, this is the root for our words 'scandal' or 'scandalous'. There *is* something about this wonderful good news, of safety and freedom in the realm of a King, which is scandalous. The New Testament writers were more than hinting at the affront to human pride that is the gospel. This is good news, which cannot be earned.

Which isn't deserved. Which cannot be bought. Which can't be stolen. It *is* a scandal in the way the gospel crosses cultures and classes, boundaries and barriers, and it's scandalous precisely because the poorest people on the edges of society, who can afford it least and need it most, can best receive it. Scandalous also because this King, this God, deliberately lowers Himself and identifies with His subjects as a servant.

HOW TO SPOT THE GOSPEL?

In searching through their religious books of the law and the prophets, the Talmud and the Misnah, the Jewish nation had identified four things that would confirm to them that the kingdom of God had arrived in their midst. They were right in all four. They were also right in thinking that these four things would be ushered in by the Messiah of God. The expected Messiah was, as the name means, one who was in special relationship to both God and His people. What many of them didn't get right was that Jesus is the Messiah. And that the good news/gospel of the kingdom of God is at one and the same time the gospel of Jesus Christ. So how did the Jews expect to spot this good news of the kingdom? And how does the New Testament confirm that in Christ this good news has indeed come? Here are the four signs of the kingdom that the Jews were looking for.

All present and correct

One sign of the good news would be that God was Himself present and immediate once again. That the God of the transcendent (distinct from, greater than but not separate from His creation) would again become the God of the Imminent. The God of the Old Testament had been constantly interventionist. He had created a theocracy. The miraculous abounded. He spoke through His prophets. His angels were encountered. The Shekinah glory of God (literally the weight of His presence) was not unknown. God's Spirit had been upon His people.

But then for 400 or more inter-testamental years God had gone silent. People had begun to think of Him as an absentee landlord. This is why, with the advent of John the Baptist, people sat up and took notice. Why they flocked out in their hundreds and thousands into the wilderness to hear him, for the rumour was that once again God was on the move. God was speaking to His people, God was promising His Messiah. It was almost as though Elijah (that great eschatological prophet who had foretold the coming of the Messiah) was back in town! And suddenly the God Who had been everywhere, became the God Who was somewhere. Became Emmanuel. God with us. So the gospel is validated by the presence and immediacy of God once again. Supremely, of course (Heb. 1:1), in His Son Jesus Christ. But also, now that Jesus has gone back to be with His Dad in heaven, through His Spirit. Could this be why every major evangelistic move of God across the ages, every revival of His church, has been hallmarked by a strong and immediate presence of God? One has only to think of the 1904 Welsh Revival, when miners would collapse prostrate in the street in repentance as they walked past the doors of the chapels. Or of the tangible presence of God, which it was reported could be felt a quarter of a mile away from the gospel hall in Azuza Street, California, during the 1906 revival, which sparked the still-raging fire of black Pentecostalism across the world.

We are the champions

The good news was also expected to demonstrate the defeat of Satan. The New Testament makes this clear in 1 John 3:8, where it's explicitly stated that Christ came 'to destroy the devil's work'. Defeat of the kingdom of darkness is complete. A defeat against Satan and all of his occult and demonic powers. A defeat over sin, both paying its penalty and breaking its power. A defeat over sickness, as healing was blood-bought by Christ as a part of the atonement. And a defeat over suffering, the kind of relational and mental torment with which the enemy would so readily afflict us. Satan's defeat was demonstrated in face-to-face, close-quarters combat at the temptation of Christ as recorded in Luke 4.

It was made manifest to the world at the cross of Christ, when every principality and power was shown to be defeated, and sin was nailed to the cross with Jesus (Col. 2:13–15). This fantastic passage draws its analogy directly from a practice of Roman conquering armies. On overrunning a nation, the Romans would gather that nation's potentates, rulers, judiciary and so on, and parade them through the streets of Rome in slatted wooden cages on wheels, while the Roman citizens pelted them with rotting vegetables. They would then be presented as defeated to the Roman emperor, who was, of course, supposed to be a deity. When Christ died on the cross this is precisely what He did with every ruling spiritual principality and power, presenting them to the One true Deity, God, His Father.

The defeat of Satan is demonstrated at the cross of Christ in three directions at once. For first, the cross works *God-ward*. Ultimately, *all* sin is against God and God alone, as only God is perfect and able both to judge and forgive sin. That's why King

David – after committing adultery, failing to lead his people into battle and arranging the murder of Uriah (the husband of Bathsheba) – could still declare to God 'against you, you only, have I sinned' (Psa. 51:4). So the cross of Christ had to be effective God-ward, as it is against Him that we transgress, Him that we offend. But since humanity is fallen and sinful, we are incapable of paying this price. Only God Himself could pay the price. Therefore the price paid on the cross had to involve God Himself. And so it did in His Son Christ.

Second, and at the same time, the cross of Christ had to be effective *people-ward*. That's because it was people who had chosen to turn against God, to sin, to offend Him. As well as the cross involving God, it also had to involve a person, and so it did, for Christ is both fully God and fully human.

Finally, the cross had to be effective *Satan-ward*. For when people turn their back on God they turn towards Satan. In sinning we played right into his hands. We gave him legal permission to affect the earth and creation. Satan is a legalist; give him space and he will invade it. So in buying back, redeeming, rescuing humanity, the God-Man had to assuage the legal demands of Satan. If this all seems rather complicated, I can do no better than recommend you read the chapter of *The Lion, the Witch and the Wardrobe* by C. S. Lewis, where the sacrifice and resurrection of the Christ-figure Aslan is dealt with. Another way to understand the totality of Christ's sacrifice is to picture the visual symbol of the cross itself. For the cross of Christ reaches upwards toward God, downwards toward Satan, and outwards toward people.

Salvation

The third sign Jews were seeking to indicate that the Messiah had ushered in His good news was that salvation would come.

In the Old Testament, in the first century and for some Jews ever since, this was interpreted as meaning national salvation, the vindication of the nation state of Israel, the establishing of the Hebrew people, the final overthrowing of all their oppressors and, specifically in Jesus' time, the complete routing of the Romans. The Jews expected a Davidic warrior-like king, who would ride in on a white charger and smite the Roman enemy.

This notion was typical of the Zealots. A small band of political activists, during the time of Christ, they believed that by waging a kind of holy war (jihad) they could attain a position in heaven closer to the right hand of the Messiah! The more Romans they killed, the nearer they got to the kingdom of God. This is a bit like Obelix in the *Asterix* cartoon stories, collecting Roman helmets, only not as amusing!

Indeed as the Jews expected this warrior Messiah to bring about national salvation, they also expected a second and more shadowy Messiah figure, who would be the suffering servant prophesied about in Isaiah. What they hadn't realised was that Christ would combine the warrior king and the suffering servant as one, would wage warfare in the heavenlies and not against flesh and blood (John 18:36), and would Himself suffer. The New Testament words used for 'salvation'/'saved' come from the root *sotereo*, and more properly mean not only 'salvation', but also 'healing', 'forgiveness', 'wholeness' – and indeed get translated this way in the New Testament. New Testament salvation is about peace with God, peace with yourself and peace with others (including extending forgiveness to your enemies). It's the nearest New Testament equivalent to the Old Testament concept of *shalom*, which is weakly and loosely translated as 'Peace be with you'.

'Once you were not a people ...' (1 Pet. 2:10)

Fourth and finally a sign of good news brought by the incoming Messiah would be that He would create a gospel people. A good news people, produced by a gospel of freedom (Gal. 5:1). This inclusive good news as taught in the New Testament was too radical for the Jews. This gospel determines the nature of the church of Jesus Christ, which takes us back to Chapter 1. This church would include Greeks and not just Jews. It would include free people as well as slaves. Scythian as well as barbarian (i.e. the extremes of cultures). Male as well as female (Gal. 3:28; Col. 3:11). This Messiah Jesus would break down the dividing walls that exist between peoples (Eph. 2:14 – where the reference is specifically to the low dividing wall in the outer precincts of the Jerusalem Temple, beyond which the Gentiles were not allowed to pass). This gospel people would form one united body in a way so unique that the Greek writers had to coin a new word to describe it: *sonsoma* (Eph. 2:16). God's presence, Satan's defeat and salvation coming was never meant to be just about an individual thing, but was always expected to create a gospel people.

These four signs are authentic aspects of what the gospel is. Can we build on this, and develop our understanding, deepen our appreciation of the gospel? Let's look at some key building blocks, or elements of the gospel.

KEY ELEMENTS

If we're to get a firm grasp of the gospel, what it involves and how it's fleshed out, we need to seriously consider each of the five following key elements. Think of it like a human hand. To work properly and efficiently all five digits of the human hand must be present and operational, working together in harmony. This is also the case with these five key elements in order to have the fullest expression of the gospel.

Presence

This is an essential part of the gospel of Jesus Christ. It's a recognition of the fact that by our very presence in the world, in difficult situations, alongside people's lives, we can have a tangible effect for the good. This presence works in at least two ways. It works, because the Bible says nothing about faith without works (James 2:14–26). It is impossible with any integrity to tell a starving child that God loves them, and we love them, and leave them in their need. Or a homeless person. Or someone suffering from Aids (Matt. 25:31–46). And so we flesh out our faith with actions, because actions speak louder than words. God loves people and so we love people. God blesses people and so we bless people. Acts of kindness are a vital part of the gospel of Jesus Christ.

Mother Teresa, a supreme example of this gospel approach, said it succinctly: 'I do everything for Jesus, with Jesus and to Jesus.' This is what St Francis of Assisi meant when he used the now famous phrase, 'By all means preach the gospel and use words if you have to.' This kind of social action has always been at the forefront of every great gospel movement. Moreover, the best kind of social action actually leads to social transformation. This can be exampled by the activities of some of the greatest evangelicals: think of William Wilberforce and the abolition of slavery, or William Booth, founder of the Salvation Army, and the amazing work that he began in the East End of London. Of Florence Nightingale and her impact on healthcare, or Elizabeth Fry and prison reform. It is why on a very much smaller scale my church is involved annually in the best-run and cheapest summer play scheme for children in Portsmouth. We demonstrate the gospel by our presence.

But presence also works in another way. A way less tangible, but just as real in its effect. The presence of Christ in and through us can change and affect the spiritual atmosphere and, in so doing, have a direct and positive consequence. Before the days of zero tolerance on the streets of New York, crime rates were soaring. For some months as an experiment the New York Police Department invited Roman Catholic priests to ride with them in the squad cars. Even though they didn't get physically involved in many of the confrontations (which were often too violent to allow them to), the very presence of people who loved God made a significant difference and, for the months that the experiment ran, crime rates plummeted dramatically.

This kind of 'presence evangelism' is dramatically demonstrated in Scripture by the healings that followed the falling of Peter's shadow in Acts 5:15, and is alluded to in 2 Corinthians 2:15, which talks about you and me being the 'aroma of Christ'. I can remember, as a young evangelist, being enormously taken by this verse and praying repeatedly that God would work this in me. My desire was that there would be something of Christ about me, which would be attractive, provocative and serve as a blessing to those around me, even if I said nothing. I can remember trips on the underground in London (I was based in the East End of London working with Youth for Christ) and looking around the carriage, praying for the individuals on whom my gaze fell, that they might be blessed and know something of Christ, even if I didn't get into a conversation with them. It's worth trying. You may see the fruit of it, or you may never know, but it's got to be better than going through life closed down to the people around us.

So, in summary, the gospel of Jesus Christ involves presence. Or, put another way, it is fleshed out by works.

Presentation

But if the gospel involves presence, it also involves presentation. If the gospel is about works, it's also about witness. Jesus, the supreme communicator, was often at pains to use everyday situations and events to graphically illustrate His explanations of the gospel. One day it might be a visual aid such as a fig tree, the next a dramatic story about a mugging, but always Christ made careful presentation of the gospel in ways visual as well as audible. He was, after all, the word made flesh (John 1:14). This is why Doctor Luke in his Acts of the Apostles could write to his friend Theophilus that the book was about 'all that Jesus began to do and to teach' (Acts 1:1). So a key element of the gospel is to do with presentation. Deliberate and careful opportunities for witness. These might include strategies and programmes of street work, of door-to-door visitation, or of specific-events evangelism – pub quizzes, cabarets, *Alpha* courses, etc. We come back to this at the end of the book.

Proclamation

The earlier quotation attributed to St Francis of Assisi is both provocative and frustrating. It provokes us towards fleshing the gospel out with our actions and challenges our apathy and hypocrisy. But it's frustrating because it has been used by Christians through the generations as a 'get-out clause'. These are the Christians who are like Alaskan rivers – they have frozen mouths! They are unprepared to back up their good deeds with good explanations. The reality is that it's not a dichotomy, works or words; it is not either/or. It's both/and. Our lifestyles should be sufficiently different and radical (not by dint of being religious and irrelevant, but rather because of values such as selfless generosity, faithfulness, honesty, integrity) to provoke attention, and demand explanation. In terms of the gospel, my lifestyle should be a demonstration which demands an explanation.

The New Testament Gospels are not just full of the activity of Christ, but also of His words. The gospel *is* proclamation. It is words. Words are important in Scripture. Jesus is the Word made flesh. God caused creation to come about through His spoken Word (Gen. 1:3). Christ calmed the storm because His spoken Word is more powerful than the elements (Mark 4:39). The New Testament uses six different verbs in connection with the gospel, so heavily does it place an emphasis on explanation. The words are to testify, proclaim, preach, herald, teach and to argue.

Power

But lest we make the mistake that we can somehow rationalise someone into the kingdom of God, the Bible is clear that the gospel consists of more than just works, witness and words. It also consists of wonders and warnings. We saw earlier that Jesus, the cross and the gospel are described uniquely as the 'power of God'. In the Gospels the arena of evangelism, the clashing of two expansionist kingdoms (more of this in Chapter 10) consists largely of healings and deliverance. The power of God is made manifest 14 times in Mark's Gospel alone (and it's the shortest!). There are mentions of healings and demonic encounters leading to deliverance. In all, 25 per cent of the entire content of the Gospels deals with such incidents. And if you add the book of the Acts of the Apostles, that percentage goes up to 30 per cent.

This is why I'm not surprised if, when I am preaching the gospel, it is accompanied from time to time by demonic manifestations. Indeed, biblically I ought to be surprised if it isn't. It's why 'healing meetings' provide a good platform for the presentation of the gospel. It's why I am as likely to pray for someone who is not yet a Christian to be physically healed as I am to pray for a Christian. Indeed in my experience it's often easier to get a not-yet-Christian healed than it is to see a Christian healed! This is because Christians often build up years of rationalised unbelief as to why God might heal others but not them! The not-yet-Christian, on the other hand, seems to adopt the attitude of 'Well, I suppose if there *is* a God, He could heal me.' God seems to adopt the attitude with the Christian of 'Show to Me that My Christ is your Lord'. Whereas with the not-yet-Christian, God seems to take the approach '*I'll* show to *you* that My Christ is the Lord.' And just as the New Testament evidences the gospel with signs and wonders following it (Acts 14:3; Heb. 2:3–4) so too it does the same thing with warnings. Perhaps the most obvious example of that is the deaths of Ananias and Sapphira (Acts 5), and another example can be found in Acts 13:6–12.

Persuasion

The final key element of the gospel touches more on attitude than on content. But then, the New Testament tends to place more emphasis on attitude than on content! Through our Western eyes we all too often put the emphasis on actions and on doctrines. But the New Testament writers (from their Jewish culture) are more at pains to talk about who we are, not what we do. And then to talk about how we do what we do, rather than merely what we do. For example, the emphasis in the Epistles on unity is based on a plea towards relationships and how we treat one another, rather than on doctrine, and so perhaps you would expect to find a similar emphasis when it comes to the gospel; the attitude which is most consistently encouraged is one of persuasion. This is in order that the gospel might win people.

So in Mark's Gospel Jesus repeatedly tells those He has healed or delivered to keep quiet. This isn't because He didn't want to be the Messiah. It's not because He didn't want people to know. There is no secrecy theory, as some commentators have imagined. Rather, it's because Jesus wanted a gradual, evolving revelation of Who He is, and a fuller understanding of the Messiah as both Warrior King and Suffering Servant, in order that *more* people might buy into relationship with Him, not *fewer*. This is about persuasion. It's not enough to simply serve people with works; it's not enough that they have power encounters of God (positive wonders or negative warnings). It's not enough that they hear our words or experience our witness and attend our presentations. We simply can't get away with dumping the gospel on people and walking off if at first they don't respond. The gospel of Jesus Christ makes it incumbent upon us to seek to win people. Paul is clear on this when he lays out his manifesto for the gospel in 1 Corinthians 9:19–23.

SAME OLD, SAME OLD?

We're still not there, though, are we? Surely there must be a sufficient number of places in the New Testament where the gospel is presented to people, to enable us to confirm its content and its consistency? Well, yes and no. Certainly Jesus teaches much about His Father and about the kingdom of God. In fact these are the two predominant themes of His teaching, both private and public. And He does teach about forgiveness. And commands people not to sin again. His teaching in the Sermon on the Mount (the largest single collected public teaching in the Gospels) epitomises the gospel lifestyle and the kingdom of God on earth. Jesus also spoke at some length about the consequences of sin and about hell. If you look at the five key elements noted above you'll find all of them present in the life and ministry of Jesus. And because in Jewish culture 'the one sent is as the one who sends' (one of the Jewish definitions of a disciple) you'd expect to find the followers of Jesus doing the same as Him as they seek to fulfil the Great Commission. And so you do.

But when you then go to passages in the New Testament to explore and examine *precisely* what constitutes the gospel, you will find quite a disparity of approach. This is because, while the gospel of Jesus Christ is the same the world over and across the ages, people are not. So the gospel doesn't change, but its application and the approach that is made does. This is about effective communication. It means that the gospel isn't confined to a particular culture. In technical terms it's called 'missiological contextualisation'! At the end of this chapter I'm going to give you four biblical passages you can work through in order to compare and contrast (sounds like a school exam!) the similarities and differences of approach. Enough to say for now that the following areas seem to apply consistently across the different contexts:

1. There always seems to be an historical and cultural context.
2. Central to the message is the person of Christ.
3. Repentance of sin (often alongside forgiveness) doesn't get missed out.

4. Neither does the cross of Christ, often with an explanation as to its efficacy.
5. The resurrection! It's amazing how many gospel explanations/preachers I've heard that stop at the cross, and fail to mention the fact that the cross is empty and that Christ rose from the dead! No resurrection, no good news!

Keep these five statements in mind when, at the end of this chapter, you check out the scriptures mentioned.

THE DETAILS

I couldn't write a chapter like this without us having a quick overview of some of the glorious statements made about the gospel in the New Testament. Obviously you don't have to look up every verse, but I've included them for the sake of completeness and, if you want to look them up, you can. There's enough material here for you to memorise or meditate on to keep you praising God until you pop your socks! But let's start with a couple of quotations. The first is from the great reformer Martin Luther.

The gospel is not in truth that which is written in books and set down in letters, but rather a spoken message and a living word and a voice which sounds out into the world and is publicly proclaimed that it might be heard everywhere.

Martin Luther knew that the gospel outworked is dynamic; it changes things. Theologian U. Becker put it this way:

This gospel is effective speech, a powerful saying, a word

which brings its own fulfilment. In the mouth of its messengers God Himself speaks. He speaks and it is accomplished, He commands and it is done.

So what happens when the gospel is unleashed?

- It releases – Acts 10:38; Matthew 12:28–29
- It heals – Luke 10:9; 4:18–19
- It creates faith – Romans 1:17
- It brings salvation – 1 Corinthians 15:2; 1 Timothy 1:15
- It brings judgment – Romans 2:16; 2 Corinthians 2:14–17
- It reveals God's righteousness – Romans 1:17
- It brings fulfilment of hope – Colossians 1:5,23
- It intervenes in the lives of people – Acts 2:37
- It creates church – Acts 8:4–14
- It produces kingdom – Luke 11:20; Acts 28:31; Matthew 6:33
- It produces new birth – 1 Peter 1:23–25; John 3:5; 2 Corinthians 5:17
- It brings peace – Ephesians 2:17; 6:15

And the effects on us?

- We receive righteousness from God – Romans 3:22
- Our sin (that word with 'I' in the middle, originally an archery term meaning 'to fall short of the target', nowadays more easily understood as selfishness), iniquity (corruption), guile, trespass (rebellion, being where we shouldn't be) is dealt with – Romans 3:23
- We are justified. To be justified in God's eyes means we are counted to have come up to His standards. Easily understood as 'JUST as IF I'd never sinned' – Romans 3:24; 5:1; 1 Corinthians 6:11
- We have redemption (just as you would redeem a

mortgage, i.e. pay off/buy back a debt) – Romans 3:24
- There was a sacrifice of atonement (making us 'at one' with God) – Romans 3:25
- Peace with God is ours – Romans 5:1
- We are safe from God's wrath – Romans 5:9
- We are reconciled to Him – Romans 5:10
- This all by way of a gift from God – Romans 5:16
- Which carries with it eternal life – Romans 5:21
- Meaning we are 'no longer slaves to sin' – Romans 6:6
- And are able to count ourselves 'dead to sin but alive to God' – Romans 6:11
- This brings us from death into life – Romans 6:13
- And sets us free from sin – Romans 6:18
- Rather making us slaves to righteousness – Romans 6:18
- Which of course ultimately means that we are slaves to God – Romans 6:22
- In Whom there is 'no condemnation' – Romans 8:1

Pretty good, eh?

And how did this happen?

- Jesus the sinless became sin for us – 2 Corinthians 5:21
- We of course had to be sanctified/made holy/sprinkled/set aside – 1 Corinthians 1:2
- So that we could be reconciled to Jesus – Colossians 1:20
- Who effected a vicarious substitution on our behalf – 2 Corinthians 5:21; Galatians 1:4
- Allowing us to receive full inheritance rights – Galatians 4:5–6; John 1:12; 8:31–36; Romans 8:15–17
- And so we are forgiven – Ephesians 4:32
- Or in classic terms, we are saved – 1 Thessalonians 2:16
- Born of God – 1 John 3:9

- That is, born again – 1 Peter 1:23; John 3:7.

IN A NUTSHELL ...

So far so good (news)! But *can* we sum it up? Can the gospel be condensed/crystallised into but a few words, to express the very core/kernel/*kerygma* of the gospel? The answer is, yes, we can. We need to, for the sake of memory and effective communication. So here it is:

For God so loved the world that he gave his one and only Son, that whoever believes in him shall not perish but have eternal life. (John 3:16)

There it is. In a nutshell. And what's more, chances are you've already memorised it. It's probably the most famous verse in the Bible. In that one verse you have all of the elements of the gospel, in a form that you know and can remember. In a way that you can use as a mental checklist to ensure that in your lifestyle and in your explanation you *are* sharing the gospel and not something else. Always remembering that the gospel is about a person, not a set of propositions. It's not rules, not regulations, not rituals. It's relationship.

For God ...

The beginning of the verse reminds us that the beginning of the gospel is God. The initiative in salvation lies with Him. Not with us. Romans 5:8 puts it this way: 'While we were still sinners, Christ died for us.' When you and I were a million miles away from God in our sin, darkness and rebellion, at that point He launched the rescue mission. Creation began at God's initiative (Gen. 1:1). So too does re-creation. In the Old Testament God began with the heavens and the earth and finished with people. In the New Testament God begins His re-creation with people and ends with a new heaven and a new earth (Rev. 21:1–4).

... So loved ...

This glorious gospel of Jesus Christ is a gospel of love. For we have discovered that at the end of the universe there is, not a monster, but Love. It didn't have to be that way. But it is that way. The gospel is about good news, not bad news. It's not about us making people feel bad. It's not about punishment, fear or condemnation. It's about love. So our job is to be good news and to have good news for people. It's not even our job to convict people of sin. That is the work of the Holy Spirit. He will make people feel bad when they are bad. Our job is to so live and explain the good news that people realise that what they have is bad news. That there is a better way to live.

... The world ...

This is translated from a Greek word, *kosmos*, which actually means 'the whole of created order'. The gospel is an inclusive gospel. It's for everyone and everything. No one who wants it can't have it. So you have never met a person who isn't 'saveable' and, what's more, you've never met a single person whom God didn't *want* to save (2 Pet. 3:9). Those two concepts combined make a powerful stimulus to evangelism!

... That He gave ...

This gospel is a giving gospel. To a world on the make and on the take, God gave His Son Jesus, which in turn means that all we can do is receive or reject. We can't earn it. It's free, but it will cost us everything. Total surrender to Christ.

... His One and Only Son ...

There it is! Smack in the middle of the verse, which is itself right at the heart of the gospel, is the Man Himself, Jesus Christ! He *is* the gospel. What is the answer to every question? Jesus. What do we want to leave people with? Jesus. This then is the ultimate, pared-down answer to the question, 'What is the gospel?' The gospel is Jesus Christ. If you remember nothing else from this chapter, but you remember that, then we're doing OK. (Could have been a very short chapter, couldn't it?)

... That whoever believes in Him ...

To the Jewish mind-set, to believe was to do. It's an alien (actually Greek) concept that you can believe something and do nothing about your belief. In the UK, the majority of us believe in God, yet the majority of us live as though He wasn't there. To Jewish writers of the New Testament, that would be a contradiction in terms. When Jesus said and John wrote, 'whoever believes in Him', they weren't talking about some philosophical and totally conceptual and rational set of propositions. The gospel isn't about making mere mental assent to an idea. It's not, like Alice in Wonderland, about 'believing six impossible things before breakfast' and then you're saved! It's about faith in action. It's about trust in a person. Believing something is very different from believing in someone. The gospel is about personalised faith/trust/action/commitment in and to the person of Christ.

... Shall not perish ...

The consequence of this gospel is that we are saved from something. There is a huge debate raging at the moment, even in evangelical circles, about the nature and longevity of hell. Does it exist at all? Who is it for? Is it a conscious state? Does it go on forever? Some of the answers are hard to come by, and cannot be validated by using a proof text out of context. But of this we can be sure. If you aren't saved, you're lost. Not merely unfortunate. Not simply misguided. But lost. And just as eternal life doesn't kick in when we snuff it, but starts here and now, so too for the many people who are currently lost. They aren't just lost when they die. They are lost here and now. They have no reason for living. They haven't discovered their destiny. They don't know why they are alive. They don't know Who made them. Only dig a little below the surface and you'll find many people are all too aware of hell. They live in it currently. But the gospel of Jesus Christ saves us from this in the here and now, and also in the there and then.

... But have eternal life ...

And we are not only saved *from* something. We are also saved *to* something. This isn't a gospel of 'pie in the sky when you die'; rather it's 'steak on the plate while you wait!' It brings a sense of perspective to any of the trials and tribulations that we suffer in the fallen world. It helps us to understand that the day of tribulation is just that – a day, a limited period of time – and that that day will end. It's a comfort for those who remain, when those who have died did so in Christ. Having just lost both my parents, both of whom were saved, this is indeed a very real comfort. It's about discovering your destiny. And your final destination. It brings perspective and wisdom to that into which we invest our lives. And excitement about the returns!

Like the original meaning of the word 'gospel', the promise of eternal life firmly establishes us on the winning side. In very real terms, we will die, but we will never end. There will come an age, a new heaven and new earth (not a disembodied spiritual state where we float around with wings on fluffy clouds with harps), when there will be no goodbyes. No sickness or suffering. No Satan or sin. When we will enjoy the inexhaustible and unfathomable God forever. And enjoy one another forever also. Where there will be eating and feasting. And the satisfaction of wise stewardship over creation. A state and a place where the wildest, most ecstatically enthralling and pleasurable experience you could ever conceive of or imagine will pale into all insignificance in the moment-by-moment light of existing with Christ. This is all a part of the glorious gospel of Jesus Christ.

PHEW!

There we are then! If all that isn't exciting, I don't know what is! Just thinking about what we've received and what we have to give away is enough to make us get on with it, I hope! In the next chapter we'll look at why we do exactly that. But we'll also look at what stops us.

GROUPWORK

1. Read the following passages together in a group: John 3:14–21; Acts 2:14–41; 10:34–48; 17:16–33; and then …
2. Draw out from each passage what you consider to be the key elements of the gospel as it is explained there.
3. Is there any overlap/similarity in these key elements across the four passages? If so, why?
4. In each case, why do you think this particular approach was taken?

Chapter 5

WHY BOTHER?

If I was teaching this kind of stuff in your church (and that forms a large part of what I do) chances are we would start off by brainstorming around the question, 'Why do we evangelise?' Then, as people fired off ideas from around the room, I would jot down their answers on one half of an acetate or flipchart sheet. After a minute we would change the question to 'Why do we *not* evangelise, or what stops us?' and I would then jot these down on the other half of the same sheet. The worrying thing is that we usually end up with more reasons why we *don't* evangelise than why we *do*! Perhaps it's just the places I go to; I'm sure that wouldn't be true in your church!

If what I said in Chapter 1 is correct – that right thinking produces right attitudes, which lead to right motivation, which stimulate right actions – then it's important that we look at our motivations. Wrong motivations rarely produce right actions. You can get a positive pragmatic end result from right actions derived from wrong motivations even in connection with the gospel (Matt. 7:21–23), but it has still got to be better to question our motives.

In God's grand scheme of things, remember, it is *who* we are, not what we do; then *why* we do what we do; then *how* we do what we do that really matters to Him. So looking at it biblically, *why* do we bother to witness? I have found the following five biblical reasons to be very encouraging, exciting and stimulating when it comes to the 'why' of evangelism. Here is the first:

BRINGING JESUS BACK

The second coming of Jesus Christ has got to be one of the most under-taught and underrated events in the Christian faith. I think in the past that I have tended to believe it notionally rather than in actuality. I could give it the nod of mental assent, I could fill in the philosophical tick box on the statement of faith, but I don't think I would allow the enormity of it to get through to me. It's rather like that bit in the film *Titanic,* where the diver on the wreck finally recognises that he'd 'Never let her get to me, never let it get in. It was just a story to me until now.'

But Jesus *is* coming back. The first disciples and the early church were so gripped by this reality that they lived their lives in the light of it. They gossiped the gospel with a sense of urgency because of it. They planted churches all over the then-known world because they expected it imminently. And when some of them died (Paul had to address this situation at the church at Thessalonica; 1 Thess. 4:13–18) before He had come back, there was turmoil. Some of this is probably because some of Jesus' words were taken out of context or misunderstood (Mark 9:1). Certainly the first disciples were eager to pin Jesus down to a time and a place (Mark 13:4–5). But look at it this way. The fact that Jesus *didn't* return to that first generation church means that He is more likely to return to yours and mine! Every generation that has ever lived since Christ went back to be with His Father has tended to think that it was in the 'end times', and yet the reality is this: every generation is more nearly right than the last one! The fact is that for you and me, this *is* the last generation; we only get the one! This is not a rehearsal. Every generation is responsible for reaching its own generation. And one day there will come a generation that actually does it. Why not yours or mine? There will be a generation who literally never dies. I wouldn't mind that; how about you?

The New Testament predominantly uses three Greek words to describe the second coming of Christ. The first is *parousia*, the second is *epiphaneia*, giving us the word 'epiphany'. And the third is *apokalypsis*, giving us the words 'apocalypse' and 'apocalyptic'. Combined together, the root meanings of these three words describe and fill out our understanding of the second coming. They indicate that what was previously invisible will be made visible to all, and that it will be the universal, visible, dramatic return of the King in full Kingly splendour and glory. What the New Testament *doesn't* do is tell us when; and indeed Jesus warns us that if anyone says that he knows then beware, as that man is a fraud (Mark 13:21–22).

But while the time is not specified, the conditions are. That is why I can categorically tell you that Jesus is not coming back the day that you read this book! When asked when He was coming back, Jesus told His disciples that only His Father in Heaven knew that. (This statement in itself casts interesting light on our understanding of Christology – how and to what extent Jesus is both fully God and fully human. The kenotic theory – from the Greek, *kenosis*, meaning 'to empty' or 'to pour out' [see Phil. 2:7] – pushes towards answers to these questions.) But what Jesus does tell us is that before His return the glorious gospel, which we looked at in the last chapter, must first be 'preached to the whole world as a testimony to all nations' (Matt. 24:14). We have already learned that the phrase 'all nations' comes from the Greek *te ethne* and more properly means 'every people group'. So Jesus isn't coming back unless and until this gospel is preached to all the people groups. But tantalisingly, in Revelation 7:9 we see a prophetic glimpse of the fact that the gospel *will* reach all the people groups, and therefore Jesus *is* coming back. Have a look at this verse for yourself. For there will be representatives before the throne of Christ from 'every nation, tribe, people and language'.

Perhaps it rests with us?

I have to say that my understanding of Scripture tends to make me subscribe to what has become known as 'the openness of God' theology. I do believe that God knows all things, but the question is, what are the 'all things' that God knows? Does He know all things because all things have been decided ahead of time and we move fixedly and inexorably towards them? Is everything definite and determined? I don't think so. Is it rather that the 'all things' that God knows consist of those that He has fixed, which are definite and determined, and those things which are definite maybes? Has God, Who is a relational being, built into the future and into our decisions the reality of relational choice, with all of its consequences? So that He knows the *outcomes* of *some* things, for He has set them thus. And He knows all *possible* outcomes of the other things, and has an eventuality plan for every possible outcome (such is the size of our God), but in doing so has left many things unfixed and indeterminate, deliberately and precisely because He wants relationship, love and trust with and from us, rather than the creation of a race of pre-programmed robots?

Now, if what I am saying is true, then it could also be true that the time when Jesus comes back *isn't* fixed and determined. Rather, that we are constantly running along the edge of eternity, waiting to flip over into it at any stage at which we fulfil the conditions for that flip. In other words, that the gospel must first be preached to 'every tribe and to every nation'? I do think so.

But you don't have to believe even that. All you have to know is that Jesus *is* coming back, but not until the gospel has gone out. And therefore the first reason why we get involved in evangelism is to bring Jesus back. Our witnessing must be seen in the light of its eschatological significance. Once you start to do that, feeble and paltry excuses like our personal inconvenience or fear levels tend to fade into the background. But is it do-able? Can we achieve it? Yes, we can! And indeed we nearly have. We are closer to it now than we have ever been. You can't be motivated by something that is unrealistic; that is why one element of a S.M.A.R.T. goal is that it is Achievable. We will come back to goal setting and faith targets when we look at friendship evangelism in Chapters 6, 7 and 8. If one of the reasons why we evangelise is to bring Jesus back, let's look at how well we're doing.

I don't know how you feel about statistics. Some people love them. Some people hate them. I certainly don't want to use the following statistics like a drunk uses a lamp post: more for support than for illumination! And I know that you can manipulate statistics to mean anything, often at the cost of common sense. That is a little like the statistic which states that if you have your head in a lit gas oven and your feet in a fridge, your overall body temperature will be comfortable!

Nevertheless, have a look at statistics relating to the remarkable growth of the gospel since the birth of the church in the first century AD. At that time there were around 360 unbelievers for every one follower of Christ. A ratio of 360:1. It took the church of Jesus Christ 1,800 years to grow from 0 per cent to 2.5 per cent of the world's population, which it reached by 1900. That's a long time. But then it starts to get exciting! For it took the church only 70 years to double in size to 5 per cent of the world's population, which it did by 1970. Then only a further 19 years to double in size again to 10 per cent of the world's population by 1989. In the ensuing 11 years to the turn of the millennium the church has more than doubled again so that there are now only four unbelievers for every one believer on the face of the earth! That is a ratio of four to 1. Even allowing for the phenomenal growth in the world's population, which actually is slowing down, Christianity continues to grow in real terms at a phenomenal pace.

Of course the distribution of Christians to non-Christians is not even. There still remains what has come to be known as the '10–40 window' (referring to latitudes), which covers much of the unconverted Muslim world. But even so! Four to one is manageable! How do you eat an elephant? Answer: a bite at a time! This task is now bite-sized!

SATISFYING JESUS

The second biblical reason why we get involved in sharing our faith is because the lost have no right to be! Jesus has already paid the price in full. Why should people stand outside of His blood-bought salvation? How dare they?! Now, you can't love God and not love people (1 John 2:9–10), but even if you do love God and struggle to love people, then at least witness for God's sake, if not for the sake of people. I know it's not either/or, and we will look at the motivation of love for others a little later in this chapter. But the reality is that none of us does anything from entirely pure motives. If we wait until our motives are fully sorted, then we will never do anything. God finds it easier to direct a moving target than a stationary one.

There is a wonderful passage in Isaiah 53:11 where the prophet paints a word picture of Jesus, more than 500 years before His arrival. Included in that description is the telling sentence, 'He shall see of the travail of his soul, and shall be satisfied.' Forgive me (if you need to) for quoting that from the Authorised Version (if it was good enough for Paul, it's good enough for me!) but, you see, I learned it in that version, and in this case I actually think it describes the scene better than some recent versions do. It is a small sentence, but its implications are enormous. In the midst of a heart-rending description of the suffering of the Messianic Servant of God, we are told that Jesus looks at the results/fruit of the pain He goes through (graphically depicted in a prophetic description of the events running up to and including the cross) and that makes it all worthwhile.

What *are* the fruits/results of Christ's sufferings? You and I, of course! But not only selfishly us. But also anyone else who we witness to and see come to faith in Christ. Each time we do that, we add to the satisfaction of Christ. For this whole created order, in all of its awful fallenness, is only kept going at enormous cost to Christ in order that more might know Him.

I think that it's this same idea of satisfying Jesus that Paul alludes to in his letter to the church at Colossae, written from house arrest in Rome around AD 60 to 62. There is a rather odd verse in Colossians 1:24, which talks about filling up 'what is still lacking in regard to Christ's afflictions'. Now this is peculiar, for what *could* be lacking? Was the cross not enough? Was it in some way inadequate and therefore lacking, that something needs to be added? Clearly this isn't the case, nor can it have been the writer's intention. So what *did* Paul mean when he wrote about filling up what is lacking in Christ's sufferings? Well, the only thing that is lacking is that there are not enough people benefiting from Christ's death on the cross! So the way that we fill up what is lacking therefore is by getting more people under the sound of the gospel, more people covered by the blood of Christ. In other words, through evangelism. It is your and my family members, neighbours, work colleagues and friends who do not know Christ who are necessary to fill up the gaps in what is lacking in Christ's suffering; in other words, the salvation of the world.

OBEYING JESUS

It is remarkable how little room for misunderstanding Jesus left in His public and private teaching. It is true that Jesus, in keeping with His Father, always leaves options. But the options tend to come down to whether we obey Him or not. There isn't ambiguity about Christ's command to witness in the Great Commission of Matthew 28:16–20. We looked at this in some detail in Chapter 3. Nor is there much room for debate in Acts 1:8, where Jesus clearly equates receiving the Holy Spirit with witnessing. He doesn't say, '*If* the Holy Spirit comes upon you.' He doesn't say, 'You might feel like being witnesses.' No, on each occasion it is '*When … you will …*'.

I think that we can be grateful that in God's kindness He is actually at pains to give us any number of reasons for sharing our faith, some of which relate to Him, some of which relate to us and some of which relate to the lost. But let's make no mistake; He doesn't need to explain. After all, His ways and His thoughts are higher than our ways (Isa. 55:8–9). Yet in His kindness and generosity He *is* knowable. Still, the bottom line remains for us: if we would name Jesus as Lord/Boss, then we must obey Him. When it comes to witnessing, our only option is obedience or disobedience. If we would be a follower of Jesus, then we must obey and we don't then have an option. But of this much we can be sure; the cost of disobedience is always greater than the cost of obedience. Both for us and for others.

Obedience because …

You will have observed from any children that you know (it's unlikely that you remember from your own childhood!) that children go through different stages and reasons for obedience. I will never forget how this lesson was borne in upon me one day when I was out driving in the car with my daughter Freddi, then aged about three, sitting in the back in her car seat. In those days I had an additional rear-view mirror suctioned to my windscreen so that I had a clear view of the little occupants of the back seat of my car. You can imagine my horror when I suddenly espied Freddi standing upright on her chair, having undone the safety buckle! At the time I was travelling quite fast in heavy traffic on a motorway, and so, unable to immediately pull over, I said in as calm a voice as possible, 'Freddi, please sit down.'

Back in response came the reply, 'No, Daddy.'

I tried again. 'Freddi, what you are doing is dangerous. Please sit down now.'

Once again, 'No, Daddy.'

By now, I confess, I was both increasingly concerned for

her safety, and annoyed at her disobedience. And so in a louder, sterner voice I said very firmly, 'Freddi, *sit down now!*'

Glancing in my rear-view mirror, I saw her sit down suddenly and re-fasten her safety harness. Potential crisis over. Then her little voice piped up with the telling phrase, 'Daddy, I may be sitting down on the outside, but on the inside I'm still standing up!'

The most immature response to obedience is: 'I obey because I *have* to.' This is where most of us start. Some of us never graduate from here. But as we grow in self-awareness, and in maturity, we should move on, to the second stage of obedience, which is 'I obey because I *need* to.' This is a recognition that goes beyond someone's authority over us, but rather begins to recognise that that authority might just be being exercised because of an inner deficiency in ourselves! But obedience because I need to can still carry a kind of grudging resentment, or even a sense of perpetual failure on my part. The third and final stage of developing in obedience is the most exciting one. However, it doesn't obviate the first two, rather it builds upon them. Now I don't just obey because I have to, or need too. I obey 'because I *want* to.' And the New Testament is clear. When it comes to issues like fasting (Matt. 6:16–18), giving (Matt. 6:1–4; 2 Cor. 9:7) and obedience in general, this is the kind of obedience that God wants. This is in line with Old Testament teaching too (1 Sam. 15:20–23).

UNDERSTANDING JESUS

My family and I have a real love affair with the nation of Scotland. Indeed, we believe that God has prophetically called us, and at some point that He will make it clear and possible to relocate there in order to serve that nation humbly with the gospel and to learn from them. It's partly for this reason (and partly because I try to live my life finding any excuse possible to turn every event into an occasion and a celebration), that in recent years a group of our friends has celebrated Burns' Night with us. It is a great thing to do in the cold and dark January that follows Christmas. So this year eight of us gathered around the table and enjoyed cock-a-leekie soup, haggis, tatties and neeps, cheese and biscuits, the odd glass of single malt whisky, speeches made and responded to, and some of Burns' poetry read out loud, complete with terrible Scottish accent!

Some of Burns' lines are memorable. Two that live with me are the following:

O wad some Pow'r the giftie gie us,
To see oursels as others see us!

Of course we can't see ourselves the way that other people view us, because that isn't dependent only on what we are like, but on the filters that other people have as well. I suppose that the more we grow in understanding of ourselves and those around us, the truer our relationships will become.

This is also the case in our relationship with Jesus. The closer we get to Him, the better we understand ourselves. Intimacy precedes revelation. All this is a roundabout way of saying that I really wish I could gain a full picture of how Jesus sees me. I want to revel more in His love for me. For it is His love for me that produces holiness in me. I know that I don't realise anywhere enough just how kind, merciful, generous, safe, secure, loving, forgiving, generous, committed, accepting, approving, affirming, sustaining, protecting and providing God is toward me through His Son Jesus. But I really want to.

Is there a way that I can grow in this understanding? Well, if it is true that intimacy precedes revelation (and it is), then I must grow *closer to Jesus* to understand more about Him. I must also *know more about myself* in order to better receive His intimacy and revelation. I must *know more about our enemy*, in order to avoid the barriers and pitfalls that he would place in the way. But I'm a pragmatist. Even allowing that these three statements are true (and I maintain they are the three pillars on which Christian maturity is based), how do we go about it? The nearest I have found to a short cut in Scripture and in experience is in one of the shortest books of the New Testament. Have a look at verse 6 of Philemon (no, I haven't forgotten the chapter, there is only one!): 'I pray that you may be active in sharing your faith, so that you will have a full understanding of every good thing we have in Christ.'

This then is the fourth reason why we share our faith; because it gives us an increased understanding of the riches of our inheritance in Christ. And the more understanding we have, the more we can give away. What's more, the better we will be at giving it. Given that the riches of Christ are inexhaustible, this is a great cycle to be on!

LOVING LIKE JESUS

This last has to be the most motivating factor when it comes to 'Why evangelise?' For it is love that drives the universe. It was love and not nails that kept Jesus pinned to a cross. And it is this same love that compels us to witness (2 Cor. 5:14). The closer we get to Jesus, the more we feel His love. The more we feel His love for us, the more we feel His love for others. The more you love Jesus, the more you love the lost. It's impossible to truly love Jesus and not love the lost. It's the summary of the law and the prophets: 'Love the Lord your God with all your heart and with all your soul and with all your mind ... Love your neighbour as yourself' (Matt. 22:37–39).

Here are a few places among many where we see love demonstrated in the New Testament. In Mark 5 Jesus does a remarkable thing. He leaves behind a whole crowd of needy and demanding people, gets into a boat, makes a two-and-a-half-hour dangerous journey across a sea, gets out on the other side, deals with one man (Legion the demoniac), gets back in the boat and sails back to the crowd! All for one person. This is the love of Jesus in action. For the sake of an individual whom everyone else had written off and shunned, Jesus spends time and effort, changes His agenda, is personally inconvenienced and is at some danger to Himself. The phrase that describes Legion restored ('clothed and in his right mind') is a technical term, which means he is embarking on a journey as a disciple/follower of Jesus.

It was because of compassionate acts like these that Jesus could teach in Luke 15 with integrity on the parable of the one lost sheep. Because Jesus never merely taught. He *did* and *then* He taught. This is the same Jesus who in Mark 1:40–42 does the unthinkable; He touches the untouchable – a leper – and makes him well. The same Jesus who mixes with tax collectors and adulteresses.

It's not surprising, then, that the shortest verse in English in the Bible is to be found in John 11:35: 'Jesus wept.' For here we see Him at the tomb of His friend Lazarus. It's important, isn't it, to get underneath those words? To actually hear the sound of a sobbing Christ? To see the tears streaming down His face? Comfortable with that? Or do we imagine a rather British, 'stiff-upper-lip' reserve? Lips compressed and a tear brushed from the corner lashes? I don't think it was like that.

The text indicates that this was not the case. When it says that Jesus was 'deeply moved' with compassion, the word 'compassion' comes from two roots meaning 'with pain' or even 'with anger'. Pain for His friend. Anger with the enemy. And the expression 'deeply moved' more literally means 'snorted violently like a horse'! Now that isn't a stiff, British upper lip, is it?

This same compassion for the lost is evident again in Matthew 9:36. Jesus looks out over people and sees them then as they are today; 'harassed and helpless, like sheep without a shepherd'. This is such a vivid picture of people fraught with hassle, scurrying aimlessly and frenetically, without a sense of proper purpose or ultimate destiny. It applied then. It applies now. And Jesus' response to this was to have compassion upon them.

In all of these demonstrations of the love and compassion of Christ we see a reflection of the tender, Father-heart of God. But God is neither male nor female. For He created both women and men, *both* in His image. And so in Scripture we *also* see revealed the tender and soft-hearted Mother-heart of God as well. In Matthew 23:37 this is made explicit. Jesus, from a vantage point above Jerusalem, pours out His heart in such a way that you only wish you could hear the tone of voice that went with the words. Wanting to gather up the people of Jerusalem protectively to Him, Jesus uses an analogy that clearly demonstrates the feminine instincts to shield and to protect.

Let me illustrate. Many years ago I used to work with Youth for Christ, based in the East End of London, and at that time I got to know Graham Kendrick quite well. He was then living on the outskirts of Wolverhampton and had one day gone for a walk in the fields with his children. He came to a burnt-out, blackened barn. On the floor before him he noticed a charred, indistinguishable lump. Stirring it curiously with his foot, Graham realised what it was as he turned it over. A mother hen at the onset of the fire had protectively managed to gather to herself several of her chicks and had sheltered them under her wings. As he turned it over, from beneath the charred and barbecued chicken there ran one or two surviving chicks. A graphic illustration of the sacrificial and saving compassion of the Mother-heart of God.

Of course we shouldn't be surprised that Jesus reveals Himself in this way in the New Testament, for in the Old Testament one of the very names of God Himself indicates the Mother-heart as well as the Father-heart of God. The name El Shaddai literally means God – 'the many breasted One', indicating the way in which He wants to nurture and succour His children.

So we evangelise because we love God, and we love God because He first loved us (1 John 4:19) and enables us to love others as He loves them. I think that supremely this is *the* motivation for witnessing; the compassion of Christ.

WHAT STOPS US?

Just as there are five demonstrable biblical reasons why we should get involved in evangelism, so too there are five predominant hurdles we have to overcome that would hinder our witnessing. For the rest of this chapter I would like to run through these five inhibitors, and then we will finish in the action section looking at first steps to assimilating the positives and getting rid of the negatives.

1. That's not right ...

Behind every action lies a feeling and behind every feeling lies a thought. Wrong thoughts lead to wrong feelings, which lead to wrong actions. Or sometimes to non-actions. So if you and I have been brought up in the kind of church, or with the kind of theological understanding, where teaching on evangelism is unscriptural, unbalanced or non-existent, then our feelings towards evangelism will be adrift and our actions or deliberate non-actions will be unhelpful. In my experience of working across quite a broad band of mainstream Christian denominations, including the new churches, it seems to me that there are three common strands of wrong teaching when it comes to witnessing.

The first strand centres around the approach that we highlighted when we looked at the old paradigm. Broadly speaking, this takes the view that evangelism is the job of the expert. It's for someone else to do. With this mind-set in your church you are really lucky if you have an evangelist in your congregation, because most such churches claim that they don't! So evangelical churches adopting this approach tend to advertise for an evangelist, or more likely employ a youth worker! At best this person is then expected to gather around herself a small posse of committed enthusiasts, which in turn becomes the church's evangelism or perhaps schools' team. But the reality remains the same; the work of the many is given to the few. Meanwhile the rest of the church can sit back with the self-satisfaction of corporate responsibility sated and personal responsibility avoided! After all, 'It's not my ministry!'

The second strand of wrong teaching is less common these days, not least because churches that adopt it tend to be dying out! This errant teaching indicates that God has already predestined those who will be saved, and that therefore, at least by implication, He has also predestined those who will be lost! This is a rather extreme form of Calvinistic or reformed theology. Pushed to its caricature, the Calvinist Christian is the one who, on falling down a flight of stairs, stands up at the bottom, brushes himself down and says, 'Thank God that's over with!'

It comes from a misunderstanding over precisely *what* is predestined in Scripture. In Ephesians 1:4,11 it is the *how* of salvation that is predestined, not the *who*. In other words, it has always been through Christ and Christ alone that it was predestined we should be saved. What was *not* predetermined was *who* should be saved. Who gets saved depends on the openness of God and the gift of free will given to us because we are made in the image of God. God Himself has a free will and uses it on occasions in Scripture to change His mind (Gen. 6:7; 18). But if you adopt the reformed position it can lead to evangelism as solely the prerogative of God! The people who will be saved will be saved anyway, notwithstanding your involvement, and witnessing to those who would be lost anyway is a waste of time! Since you can't tell the difference between the two and only God can, what is the point?

Of course, this is not the God of the Bible. It is not the God of dynamic relational faith. It is a kind of *che-serà-serà*, fatalistic theology. It needs to be said that reformed theology doesn't always lead you to this conclusion. Indeed there is a whole network of new churches that are reformed in their theological position, but which are doing an excellent work of church planting around the UK at this time. I wouldn't agree with their view on predestination, their position on women in ministry and leadership, their hierarchical approach to church leadership, nor would I agree with their rather Platonic approach to spiritual warfare (see Chapter 10), but I envy them their enthusiasm and effectiveness in evangelism. Easy to criticise. But at least they are getting on with the job!

The third strand of wrong teaching that hinders evangelism is more prevalent among the newer churches, of which I am a part. This is an altogether cosier error. It makes the mistake that evangelism is only one of many reasons why we are here on the earth. And is probably not that high up on the list of priorities. So while to these churches evangelism is *on* the agenda, it is not *the* agenda. Once this approach is adopted, it isn't long before evangelism sinks down the ratings of priorities and eventually slips into the abyss beyond! Once the focus starts to move from the outward to the inward life of the church, a strangely self-indulgent and rather incestuous thing starts to happen. Maintenance starts to replace mission. People start to 'spiritually introvert'. They disappear up their own spiritual navels! And the result of this evangelistically? First the cry goes up 'When we are loving enough to one another, and have built the nest sufficiently carefully to receive the young, then we will evangelise!' This is usually shortly followed by the cry, 'God, of course, will tell us when we are to witness, we could fish all night and get no catch. He will tell us where to drop the nets!' Both of these statements sound reasonable at first glance. But actually they are little more than excuses. They are a super-spiritual approach that runs counter to Scripture and deny the heart of God, both for His children and for those not yet in the family. After all, what does 'love one another *enough*' actually mean? What will it look like? How do we achieve it and when?

Antidote

Isn't Scripture clear that we *can't* attain maturity unless we are sharing our faith (Philem. 6)? Hasn't God told us in the general when, where and how to evangelise (have a look at 2 Tim. 4:2; 2 Cor. 6:2 – hard to argue with!)? And in the specific, through the ministry of the evangelist (Eph. 4:11–13)? I think so. Any of these strands of wrong teaching will seriously debilitate your desire and your actions in evangelism.

2. 'I don't believe it!'

It's hard to write that phrase without hearing it in the strangled rising inflection of TV comedy character Victor Meldrew! Unfortunately, in the context of evangelism, it isn't funny. The second barrier to effective evangelism is unbelief. Sometimes this can be born of our past experience in evangelism. It's a 'We tried that once before and it didn't work then, so why should it work now?' approach. It's remarkable how quickly disappointment can lead to disillusionment, which ends up in cynicism or even despair. It's very hard for God to use a disillusioned Christian. Sometimes our disappointment and disillusionment have more to do with measuring our witnessing against the wrong criteria, as we saw in Chapter 2. Sometimes our view that evangelism doesn't work is formed because we have too narrow a definition of evangelism, or because we expected to reap where actually we should have been sowing.

Perhaps our unbelief is a reflection of the way that we view God. Perhaps we are not clear that He wants to see people saved. Or possibly we believe that that is true in the general, but not with this specific person. Perhaps for us the revelation of 2 Peter 3:9 – 'The Lord is … not wanting anyone to perish' – has not yet made the vital 18-inch drop from our heads, where we *know* it, to our hearts, where we *believe* it. Or maybe our unbelief is not so much rooted in past negatives, or in our view of God, but in our view of ourselves. Some of us don't believe that God, Who does desire to save people, could ever possibly use us to see it happen. Lack of self-awareness, negative self-image and lack of self-worth can all combine to freeze us into immobility and to bury us under a mountain of unbelief, when it comes to witnessing. Unbelief can become a negative version of or opposite to faith, and works on the same principle; we could have so much unbelief that something *won't* happen, that it actually *doesn't*.

Antidote

The Bible, in two remarkable parallel statements, makes it really clear. Without faith it is impossible to please God (Heb. 11:6) and whatever is not of faith is sin (Rom. 14:23). So if you and I would please God, and would not sin, we *have* to break free of the grip of unbelief on our lives, wherever it comes from.

3. Hypocrite!

I don't know of any other single barrier or block that is more effective in preventing a Christian from actively sharing their faith than sin. For if we are wilfully, deliberately and rebelliously disobeying Jesus in one area of our lives, it is a lot less likely that we will want to be wilfully, deliberately and obediently obeying Him in another.

At the end of the day, sin is sin. But I should be clear about the kind of sin I am writing about here. Before we were saved, you and I were slaves to the law of sin and death. We lived under the rule of fear, under the boss-ship of Satan. He called the tune. When he played, we danced. Satan would tempt us with the external (things that can be seen, touched, tasted, felt, heard, etc), which would then produce an internal response within us. And when we indulged that internal response, temptation led to sin. And sin gave way to death (James 1:13–15).

Let's use the analogy of a piano. Before we were Christians, Satan could flip the lid of the piano of our lives any time he chose and yell into it with horrible, snarling discord. Of course, that's not the way a piano is meant to be played, but if you do that to a piano, you will evoke what is called a sympathetic response. Your shout will produce a musical discord from within the piano. And so it was with Satan, producing discord in, through and from our lives. Then we became Christians. To continue the analogy, that was like slamming the lid down on Satan's fingers! And handing the key of the piano of our lives over to Jesus, the Master Piano Player and Tuner. Now Jesus unlocks the piano and plays beautiful music on our lives, not only individually, but in harmony with those around us, so that our lifestyles become a corporate symphony of praise and worship to Him. Now we are no longer slaves to the law of sin and death, but rather the law of Spirit and righteousness (Rom. 8:1–2). Where once when Satan yelled we had to respond, now we don't. So now in our lives it is not a matter of *when* we sin, but rather *if* we sin.

Please don't misunderstand what I am saying here. I am not advocating 'sinless perfection'. That is a hallmark of some cults and sects. It's a direct route to unreality, super-spirituality and ultimately condemnation. For we do still sin. At least, I do! But it is no longer automatic. We don't have to. And indeed now when I do sin, it actually goes against what has become natural to me. I have to actually choose to grieve the Holy Spirit within me. For I know better. And I am empowered to live better. But because I live in a fallen world, because I am still being changed from glory into glory (2 Cor. 3:18) and because I make stupid and sinful decisions and still live in the consequences of some past sins, I do still sin.

But this is *not* the kind of sin I am talking about here, not the kind of sin that stops you witnessing. I see a pretty girl in the gym, and my mind strays. My children do something wrong, and I react irritably. These are the everyday sins that you and I are called to combat. And so we do. We respond to conviction and repent with increasing speed. One of the hallmarks of maturity is the extent to which we lessen the time gap between conviction and repentance! This is the stuff of life. No, I am talking about the kind of sins that we hide. That we haven't shared with anybody else, except possibly God. (Sin shared with God alone isn't scriptural.) *Sins in which we deliberately and repeatedly indulge.* What the Bible calls 'besetting sins' or 'the sin that so easily entangles' (Heb. 12:1). These are the sins that Satan will use to clobber us. The difference is this. With the first kind of 'everyday sin' (you know what I mean, I hope!), the enemy perches on our shoulders and whispers into our ear saying, 'You can't share your faith, you hypocrite. How can you talk about a gospel of love and forgiveness and the power to break sin, when you are still doing "that"?' These are the condemnatory lies of the enemy and they are relatively easily dealt with. We have to 'submit … to God' and 'resist the devil, and he will flee from you' (James 4:7). For we don't witness because *we* are perfect. But rather because *He* is perfect.

But where our lives shelter secret, hidden, wilful and repeated sin, it is these unshared areas of our lives that Jesus isn't Lord of. The blood of Christ will cover only what we will first uncover. And now when the enemy sits on our shoulder and says, 'You hypocrite!' he is unfortunately correct. He is a legalist. He will take whatever legal turf we give him. This will necessarily debilitate our desire and our fruitfulness in sharing our faith, like almost nothing else on earth.

Antidote

All sin, even besetting sin, is dealt with in the same way. The only way that sin leaves our bodies is through our mouths. The biblical principle is that if sin is stopping you sharing your faith effectively, then confess it. In 1 John 1:9 it is clear that the result of confession of sin is that the God Who is both faithful and just will both forgive us and cleanse us. This is fantastic good news. God is 100 per cent committed to us. But because of His justness, He will not overlook sin. Because of His generous faithfulness He will forgive us, and because of His justness He will not leave us in our sins, but will cleanse us from them. Fantastic!

One last word on confession, however. Confession is not for God's benefit; He knows our sin anyway. It doesn't take Him by surprise. It never makes Him disillusioned with us, for He had no illusions in the first place. No, confession is for *our* benefit. And the Bible knows nothing of confession to God alone. John the Baptist preached a radical gospel of repentance of sins and forgiveness. It was radical because the Jews felt they didn't need to hear this. After all, they were 'sons of the promise'. They were included in the covenant of God by birthright. They thought that as sons of Abraham they were automatically free (John 8:31–36). But John the Baptist's insistence was that the gospel he preached in preparation for the coming of Christ *should* include confession.

In Mark 1:5 we read of how this confession was to be outworked. As the Jews were being baptised, the Scripture says that they confessed their sins. The word which is used for 'confess' is not the normal word *homologeo*. Rather it is the Greek word *exhomologeo*. This doesn't *just* mean to confess. It means to tell or shout out. It's a public thing. This same word is also found in the command in James 5:16 to confess our sins to one another, to tell or speak them out. Scripture insists upon this because its Author is a realist. God knows that if we confess sin to Him alone we tend to leave the 'back door' open for us to commit those same sins again. After all, God must forgive us, for He is love, and nobody else knows about it anyway! However, if we confess our sins to God *and* to one another (as Scripture insists), then we are helpfully surrounding ourselves with people who should be prepared, out of faithfulness, to ask us the awkward questions. If I am honest, the reality is that sometimes I have not sinned again in a particular area, not because of what *God* might say, think or feel, but because of what others around me that I have confessed to would say, think or feel! How about you?

4. Be afraid! Be very afraid!

Fear is a great inhibitor of evangelism. It always comes up in my training sessions when people are brainstorming about what stops them sharing their faith. It's very likely that you have experienced this. Certainly I have. And I'm an evangelist! There are two main kinds of fear inhibitive to witnessing. The first is a wrong fear of God. Scripture teaches that 'fear of the LORD is the beginning of knowledge' (Proverbs 1:7) but that kind of fear is more akin to a healthy respect, a sense of awe, an awareness of His burning holiness, and an acknowledgment of the consequences of sin. Remember that section in C. S. Lewis's *The Lion, the Witch and the Wardrobe*, where Lucy asks Mr Beaver a question about Aslan, the Christ-figure?

'Then he isn't safe?'

'… 'Course he isn't safe. But he's good. He's the King …'

But a *wrong* fear of God is usually more rooted in how we view authority figures in our lives, perhaps because of bad experiences at school, or with a demanding parent, whose affection and approval we felt we had to win. Whatever its roots, a wrong fear of God tends to close us down to possibilities. We fear taking risks. We fear getting things wrong. We fear disapproval, or even rejection. We haven't understood that mistakes are not sin. That mistakes can become doorways to maturity, instead of trap doors to obscurity! This fear of putting a foot wrong, of letting God down, can loom all the greater when it comes to sharing His gospel. Here we imagine the consequences of getting it wrong could be that someone won't be born again!

Think back to the blind panic I got into when my school friend asked me what he needed to do to become a Christian, and I wasn't sure of the answer. My concern was that I would get it wrong. That I would only give him part of the gospel. That he would be only half born again! As though somehow God couldn't cope with my inadequacies. Couldn't circumnavigate (or even circumvent) my mistakes. As though the eternal salvation of a school friend who wanted to know Jesus depended upon my accuracy of communicating the gospel. Put like that, I hope you can see how ridiculous this wrong fear of God is. It really flies in the face of a gospel of grace. And of a God who is unwilling for any to perish.

The other kind of debilitating fear is what the Bible calls 'fear of man' (Prov. 29:25) and this is extremely common. The Bible calls this a snare or noose. It often takes the form of 'What will they think of me if I tell them I'm a Christian?' We worry that we might come across as cranks. Or as naïve and gullible. Or as harsh and judgmental. We worry about how others will perceive us. We may lose face. Kudos. Perhaps we'll get embarrassed. Go red in the face. Get sweaty palms. Maybe our witnessing could jeopardise our job prospects. Or our social inclusion. Because our witnessing might be at the cost of humorous comments, sarcastic remarks, or even spiteful insinuations, we can choose not to witness at all. Fear of people takes all of these guises. We may not only be fearful of how people perceive us, but fearful also of jeopardising our friendships with them. Scared that we will damage a good friendship. Concerned that the mention of Jesus might drive a wedge in an otherwise blossoming relationship. Frightened to offend. We seem to forget that we are not so very different from everybody else. That if this glorious gospel of Jesus Christ can work for us, then it can work for anyone.

Antidote

Ultimately fear isn't rational. Fear is irrational. Fear cannot be avoided. We never get to a place where we will never fear again. You cannot get over fear. You cannot get under it. You cannot get around it. You have to go *through* it. Ultimately fear is to do with punishment, with negative consequences (1 John 4:18–19). But for the Christian the ultimate consequence is a positive, not a negative one. This the gospel promises us. So for us the issue isn't whether we are afraid or not. The issue is whether we will allow fear to stop us witnessing. Only push through the fear and we will find, instead of it being the mountain it appears, that in fact it is more like a stage prop made out of papier maché.

It's interesting to note that in 1 John 4:18, which is the nearest to a solution to fear – fear is driven out by love – we find the present continuous tense being used in the verb. And it's God's perfect love for us, not our perfect love for Him. The verb doesn't just mean 'to drive out once', it means 'to drive it out, and when it comes back to drive it out again, and then again, and then again'! As many times as needed. It is a very strong verb at that. And it's the same verb as is used when Jesus drives out the money-changers from the temple (John 2:15). And to describe Jesus' actions when He is driving out evil spirits. And interestingly enough it's the same verb used in Matthew 10:5 when Jesus sends/drives out the disciples into the task of evangelism. So the antidote to fear, which is love, has to be taken as a regular and repeated dose. This is realistic. Perhaps that's why the Bible says 366 times (one for every day including a leap year!) words to the effect of 'Do not fear/do not be afraid'.

5. I can't be bothered …

Last, but far from least, one of the greatest barriers to our witnessing is that we can't be bothered. I am fairly confident that I can say 'we' because many is the occasion when this is true of me and I am the 'professional'! I get paid to evangelise! Apathy is what often remains when all of the other excuses have been expended.

Just before his public execution for murder in the nineteenth century, notorious criminal Charles Peace was visited in the condemned cell by the prison chaplain. Peace was a profligate, a violent man and an avowed atheist. But his remarks in those circumstances remain very telling to this day. Turning to the prison chaplain, Peace is reported to have said, 'I don't believe all that stuff. But if I did let me tell you this. I would crawl on my hands and knees the length and breadth of England over broken glass to tell just one person what you are telling me.'

I think that sometimes apathy is the result of the Greek dualism that we looked at in Chapter 1. In other words, we believe stuff in our heads, but it has never made it down to our hearts. We believe it in theory but we don't believe it in practice. In theory we believe that people who die without Christ are hell-bound for a lost eternity. But in practice we don't live as though that were true. Apathy is the result of dislocating our head from our heart. Perhaps of sometimes shutting out painful realities.

But apathy can also be the result of over-busy and over-burdened lifestyles. I know that in the last few years, dealing with the difficult circumstances of the death of both of my parents, there were many occasions when I felt I had no extra physical, spiritual or emotional energy left to do much else at all. A kind of ennui or apathy would creep in. So sometimes passivity in front of the TV, or even sleep on the sofa would become an escape, in exactly the same way that people will use drugs or alcohol as an escape from reality, or to obviate responsibility or the need to expend emotional, relational, social, or psychological energy. Any or all of the above will produce apathy.

And sometimes apathy is plain and simple. It's not because we don't believe stuff in our hearts. It's not because we have run out of sufficient energy. It is simply because we don't love people enough. Real love always outworks itself in actions.

Antidote

One of the problems with apathy is how to overcome it. Because if you can't be bothered in the first place, how can you be bothered enough to stop being not bothered? I have a friend who, on holiday in Ireland, wound down the window of his car to ask directions from a local. On being asked how to get to a nearby village the local replied, 'Oh, if I were you, I wouldn't start from here. You can't get there from here!' Is this the case with apathy? Can we get from apathy to action, or can't you get there from here? Is it possible? Yes, it is.

I would suggest that the opposite spirit to apathy is the spirit of compassion. Now, if asked the question, 'Which of us is compassionate enough?' I know I wouldn't have my hand up. How about you? We *all* need to be more compassionate. How is this possible? I would like to share two biblical principles with you if you are keen to combat apathy by growing in compassion. But please be aware that, the more compassionate you get for people, the more involved you will become with them, and the more it is incumbent upon you to share your faith with them.

The first principle of expanding compassion is found in John 6:1–13. This is more likely to have been the feeding of the 10,000, because the Bible, in and of its culture, tends to make lists and count numbers of men and not to include women and children. Either way, we are dealing with a pretty major miracle here! What prompts it? Certainly it's not the actions of the disciples. In fact they appear to lack considerably in compassion. Their solution to dealing with an increasingly hungry crowd is simply to send them away! No, the initiative in this story comes from Jesus. It is He Who has compassion on the people. No change there, then!

But the lesson is reserved for the disciples. Ultimately it is they who will feed the crowd. Searching around among their own resources they come to a conclusion often seen in Scripture: 'We haven't got enough. We can't do it. We have only got this ...' Heard this sort of thing before? Have a look at Moses' response to God in Exodus 3:11, or the widow's response to Elisha in 2 Kings 4:2. In John 6, all that can be found is one small boy (note God's involvement with children and youth) with five loaves and two fishes. What does Jesus do? He takes the bread, breaks it, gives thanks to His Father in heaven, looking upward as He does so (Matt. 14:18). This would be blasphemy for the Jew who, in imperfect relationship to God, would always give thanks for food, but always look downward while doing so. Not so with Jesus, Who was in perfect relationship to His Father.

Jesus then gives the food to His disciples, and it is they who distribute it to the crowd, according to the earliest account in Mark 6:32–34. The tense and the verb is again in the present continuous; they *kept on* giving the bread out. You can imagine them giving it away and thinking, 'Where on earth (or heaven) is all this coming from?' There is no noted reaction from the crowd, as it appears that the lesson was aimed at the compassionless and apathetic disciples. Once everyone had enough there were 12 baskets left over, and it is probably more than preachers' license to say that this was one for each of the disciples! That's because the word used for 'basket' is a technical term for a small wicker basket that would normally be attached to the belt of a traveller, a little like a 'bum bag'!

How does this story help us grow in compassion? Well, the principles are all there. A bad reaction is often a result of running out of our own human resources. But the lesson? Turn to Jesus. His response? That we should give Him the little bit that we have left, just as the disciples took the boy with the food to Jesus. So when it comes to compassion, if we will give the little bit that we already *do* have to Jesus, He will take it from us. He will break it. And I warn you, that may hurt. You will begin to get a glimpse of people the way that God sees them. To feel His heart for them. It won't be so easy to stand in queues at Tesco's and plan tomorrow's meal, while ignoring the checkout person. Or stand in the bank queue with faceless anonymous people, while only working out what denominations you would like your notes in. Or climb on a crowded bus, avoiding eye contact, while thinking only about what is on TV that night. We have all done it. But each time we do, we fail to see people around us; fail to see them as God would see them, made in His image, and lost.

But what does Jesus then do with the little that we have given to Him? He gives it back to us. And with the little we feed the many. That's because a supernatural multiplication miracle has to take place, and this is exactly what Jesus will do with our compassion. He will take it. He will break it. He will cause it to supernaturally multiply. He will give it back to us. And *in our giving of it to others*, it will be supernaturally multiplied. Please note that it is *as we give it away* that the miracle takes place. We don't wait for the miracle and then give it away. Compassion is not essentially a warm, cuddly feeling. It cannot be stored up, banked or invested. It is predominantly a verb. It is about *doing* the compassionate thing. Not having the compassionate feeling. Actually the compassionate act provides the framework for the compassionate feeling to follow and fill. This is the first principle to actively adopt if you and I would grow in compassion.

The second principle can be found in Romans 12:8. This is very encouraging! According to this passage there is a *spiritual gift* of compassion. Romans 12 is one of a number of places in the New Testament where the spiritual gifts of the Holy Spirit are listed and in part explained. None of the lists is exhaustive. For others, have a look at 1 Peter 4:9–11, and 1 Corinthians 12–14. While there is overlap, the lists are not identical. But they all deal with what Scripture calls the *charismata*, from two Greek words, *charis*, which means 'grace', and *mata*, which means 'gifts'. So the spiritual gifts (also sometimes called *donata*, meaning 'things given'; or *pneumatikon*, meaning 'things/manifestations of the spirit') are *grace gifts*. In other words, they are not given on the basis of our deserving; they are given on the basis of God's desiring.

Too many of us in the past have got hung up on trying to find what our specific spiritual gifts are. We have wondered if God has this or that particular gift for us. And in being unsure, we have often not used any! We have understood that the Holy Spirit gives these gifts to us, according to His decision. What we have *not* understood is that while He gives the gifts where He wills, the fact is, He *does* will! He wants us to be maximum Christians, not minimum Christians. He doesn't want us to be content with one or several of the spiritual gifts. He wants us to have them all. He wants us to go for broke! That's why Paul uses such strong language in the New Testament when he exhorts us to 'earnestly covet' the spiritual gifts. Go for it! This is the only thing in Scripture that you are allowed to covet! Make the most of it! You don't have to be old enough. You don't have to be mature enough. You don't have to be spiritual enough. You just have to be greedy!

The gifts of the Holy Spirit are not an end in themselves. Rather, they are a means to an end. View them as tools. The best tool you could have in your hand is the tool appropriate to the job. So if someone confronts me in agony because they've twisted their ankle, it is no good saying to them, 'That's OK. I'll just ask God for the gift of administration'! No, what they need is a gift of healing, the best possible gift of all in that context. The gifts are not hierarchical. They are functional. Nor do the gifts reside in us. They are not fixed and static. I have seen too many churches where the same person week in and week out gets up to give the same tongue, and then the same person gets up to interpret it. This runs contrary to Scripture. In 1 Corinthians it is clear that every time we come together there is a different manifestation of spiritual gifts among us. Indeed the word that is used for manifestation here is *phenerosis*, which literally means 'the dancing hands of God'. What a wonderful image! The hands of God playing over our corporate lives together to produce the free play of the gifts of the Holy Spirit, to bring glory to Him, and to be used as tools in the lives of unbelievers and believers alike (1 Cor. 14:22–25).

So, if the Holy Spirit lives in us and not the gifts, we can have whatever gifts He wants to give us and He does want to give them to us, and if the best gifts to have are the gifts that get the job done, how do we get them? Well, obviously first of all we must be filled with the Holy Spirit (Eph. 5:18), which can be effected through the laying on of hands and prayer from those already filled, as a symbolic gesture of our interdependence one upon the other (Acts 8:18–19). Even Simon the sorcerer realised this, although he offered money for what you cannot buy! Being filled with the Holy Spirit is an ongoing matter and not a one-off experience. The reference in Ephesians 5:18 is in the present continuous tense: 'go on being filled with the Holy Spirit'. We must then ask for His gifts (Luke 11:13), and having asked we must receive in faith. But how do we know that we have received? By putting the gift into action. How do I know I have the gift of tongues? When I speak in tongues.

And so too with the gift of compassion. There! I knew we would get back to it in the end! The principle is the same. Just as surely as there are gifts of tongues, of prophecy, of administration, so too there is a gift of compassion. Your Bible (in Rom. 12:8) may call it the gift of 'mercy', but be assured that it's exactly the same word as 'compassion' in Matthew 9:36. We go on being filled with the Holy Spirit. We ask for the gift of compassion in faith. We receive it in faith. And then we do the compassionate thing. That's how you know you have the gift. And because the gifts operate by faith, and faith is like a muscle, the more you exercise the gifts, the more you get familiar with the things of the Holy Spirit, the sharper and stronger they grow. Try it!

So there you have it. Two biblical principles for us to grow in compassion. You can't *make* yourself more compassionate. Poking your finger in your eyes, or peeling onions to make yourself cry over your town won't do it! So you might as well try this method. Ask God to take, break and supernaturally multiply the little that you *already* have of compassion, but at the same time be greedy for more and ask Him for the *gift* of compassion.

With these five chapters as a backdrop, we're now going to start looking at increasingly practical ways of how to be more fruitful in evangelism. But I couldn't pitch in there, because to do so would be to miss the point. It's not that so far we have had the theory and now we are heading to the practice. It's that head and heart must work together for the sake of the gospel if we are to reach the lost.

But before the next chapter, some homework!

GROUPWORK

1. In your group discuss which reasons you found the most compelling for sharing your faith. Can you find and discuss other reasons?
2. Identify one (or more) of the reasons outlined for sharing your faith that you *haven't* thus far embraced or experienced. Pray for one another for God to reveal this motivation to both your head and heart.
3. Which barriers to effective evangelism can you identify with and why? Discuss this together in your group, with honesty. Can you find and discuss other barriers?

4. Using the references given under each barrier, confess the barrier and pray to bind down its effects and to loose its antidote, in effect coming against the barrier in the opposite spirit (e.g. wrong teaching versus 2 Tim. 4:2, 1 Cor. 10–12, and specifically to correct the notion of inappropriate timing, 2 Cor. 6:2; unbelief versus Rom. 14:23, Heb. 11:6; sin versus 1 John 1:9; fear versus 1 John 4:18; apathy versus Mark 6:32–44, Rom. 12:8).
5. Memorise and meditate on the antidote verses.

Chapter 6

THE JESUS WAY

It has rightly been said that evangelism is simply 'one beggar telling another beggar where to get bread'. What I particularly like about this quotation is that there is an inclusiveness about it. A mutuality. It smacks of the new paradigm of evangelism rather than the old (Chapter 2). Put simply and logically, we will communicate best with those to whom we are closest. As we saw in the previous chapter, the gospel of Jesus Christ is not essentially informational, but is at its heart relational. The simple answer to the question 'How do we witness?' is 'To our friends through our friendships'.

A FEW STATISTICS ...

Statistics really are a bit like Marmite. You either love them or you hate them! I took an A level in pure maths and statistics at school and failed it, so I guess I ought to hate statistics, although in fact I don't. The effectiveness of friendship evangelism can be demonstrated through a couple of surveys, which make a dramatic and encouraging point.

In the latter part of the twentieth century a survey of

15,000 Christians on the west coast of America was undertaken. The purpose was to understand what the primary influences on conversion were.

- *1 per cent of those surveyed* maintained that the primary influence on their conversion was attendance at a major Christian evangelistic event, which are sometimes called rallies or, more unhelpfully, crusades. These would typically involve town- or city-wide presentations in a stadium or large tent, and be the result of inter-church co-operation. They also frequently revolve around anointed evangelists such as Billy Graham or Luis Palau or, in the UK, evangelist J. John. Such evangelistic missions have 'fished' in the fringes of the Anglican and Baptist denominations. They would fairly typically see a response rate of between 5 per cent and 10 per cent of those unsaved present at the meetings, and around a 1 per cent to 10 per cent retention rate approximately one year after the event has finished.

- *A further 1 per cent of those surveyed* attributed the primary cause of their conversion to visitation. Although it would be nice to ascribe this to angelic visitation(!) this refers to some form of door-to-door strategy. Over the years very many of us have been involved in such visitation programmes. And most of us (certainly including me, and I am an evangelist!) have hated the experience. For it carries with it the uneasy feelings of invasion of privacy. A higher-than-usual potential for confrontation. A possibility of confusion with other 'door-to-door practitioners' who, certainly in my road, are more likely to be Jehovah's Witnesses or Mormons. I cannot tell you how many times I have embarked on a door-to-door visitation programme and found myself fervently praying on the doorstep, 'Oh Lord, please let them be out!' Or how many times I wanted to knock on the meter cupboard door in order *not* to elicit a response! Nonetheless, 1 per cent of those surveyed (that's 150 individuals!) were saved as a result of this kind of programme, so we would be foolish indeed to ignore its potential. The apostle Paul's approach was 'by all possible means … save some' (1 Cor. 9:22) and, with effective strategy, I have seen this 1 per cent go up to 17 per cent under circumstances we will explore in the final chapter of this book.

- *A further 1 per cent of those surveyed* rated crisis or trauma as the principal ingredient in their conversion, although the survey didn't go into details as to what these might be. People *are* more open to the gospel at certain vulnerable times of their lives. We will come back to this in Chapter 8. This is nothing that we can plan for, but it is something that we can pray into, in the expectation that God will work 'in all things … for the good' (Rom. 8:28). In their desperation, 1 per cent of those surveyed turned to God and to their surprise found Him to be there!

From here the statistics begin to rise.

- *The next category of respondents (3 per cent)* indicated that 'cold' church contact was the main cause of their conversion. I don't think that this is a justification for turning the heating systems down in our church buildings! These were people who, outside of the normal run of their lives, came into unusual or unexpected contact with the church gathered. This would most likely be through some of the 'rites of passage' where, even in a post-Christian society, church still plays some part. So we are looking here at baptisms and confirmations, marriages and blessings, and funerals. Hatching, matching and despatching!

Our own wedding would serve as a good example. Aware that most of Nikki's family who would be present were not-yet-Christians, we began to pray months in advance that God would use our wedding ceremony as a means of reaching them with His love. And because He was keener to do this than we were to pray it, that is precisely what began to happen. A month or so before the wedding Nikki's chief bridesmaid, her cousin, came down to see the church for a weekend and to talk through the details, during the process of which she was impacted by the love of God, surrendered her life to Christ, got delivered of some demons and filled with the Holy Spirit! There then followed a series of ripple events over the ensuing months, which saw another of Nikki's cousins converted, two uncles and aunts, grandparents, plus some excellent conversations with her parents.

When both my parents died recently my prayer was that the eulogy I gave in both cases would not only be a testimony to their wonderful parenting, but also to their personal faith in Christ, and that as a result of that many would be deeply affected. From conversations I have had since, that seems to have been the case.

- *Another 3 per cent of those surveyed* indicated that event evangelism was the predominant factor in their conversion. This is as distinct from large-scale missions. This might include things such as healing meetings, wine and wisdom evenings, concerts with Christian bands, school concerts at the end of a week's activity and lessons in a local school, evangelistic cabarets, etc.

- *For some 5 per cent of those surveyed*, Sunday school was seen as of primary importance in their conversion. In many of the 'new' churches, consistent children's work is in danger of being neglected. I am not an advocate of the old paradigm of Sunday school, where children are hived off out of the main meeting so that the adults can get on with the 'real' stuff, more out of a sense of convenience and quiet than out of a desire to reach the children with their own personal access to Christ. Those days should be long gone! Indeed the very concept of Sunday school is old paradigm; it once carried great relevance and attractiveness evangelistically at a time in the UK when education was not the right of all. Perceiving a void where the church could serve and demonstrate good news, Sunday schools were set up all over the country not only to educate children, but also to see them saved. And so they were. But with the advent of the various Education Acts, it is enough now to try to get children to attend school Monday to Friday, let alone encourage them to come to a different kind of school on a Sunday! Another example of what once was relevant, radical and served its purpose being perpetuated from the mists of antiquity into irrelevance in our modern culture.

But church as an expression of family, working across the age ranges, and giving a particular and personal emphasis and access to children, in the same way that Jesus did (Mark 10:13–16), is not only viable but also reflects much of God's heart for young people and children. I suspect that this is one of the reasons why as many as 5 per cent found Christ as a child through a church's children's work.

If you wanted to explore this further you could do no better than read Ishmael's book, *Angels with Dirty Faces*, and flick through the following Bible references, which indicate God's concern for young people: Exod. 22:22–24; Lev. 20:1–5; Judg. 13:24; 1 Sam. 2:21–26; 3:1–21; 17:33; Psa. 8:2; 103:1–5; 127:3–5; 139:13–16; Jer. 1:5–7; Zech. 8:5; 9:17; Matt. 11:25–26; 18:10; Luke 1:15; 2:11,41–52; 11:11–13;

John 6:9; Acts 7:20; 23:16–22; 1 Cor. 16:10–11; Eph. 6:4; Col. 3:21; 1 Tim. 4:12; Titus 2:3–8; Heb. 12:5–13; 1 Pet. 2:2. Certainly it is a sobering thought that in the Old and New Testament God seems to have judged nations by the way that they treat their children. As you can see, God has a lot to say about children and youth!

- *6 per cent of the survey* cited contact with church leaders as of first importance in their finding faith. Again, not an argument for a clergy/laity split. But certainly an encouragement for anybody in the privileged position of serving the body of Christ in a 'full-time' capacity (we are all full-time for Christ, but I think you know what I mean) to be actively involved in sharing their faith, irrespective of whether or not their primary ministry is that of an evangelist, since these statistics do indicate their potential effectiveness. Or maybe it's just that church leaders know an awful lot about sin!

But it is the final category that is the most revealing. In reading this, some of you will have already worked out the percentage (if you have, you probably need to get out more!). But the fact of the matter is that *the survey indicated that a staggering 80 per cent* of people stated that the primary cause of their conversion was friendship evangelism. That is an enormous weighting. But I suspect some of the other categories hide a truer and even higher figure. For of those attending major mission events and smaller event evangelism, it is surely likely that they had been in the first place invited by friends?

A LITTLE CLOSER TO HOME ...

About ten years ago another, smaller, survey was undertaken in the UK for the same purposes; to elicit what the predominant factors in conversion were. This survey was undertaken by the British and Foreign Bible Society and resulted in the publishing of a book by John Finney, *Finding Faith Today*. If you can get hold of this book, it is worth doing so. It is a seminal work and one that, in the UK, began a debate on 'process evangelism', in contradistinction to 'crisis evangelism'.

The results of this second survey were no less startling than that of the one conducted in the USA. In answer to the question, 'Was your journey to faith gradual or sudden?!' (*of the 500 UK Christians interviewed*), 69 per cent described their journey to faith as gradual, with only 31 per cent describing it as sudden. This was *not* what was expected. Where were all the 'Damascus road' experiences? At first it was thought that the survey itself might be skewed. Perhaps there was a predominance of 'liberal' Christians? People who didn't really understand about 'new birth'? For whom 'conversion' was an unfamiliar or uncomfortable term? And so the analysts went back to the statistics and checked the figures among those who specifically identified themselves as evangelicals. These were people who certainly should know about the conversion experience, and who probably could give the time, date and place when this had happened to them. Yet even among specifically evangelicals the figures were little different. Here, 63 per cent described their journey to faith as gradual, with 37 per cent describing it as sudden.

As if to underline the reality of this gradual process, the next surprise that the survey revealed was that on average it took *four years* for a person to make that journey to faith! Now, we can either be discouraged or encouraged by that fact. Personally I am encouraged by it. It means that among my friends there will always be some who are already in process along that journey to faith. Some will be just embarking on it.

Some will be nearing its completion. Some may be mid-term. But certainly it means that all of them require more time, diligence, persistence, prayer, befriending and effort on my part than I am usually, at least initially, prepared to give them. Most of us give up too soon and too readily. Or may even, with an enormous lack of integrity, be prepared to 'drop' friends who don't look like promising converts, as we move on to the next target! This is *not* friendship evangelism.

TABLE 6.1. FACTORS IN COMING TO FAITH IN THE UK

Factor	Male	Female
Spouse/partner	22%	10%
Children	3%	13%
Parents	7%	5%
Other family	1%	1%
Christian friends	15%	29%
Lay person	4%	4%
Church activity	3%	8%
Dream/vision	3%	3%
Minister/church leader	16%	17%
Evangelistic event	3%	5%
Bible	7%	5%
Literature/drama/music	4%	2%
Christian TV/radio	0%	0%
Other	14%	9%

Note: Percentages all approximate; taken from *Finding Faith Today* by John Finney (Bible Society, 1992). Used with permission.

In comparison to the US survey, the UK survey outlined a greater number of primary factors in the journey to faith. These are shown in Table 6.1. Whatever else it does, Table 6.1 clearly indicates yet again that the predominant factor in conversion was friendship evangelism. The first five categories in the list (Spouse/partner, Children, Parents, Other family, Christian friends) could all be legitimately grouped under the general heading of friendship evangelism. Thus 48 per cent of all males and 58 per cent of all females surveyed indicated that this was the single most important factor in their journey to faith.

Two observations. First, the UK friendship-evangelism factor is considerably lower than that indicated by the US survey. I wonder if this says something about the nature of the two respective cultures? Perhaps British culture is generally more reserved, more class-ridden (and therefore potentially less inclusive), more cynical and less friendly than its American counterpart? If there is any truth in this, then it means we have something to be praying into, working at, repenting over, learning from and being humble about.

Second observation: the fact that a higher percentage of females than males identified friendship evangelism as a primary factor in their journey to faith might indicate that UK men have something to learn from women here. Without wishing to unhelpfully stereotype, it does seem to me that women are quicker and better than men at forming and maintaining friendships. Perhaps because of cultural stereotypes ('Big boys don't cry'), and so on. Men seem more reserved, less in touch with their emotions, less ready to share them. And more inclined to form friendships around common activities. On the other hand, women need little or no excuse to share their emotions, engage in open dialogue, offer support and understanding; they are often less embarrassed and inhibited about the nature of friendship and intimacy, and need not build that around common interests. Again this may be something that the men among us need to pray into, work at, repent of and humble ourselves over.

God is a God of love, and the power of love is the most potent force in the universe. Love is expressed through friendship and intimacy. Through relationships done properly. Even one of the most despotic rulers in history had it right: 'There is only one way not to be won over by love, and that is to flee from it' (Napoleon Bonaparte). But enough of statistics.

IS FRIENDSHIP EVANGELISM BIBLICAL?

The answer to that question has to be 'Yes'. The best proponent and example of friendship evangelism in the New Testament is Jesus Christ Himself. We have considerable detail of His miraculous birth and the attendant events, but we don't have too many recorded details of His early life. We are assured that Jesus grew in grace and wisdom and favour with people (Luke 2:52). It is hard to see how He could do this without adopting a friendly approach! Doubtless Jesus understood and practised the truism: 'He who would have friends must prove himself friendly.' We see another snippet of Jesus relating explicitly to His family at the age of 12 in the Temple (Luke 2:48–51).

But the majority of Jesus' recorded history involves the last three and a half years of His life, spent in the public arena. And it is in this context that we have a clear demonstration of friendship evangelism. Of the incidents in the life of Christ recorded for us in the Gospels, some 50 per cent of His time seems to have been spent winning and wooing individuals. When it came to the disciples, before they were ever called to *do* anything *for* Him, they were called to *be with* Him (Mark 3:13–15). There are a significant number of references in the life of Christ to the things that go towards creating friendships. Jesus spends time with His disciples (Mark 6:30–31). He shares His thoughts with them (Mark 4:10–12). He answers their questions (Mark 7:17–23). He asks them questions (Mark 8:17–21). He helps them (Mark 6:48–51). He asks for their help and He is emotionally open and vulnerable with them (Mark 14:32–34). He shares meals with them (Mark 14:3). He extends His activity and interest to their families (Mark 1:29–31). Nor does He neglect His own family (John 19:25–27). From a position of incredulity and unbelief (Mark 3:21), Jesus wins and woos His family to a place of faith and fruitfulness (Acts 1:14, 1 Cor. 9:5).

Jesus starts with His own family and disciples, whom He specifically defines as friends (John 15:14–15). So it's not surprising that in Luke 15:1–2 we are told that Jesus became known as a man who 'welcomes sinners'. It is the ultimate irony that Jesus was called a 'friend of sinners' in a pejorative sense among His enemies and the religious leaders. Religion mitigates against friendship! A relationship with Jesus, on the other hand, promotes friendships. As is so often the case, a closer look at the Greek word sometimes translated 'friend of sinners' paints a fuller picture of how Jesus operated. The word is *prosdechomai*, which literally means 'to personally receive someone to yourself'. It carries connotations of openness and vulnerability. Of letting people in, and giving yourself away. Of risk and responsibility as well as benefit.

All of this is demonstrated in another use of the same word found in Mark 10:21. Here the rich young ruler has come to Christ, asking what he must do to inherit eternal life. Jesus, perceiving the man's stumbling blocks to lie in the area of materialism and accumulated wealth, advocates that he gives away what would hinder him. This being too high a price, the rich young ruler goes away sadly. His rejection of Christ is real, but it is more than a rejection of principles and values. For

Jesus had extended to this rich young ruler personal acceptance and intimacy. The little phrase in Mark's Gospel, so easy to miss, is that when Jesus looked at the rich young ruler, 'He loved Him'. The word is *prosdechomai* and probably literally means that Jesus 'personally embraced' the young man. Nor was this unusual behaviour for Jesus. So much so that He was consistently accused of spending social time eating and drinking in the company of tax collectors, publicans and other such sinners. He even on occasions took the initiative to invite Himself around to theirs for supper (Luke 19:5)!

REMEMBER THE GREAT COMMISSION?

We looked in some detail at Matthew 28:16–20 in Chapter 3. So it is enough to remind ourselves that the Great Commission is a command to go to all the 'people groups' (*te ethne*). Definitions vary, but it has been estimated that there are some 60,000 people groups in the world with some 10,000 of them as yet unreached, and 1,500 of those in the UK. However you define people groups, certainly your friends are a distinct people group in their own right. *You* are the common denominator. *You* may be the only Bible they ever get to read! In Acts 1:8 the Great Commission gets further unpacked with some hints at strategy, which we also looked at in Chapter 3. The principle seems to be: begin to be witnesses, where you are currently, in terms of both geography and culture (Jerusalem). Then move on to near neighbours, where there is some common ground and mutuality (Judea), before moving on to perceived 'enemies' and those who have nothing in common with you (Samaria and the ends of the earth). If this is a right reading of Acts 1:8 then at least half of the strategy and people groups are to be defined through friendship (Jerusalem and Judea).

AND ELSEWHERE ...?

Apart from Jesus and His Great Commission, do we find friendship evangelism evidenced anywhere else in Scripture? Yes, we do! The New Testament is full of it. When Andrew is called by Jesus his response is to find his brother Peter. When Philip is called his response is to find his brother Nathanael. The paralytic in Luke 5 is brought before Jesus by his friends. It's Peter who summons Jesus to Peter's mother-in-law in Mark 1. It's friendship which affects Levi's household in Mark 2, and in Mark 7 it is friends of the deaf and near mute man who bring him to Jesus. In Mark 8 it's the blind man's friends who access Jesus for him. In Mark 9 a father brings his son, in Mark 10 babes at arms are brought to Jesus by their older siblings (indicated by the literal meaning of the Greek text) and so on and on it goes. It is quite a salutary exercise to read Scripture through the lens and focus of friendship evangelism. To do so is both encouraging and challenging.

We have seen in this brief introductory chapter to the subject of friendship evangelism that statistically friendship evangelism is the single most effective means of witnessing. And the reason why that is statistically true, is because it is the *Jesus method* of evangelism. And that consequently *Scripture* is full of examples.

But as we close this chapter can we be clear about one thing? Friendship evangelism is *not* simply a sneaky way of reaching the lost. It is not an undercover way of adding notches to the back of our Bible! We don't make friends in order to see them saved. Rather, we want to see saved the friends that we have. For true friendship must mean that we want the very best for our friends, and the very best is Jesus. We must not get into the situation where we are so friendly with someone that we daren't mention the 'J-word'! I know many Christians with friendships like that. And the fact is, the longer you leave your friendship without introducing Jesus into the friendship, the harder it gets. The greater the pain barrier to push through. So if I am describing you, start now! But however many times on their average four-year journey to finding faith our friends apparently reject Christ, they still remain our friends. Ultimately, if they continue to reject Christ, they *still* remain our friends. My friends have to be able to ask me the question, 'If I reject your Jesus, will you still be my friend?' And, my answer has to be, 'Yes, of course'. Did Jesus withdraw acceptance and affirmation from Judas at any stage in their three-year journey? I don't think so. Did Judas (or the rich young ruler for that matter) withdraw from Jesus? Yes, they did. All friendship carries that risk.

Real friendship evangelism places the emphasis on friendship, with the consequence of evangelism. It doesn't place the emphasis on evangelism, with the consequence of friendship. That is to lack integrity, in the same way that to have a friendship and not to share Jesus with that friend is to lack integrity. The next two chapters will concentrate in very practical ways on how we can best share Jesus with our friends, now that we are hopefully biblically and statistically convinced that this is indeed the Jesus way.

GROUPWORK

1. Read together the following three passages: John 1:40–50; Luke 5:17–32; John 9:1–41.
2. Discuss together what circles or networks of contacts are involved in each story.
3. Together, what do you consider to be the advantages of this friendship evangelism?

4. In the stories you have read together, what are the specific results of this friendship evangelism?
5. As a group *and personally*, what do you feel that we can learn from this for our witnessing today?

Chapter 7

SO HOW?

I almost feel like this and the next chapter should carry a *caveat emptor* – a 'buyer beware' warning – attached to them! I say that because I am about to outline a five-point strategy for friendship evangelism. It is a strategy which I personally use and have done for many years. It is also a strategy which I have taught in literally dozens of churches over the last dozen years. I know it to work. It is not *the* way. It is only *a* way. But it *is* a way! I have seen people saved through it. I have seen churches grow through it. So why should it carry a warning?

PRACTICALLY SPEAKING ...

Because it is intensely practical. And not uncommonly I have seen some Christians react to any kind of perceived strategy. As though strategy and the Holy Spirit were opposites. But my problem has been this; wherever I have found Christians without a personal strategy for witnessing, I have almost without exception found them to be ineffectual in their evangelism. All too often Christians who simply 'let go and let God', who rely on the wholly intangible and indefinable work of the Holy Spirit in their evangelism, are Christians who *don't* see people saved. If you are the kind of Christian who finds yourself reacting to the concept of thinking, planning and praying towards seeing your friends saved, then you are probably exactly the kind of Christian who needs to embrace this five-point strategy! So please don't react. Put these next two chapters into practice and over a good period of time, see what happens.

For the truth is, God Himself is the Master Strategist. If it were not so He would not have been able to map out for us good plans, good works, good gifts (Eph. 2:10; Jer. 29:11; James 1:17). If the Holy Spirit were not a strategist, why then should He prompt Paul to go to one place rather than another (Acts 16:6–10)? And if there were no value to be found in strategies, why then are we commanded to be aware of the strategies of the enemy (Eph. 6:11; 2 Cor. 2:11)? If strategies are ineffectual, why does the enemy use them at all? If God is not a strategist, what on earth do we suppose it to mean that Jesus was sent 'when the time had fully come' (Gal 4:4)? And isn't the Great Commission itself God's master plan and strategy for the salvation of humanity? We'll return to the importance of strategy in Chapter 11.

IDENTIFY YOUR NETWORKS

This is the first part of our five-point strategy for friendship evangelism. The idea of networks, or people groups, is not merely a sociological one. It is to be found in the pages of the New Testament. There, a people group or network of relationships was often referred to as a 'household'. The Greek work is *oikos*. It never literally meant those who lived under your roof, although in New Testament culture the idea of a 'nuclear' family was unheard of (husband, wife and 1.8 children!). Families in the New Testament culture were invariably extended families. In a more rural, more relational culture, it was not uncommon for your extended family to consist of mother, father, siblings and grandparents, and even to extend to uncles, aunts and cousins. But the concept of the New Testament household also included those with whom the household were in regular contact. So the household would extend to genetically more remote, but relationally still meaningful family members, and to hired servants, workers and close family friends. The best estimates indicate that in New Testament times the average *oikos* consisted of around 120 people. In our increasingly impersonal, isolationist cultures that number has now decreased to around six! The cry of the human heart is for community; but the experience of human kind is of relational breakdown.

Over the next ten years the British government is committed to building 4.4 million new, single-tenant homes, often on brown or greenbelt land. This is because the numbers of those not marrying is increasing exponentially, while 41 per cent of all UK marriages now end in divorce. The emergent Generation X yearns for community and relational intimacy, and is sexually satiated but relationally stunted. Technology has pushed us as a society so far towards isolation, with its online shopping, banking, automated telephone answering systems, etc, that we need never see another human being in the course of our day-to-day living unless we choose to. Yet even business is recognising that this drive towards efficiency is at a high price; the relational factor. And so businesses the world over are retraining their employees in the skills of people contact, of meaningful gesture and touch. Even in corporate management, the drive is now on to re-establish the importance of effective networks. Your networks may be small, but they are important.

One of the great things about this strategy for friendship evangelism is that it doesn't involve us finding extra time or doing extra things in our busy lifestyles. Rather, it is about getting more of God into our existing contacts. I would like to suggest that you already have five networks or spheres of contact which God has given to you, and is giving you to. Indeed, you may come up with others. These are the five that I have come up with.

1 *Your family* – It is highly unlikely that everyone in your immediate family, let alone your extended family, is already saved. For most of us the reality is that we live among a mix of saved and unsaved. Our family are usually those that we are closest too, those that we most love and yet, paradoxically, can often be those that we find the most difficult to see saved. Or even have faith to see saved. Why is this? Sometimes it's because we perceive the stakes to be higher; we so want them to be saved that we never present them with the options for fear that they might reject them. Sometimes it's because they are so close that we take them for granted, like no longer being able to hear the familiar ticking of a clock in a room. Sometimes it is because we fear the cost of their rejection of *us*, rather than of the gospel. We fear being ostracised or rejected or, in extreme cases, even being relationally and financially disinherited.

More often it's because our family have seen the very best about us, but also the very worst. They have seen us at our most godly moments, but also at our most devilish! When the gospel appears to be working for us, and when it appears not to be! Or they may have already adopted the view that 'it's just a passing phase'. For whatever reason, the salvation of our family can sometimes seem a distant and remote dream. And for some, of course, dysfunctional families of separation, divorce or even abuse provide their own set of familial evangelism challenges.

And yet ... And yet God is into families. He is the original family: Father, Son and Holy Spirit. Indeed, we don't understand God as family because we have families on earth. No, it is the reverse. There are families on earth because essentially God is family. Our families are meant to be made in His image, not the other way round. According to Ephesians 3:14–15, God is 'the Father, from whom his whole family ... on earth derives its name'. He is the *pares patria* – the Greek for 'daddy of all daddies!' So God does want to save whole families, and God can. When it comes to your family's salvation, God is on your side. It *is* the will of God. Remember our UK survey? 33 per cent of all males and 29 per cent of all females came to faith predominantly because of members of their family.

2 *Your church* – Just as it is unlikely that everyone in your immediate family is already saved, so too is it unlikely that everyone in your church network actually already knows Jesus. This is particularly likely to be true if you are from one of the more established denominations.

The so-called 'new' churches (of which I am a part) have much to learn here from the more established denominations. God has been kind to new churches over the years and has shown them something of the nature of church, the family of God, the multiplicity of leadership, the priesthood of all believers, the diversity of the gifts within the body, Christianity built on relationships, and so on. One of the results of all of this has been that new churches have a relatively clear understanding of the expectations a believer can have of church. And the expectations church can have of believers. Even as I write, much of this is being challenged for the new churches (see Chapter 1). But the result evangelistically has tended to be negative when it comes to working the church's fringe. All too often new churches do not have a fringe! You are either in or out. Too many new churches can be like express trains whizzing through the station; it is hard to get on!

The more established denominations, which have been around for longer, have less to prove and have felt under less threat, and have been better at finding or developing a fringe. Of course there are negatives to this, particularly in terms of commitment to body life, church expressed holistically outside of meetings, and so on. But the positive is that evangelistically it gives you a bigger pool to fish in!

Whatever your church background, you should be able to identify those on the edges or fringe of church life who have not yet made their own personal commitment to Christ. They may be partners of those who are already saved and a part of church. They may be 'high days and holy days' church attenders (usually Christmas, sometimes also Easter), or they may be consistent but religious attenders. Whatever the reason for the contact I would suggest that this is the second network that you need to be aware of for the purposes of friendship evangelism.

3 *Your work* – It is appalling (and thoroughly unbiblical) how many Christians seem to view the workplace as a necessary evil. As we saw in Chapter 1, this derives from a Greek mind-set, which separates out the sacred and the secular. But the church of Jesus Christ is meant to fill out all things of Christ in all things of creation in every sphere (Eph. 4:10). And this includes the sphere of the workplace (Eph. 6:5–9). Work is a creation principle, not a consequence of the fall.

Does God want to inhabit and invade your place of work? Yes, He does! How will He do that? Since church is the primary agent for the advancement of the kingdom of God in evangelism and discipleship (see Chapters 1 and 2), He will predominantly do that wherever He finds aspects of the church in your place of work. In other words, through you! It isn't that we merely go to work in order to witness to our work colleagues. Anymore than we merely go to work in order to raise money so that we can do the really spiritual stuff on a Sunday or at a midweek meeting! The workplace, our attitude to it and our presence in it is merely one of the ways that God wants to fill all things of creation with all things of Christ. Evangelism is a part of that.

It really is time to develop a more coherent theology of the workplace that goes beyond merely 'Don't steal the paper clips and witness to your colleagues'! But, since the average person will spend at least 60 per cent of their life at the workplace, it is also incumbent upon us to use this as an opportunity to build friendships and within those friendships to share the gospel.

It may be that, for you, your school, college or university constitutes your workplace. That's fine. Or it maybe that you are predominantly a homemaker, in which case your workplace would include all those that homemaking brings you into contact with: your butcher, the newsagent, the girl at the local corner shop, the guy behind the checkout counter at the local supermarket, the man who services your car, or the bank clerk, and so on. Even if you are currently unemployed there will be a sphere or circle of contacts that your unemployment will bring you into (DSS, job seekers' club, disability or pensions collection, and so on). The very stuff of life demands that we *all* have such contacts, which do not fall more readily into any other sphere of life.

4 *Your neighbours* – I firmly believe that God knows all things. By that I mean that He knows certain things which *will* happen. And that for very many other things He knows what *might* happen. And that He knows the consequences of every possible choice that we might make. This gives me a tremendous amount of confidence and faith when it comes to thinking about the people whom I live near, my neighbours. I don't believe that it all has just happened by chance. I do believe that if I will co-operate with God (Rom. 8:28) then He will in all things work for good, including my relationships with my neighbours. With this in mind, one of the things that intrigues me about my neighbours, and one of the first things I ask myself when I move into a new area, is 'What is it about me, my family and our testimony in God that will exactly fit the needs and experience of our unsaved neighbours?' That is a good way to view your neighbours!

An example: when we moved to Portsmouth ten years ago, we received a prophecy indicating that there would be a strong naval connection with the house that we bought. Also, strangely enough, that roses would have some prominent feature in the property we were to buy! Now, we must have looked at more than 60 houses before we bought the house where we now live. In fact, we put an offer in on a property we liked whose back garden was oddly but entirely planted out with roses. But that offer fell through when we were gazumped. We had had the details about the house we now own for many months before we looked at it, because it wasn't the period of house we wanted. When, with a measure of desperation, we finally agreed to look at the house (we didn't like its exterior) it came as something as a surprise to notice immediately by the front door was an unseasonably early flowering rose bush! Even more of a surprise that, on going into the house, we noticed it decked out with naval ephemera: there were cutlasses, telescopes and sea pictures everywhere! We soon came to realise that the property was owned by the (then) youngest merchant navy captain in the fleet. Indeed, so strong was the naval association that we never actually met the male owner since he was away at sea all the time, and we did all of our business with his wife.

Now, did we *have* to buy that house? No, we didn't. Was it foreordained and predestined that we should? No, it wasn't. Was God indicating to us that it would well suit our purposes as a family who liked to entertain a lot, often have people stay with us and run lots of meetings from the property? Yes, He was. Was He also indicating that our personal testimonies might well fit those of our immediate neighbours? Yes, He was, as events were to prove. Shortly after moving in we threw a housewarming party and invited the newly planted Portsmouth church and many of our neighbours. During the course of the evening, one of our neighbours collapsed on the floor, much to her dismay and embarrassment. (She was concerned that everyone would think that she had drunk too much!) Her husband and I had to physically carry her down the corridor and across the front of the house back to their home. In popping round the next day with a bunch of flowers, a card and box of chocolates to say that we wished her well, it transpired that she was undergoing various 'female problems', which my wife through her own personal experience could readily identify with. Here's how (and probably why!) God works all things together for good, and threw out those prophecies at us!

So what is it about your personal testimony which exactly fits the needs of your neighbours? I guarantee you if you look for it you will find it. Being good neighbours is a part of being good news to people. It's remarkable how often I have taught this in churches and elicited groans of challenge and conviction around the room. If for any reason *you* are at odds with your neighbours, let this chapter provoke you into seeking reconciliation. Perhaps the arguments and the issues need to be dropped. Maybe what's called for is for you to humble yourself, pop round with a bunch of flowers and a card, and apologise for any ill feeling or lack of communication in as much as it has depended upon you. For one thing is for sure; God *will* want to reach your neighbours through *you*.

5 *Your socialising* – There are those Christians for whom the concept of socialising is an alien one. The idea of having enough time outside of work, church and sleep to socialise with people seems foreign and remote to them. Sometimes fear of contamination, lack of mutuality, and/or sheer apathy can keep us restricted to the enclave of the Christian family, and so all our socialising is done with Christians. Sometimes the sheer demands involved in internal (and ultimately incestuous) efforts to maintain the construct of church means that we literally have no time to socialise. We may have reached the dizzy heights of super-spirituality whereby every time we put our foot outside our front door it is to go to another Christian meeting! Whatever the reason, if you haven't got a social life, get one! This is one of those occasions when literally you ought to 'get out more'!

Developing a social life is not only good for you in as much as God is interested in the whole of your life (and not just the 'spiritual' bit), but it also means that, in a social context, which is likely to be conducive to building friendships, you will rub shoulders with the as-yet-unsaved. How do you do this? Do it in consultation with friends in the church. With leaders or cell leaders if necessary. Get them to help you strip your diary back to make time for relating to the unsaved.

And if you are a church leader this particularly applies to *you*! As I said before, it *is* time to recognise that 'example is not the best means of leadership, it is the *only* means', as missionary Albert Schweitzer said. Time to realise that those whom we lead *will* attach importance to those things that we give priority to. So if you're a church leader you can't preach and teach about evangelism, and not do it yourself. If you are not going to do it yourself, don't preach about it! It's time to measure our values against our priorities. No longer good enough to espouse the value of witnessing and then to make everything else a higher priority. Developing a social life begins with ruthless prioritisation.

I, like you, am busy. I have to carve time into my diary to connect with the community of Portsmouth. I have to write in (sometimes months in advance) when I will be spending time with other members of the board of governors for my children's school, of which I am a part. Governors who are, as yet, unsaved. I have had to plan a year in advance when I am able to sit on the Bench as a local magistrate and thus rub shoulders with other magisterial colleagues, as yet unsaved, and in so doing become more realistically acquainted with the criminal underbelly of Portsmouth. We have to diary in meals with unsaved friends and neighbours. But do it we must. And so must you. Once you've dealt with the time pressures, developing a social life is relatively easy. Just think about the things which you like doing the most, then do them with not-yet-Christians. (Obviously within the bounds of moral propriety!) So if you like doing drama, *don't* start another church drama group! *Do* join the local amateur dramatic society. If your social conscience prompts you towards charitable fundraising, *don't* start another charity. *Do* find out what the Mayor's annual charity is, and join in that.

So there you have it. Five networks, already in existence, where you can begin to identify friendships (current or potential) and see what God would do.

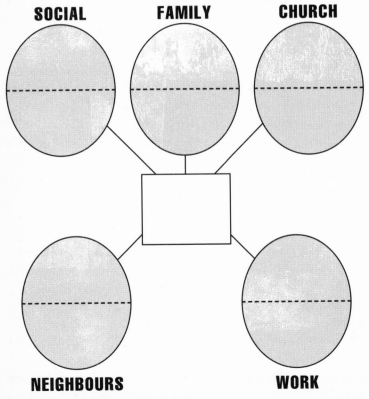

FIGURE 7.1 – FRIENDSHIP NETWORKS

Name, names …

Before we move on to the second part of the five-part strategy, can I push you further to be practically ruthless in the application of this first point? At the centre of Figure 7.1 you will see a box. Would you write your name in that box? Then ranged around the box, like spokes of a wheel, you will see a number of spheres or circles of contact, as outlined above. Each of the spheres is divided in half by a horizontal dotted line. In the top half of each could I ask you to write the names of one or more people who fit in that sphere with whom you are already well acquainted? Then in the bottom half could you write one or more names who fit in that sphere, with whom you are less well acquainted?

This way you will have names in each sphere who represent two kinds of evangelistic 'fishing'. The first list (those in the top part of the circles) represents those where there is an already established line of friendship, contact and communication. It is like fishing with a rod. Those in the bottom half of the circle represent a more nebulous relationship; this is more like fishing, a little less specifically, with a net! But either way, they are friendships or potential friendships.

A word of advice. It is more meaningful to write down names of people with whom you have real friendship, or a real potential to build friendship, rather than simply make yourself feel better with lots of names of people you may never see again or even speak to! So don't put down the name of your wife's maiden aunt's budgie's vet's assistant! Or the milkman, whose name you don't even know, and whom you may never speak to! It's better to have fewer names and a real chance of building friendships, than many names and little chance at all.

One other thing. This is not a paper or administrative exercise. Please don't put down any names *unless* you are prepared for God to both challenge and help you to deepen your relationship and share Jesus with them. For these are not just names. They're faces. They're real people. Behind every name and face lies a life history, an accumulation of hopes and fears, purposes, mistakes and sins. Of pains and pleasures, of potential, of privilege and responsibility. Please *don't* do this exercise, unless you are prepared to be the answers to your own prayer, and for God to use you in reaching these specific lost people.

What might this mean?

When I teach this in church training sessions, it is not uncommon to find that a room of 100 Christians will have pre-existent real relationships with between 300 and 500 not-yet-Christians. This is incredibly encouraging. You could try this yourself among your own friends in your own church.

Let's explore the scenario. Let's say you are in the early stages of exploring and identifying your networks, and from the five spheres of contacts you have been able to identify only five names. Suppose you then share those names with the nine other people who make up your house group/cell in your church. If each of them had also found five names, that means that you are now looking at 50 named, not-yet-Christian contacts. Because you already know the people in your house group/cell, it's likely that some of the people that you have all named will be the same; there will be some overlap. Let's say that each cell member has one of their five names overlapping with those of some other cell member. That means that you have a list of 40 *different* names.

We have already seen that most people come to faith in Christ as part of a process rather than during a crisis, and that for most people that process can span four years. So some of those 40 people will already be on that process and some of them may be near to completion! I wouldn't find it a great strain of faith to believe that of those 40 perhaps 10 per cent might come to faith in Christ over the course of the next 12 months. That doesn't seem to me to be a lot to believe for, or a lot to pray for. Particularly when you know that God is unwilling for any to perish. This would mean that your cell alone could perhaps believe, pray toward and work for four of your contacts to become Christians in the course of the next 12 months. That would represent 40 per cent growth in a year! It would necessitate your cell having to multiply in order to effectively disciple and empower its members! That wouldn't be bad, would it?!

EVALUATE YOUR NETWORKS

The second part of our five-point strategy for friendship evangelism is the evaluation of our existing networks. This stops us assuming that a friendship is stronger or deeper than it actually is, or helps us avoid the fear that the friendship is more fragile than is the case. As has been accurately said, to assume makes an 'ASS' out of 'U' and 'ME'! I need to know what the nature, extent, scope, strength and depth of my relationships with not-yet-Christians really are, if I am to properly pitch any gospel content and exercise any relational integrity.

For a very brief period of time I was fortunate enough to drive a Volvo B121 saloon car, which was resplendent with a leather interior, lots of chrome, an 1800cc engine and fitted twin Webber carburettors. The car had been given to me in my early days of working with Youth for Christ in the East End of London, and within a year someone had driven into the back of it and written it off! But during the time that I was its proud owner, I had occasion to take it up to Scotland on holiday. Exploring the single-track roads of the Scottish highlands and crossing freezing cold burns on rather rickety bridges, I suddenly became very aware of the weight of my vehicle, for it weighed well in excess of a ton! There were some bridges I had to make a detour around and avoid all together, because otherwise I would have been at risk of putting too much car across too weak a bridge!

And that's the point. We need to spend some time evaluating the nature of our network of friendships, in order to avoid trying to drive a ten-ton gospel message across a five-ton relational bridge! To do so might place too great a strain upon the friendship. It could even damage or destroy its relational integrity.

The other good thing about evaluating your networks of friendships is that by giving you a snapshot of where you are *currently* at, evaluation can also give you an indication of where next to 'point the camera'. It can both highlight and answer the question, 'Where do we go to from here in our friendship?' And evaluating your networks will help you to meet people at the appropriate point of their need. It's evaluation that will show you what their primary need is. We know that their *ultimate* need is to find Jesus. But often that is not their perception. Often that is not their *primary* need.

Jesus was very good at doing this. Have a look at Luke 19, the story of a hated, feared and despised tax collector. Then being a tax collector was synonymous with being a sinner! Leper-like, they were banned from the Temple and from giving witness in court. As Jews they collected taxes from their fellow Jews on behalf of the Romans, and were therefore viewed as traitors, always creaming money off on top for themselves. So as a corrupt tax collector you might have money, but you wouldn't have friends. Zacchaeus was one such. Added to this, he was small in stature. As like as not, this was a man full of insecurity, carrying at heart a sense of guilt, almost certainly with a low self-image and a projected anger toward others, experiencing hefty doses of rejection and isolation. Yet so desperate is he to check out Jesus, that he climbs up into a tree to gain a better view over the heads of the crowds. And Jesus' response? He doesn't target Zacchaeus' *ultimate* need, for forgiveness, for repentance, for salvation. Rather, Jesus homes straight in on Zacchaeus' 'felt' need. A need for security. A need for self-worth. A need for friendship and acceptance. How best to demonstrate this? Why, invite yourself round for a meal, of course! And that is exactly what Jesus does. It's significant that it is this offer of acceptance and friendship that evokes a response of repentance and restitution in Zacchaeus.

Another good example sees Paul and Silas singing hymns of praise while incarcerated in the local prison (Acts 16). God shows up, big time! An earthquake opens the doors, the chains fall off. Not just off Paul and Silas, but off all of the other prisoners too! The penalty imposed on a jailer who lost a prisoner was that they be executed, often burned alive in the clothes they stood in. Understandably this jailer is about to fall upon his sword, a noble Roman suicide. His primary need is for comfort and reassurance. He needs to know that he has not lost his livelihood, his prisoners or his life! And these are the needs that Paul and Silas meet. Rather than escape following divine intervention, Paul and Silas are at pains to encourage the jailer that they and the rest of the prisoners are still there safe and sound! They meet his *primary* need. And the subsequent result? The jailer and his family turn to Christ for salvation. Evaluating your networks helps you to learn to meet people at the point of their appropriate need, in order then to meet people at the point of their ultimate need.

So how do we do this evaluation? Here are two tools to help you. Use either or both. I would encourage you to use both at first to see which you get on best with.

Maslow's triangle

Maslow was an interesting guy with not a few wacky ideas, but one of his sociological innovations was the construction of a social hierarchy of needs. Everyone is created with an inherent desire to both love and be loved, to both give and to receive. Maslow's assertion was that humans are social animals whose needs must be met in a relational context. These needs have an order or priority about them. This is best represented in pictorial form, as shown in Figure 7.2.

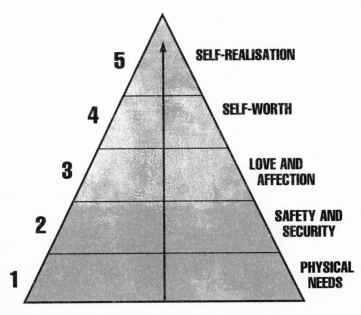

FIGURE 7.2 – MASLOW'S TRIANGLE

- According to Maslow our primary needs are *physical*. Among other things, we need to eat, sleep and breathe. So in terms of the early stages of friendship, hospitality comes to the fore. Good hospitality makes excellent provision for physical needs. Physical provision is a good measure of the level of your friendship. It's one way of evaluating its extent. It's why meals and shared food and wine are so important. Why opening up your home, or offering a bed for the night when someone has had a meal with you are important steps along the way to friendship, and a marker when it comes to evaluating it. It's also why servanthood evangelism and the offer of practical help are often important in the early stages of building friendships. If in some measure you are providing these things (or things like them) in your friendships with not-yet-Christians this will tell you something of the nature and extent, the depth and reality of those friendships. If you are not, it will also tell you something!

- *Safety and security* come next in Maslow's hierarchy of needs. While these are physical needs (i.e. you are not about to hit one of your not-yet-Christian friends, or poison them with your cooking, which would certainly tell you something about the state of your friendship!), they go much beyond this. They also involve emotional safety and security. Is your friend emotionally and relationally safe and secure in your absence as in your presence? Can they trust their wellbeing and their reputation to your words and your actions? If so, then you have gone beyond mere physical provision; evaluation indicates that trust, an important part of friendship evangelism, will be developing.

- Next on the way up Maslow's Triangle come *love and affection*. The British culture may not be very good at verbally or physically expressing love and affection, encouragement and approbation. Yet at the same time we all need it. If this is missing from your current relationships with not-yet-Christians then the process of evaluation will show you this, and give you something to aim for.

- Then comes *self-worth*. Without a proper sense of self-worth we have very little to give away to other people. For the Christian, self-worth is not based upon narcissistic self-love, but rather upon a realistic assessment of our own sinfulness and yet of God's grace and love. For many who are unsaved, self-worth is an elusive dream, which many seek to achieve through the delusion of performance and perfectionism. If your relationship with those not yet saved helps them realise they are something other than a mass of unplanned molecules, more than an evolved animal, and that there is a unique value and dignity about each individual human, then you have strong relationship capable of carrying considerable gospel content.

- At the peak of Maslow's hierarchy is the need for *self-realisation*. Outside a Christian mind-set, 'self-realisation' is a very nebulous term, and sounds somewhat 'New Age'. Much Eastern mysticism and most cults seek to find self-realisation through a process of journeying within the individual. The search is on to find the god who is within you, or even to realise your potential to become a god! But the Christian has realised that self-realisation is impossible outside of a personal relationship with the Creator God, Who realised us in the first place. In many respects Maslow's ultimate hierarchical need is every individual's ultimate need: true salvation, realising our destiny and identity in Christ. If in evaluating your relationships you feel they have reached this point, then well done! It should mean that your not-yet-Christian friend is now a Christian, or very close to becoming one!

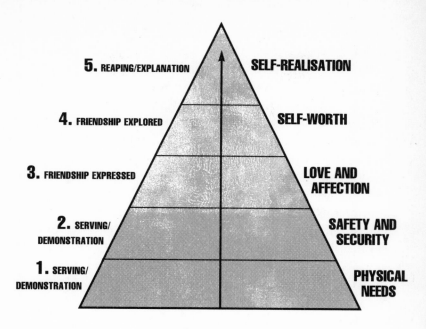

FIGURE 7.3 – EVALUATING RELATIONSHIPS TRIANGLE

Let's look at that triangle again, but this time down the left-hand side. In Figure 7.3 I have written in what I think are the main hallmarks of our friendships with not-yet-Christians. This gives us a hint on how best we might proceed. The best way to use this evaluation tool is to write names from the exercise on page 188, where you identified your networks, into the appropriate levels on the triangle in Figure 7.3. This will not only help you evaluate where your relationships are currently, but also how you can move them on.

Get the picture?

The second tool to help evaluate your friendships involves profiling to build a picture of the relationship. The great thing about the profile chart is that every part of it can be useful in your evaluation, even the bits you *can't* fill in. All of it has the potential for telling you something about how strong (or weak) your relationship is. The chart is shown in Figure 7.4.

Most of the headings are self-explanatory, but here are a few hints on some of them. Please don't restrain your entry under 'Occupation' to details of paid employment; being a homemaker is as much an occupation as is being a student or a car salesman. Under the heading 'likes', it will be helpful to jot down things like 'curries' and 'red wine', but please don't restrict it to this, as things like 'people of integrity' or 'justice issues' will also prove useful. Similarly with the column entitled 'Dislikes', please don't *just* include things like 'dogs', and *do* include things like 'hypocrisy'. Clearly we are going for the conceptual here as well as the material. Under the heading 'Qualities', *avoid* generalities like 'an all round good bloke!', but *do* include 'good sense of humour', 'honesty', 'sociable', 'generous', 'expressive', etc. When it comes to 'Needs', again let me urge you to be specific and practical. Don't put down 'they need Jesus'! Rather, include things like 'a lift to work on Wednesdays', 'a baby-sitter on Thursday evenings', 'a job', 'emotional support at a time of divorce'.

The column entitled 'Idea of Jesus' will instantly tell you whether you have reached that place in your relationship to even mention Him. If you have no idea what they think about Jesus, please put that down. On the other hand, some of your friends may believe Him to be the Son of God, but have done nothing about it. Some may think He was a good teacher, a political interventionist and so on. The final column, headed 'Relationship to you', should again contain some detail. Don't just put down 'my friend'. Include stuff like how often you see them, in what areas they receive from you, in what areas they

NAME	AGE	OCCUPATION	FAMILY SITUATION	LIKES	DISLIKES	QUALITIES	NEEDS	IDEA OF JESUS	RELATIONSHIP TO YOU

FIGURE 7.4 – PROFILING FRIENDSHIPS CHART

give to you and any areas of mutuality.

Taken together these two tools will give you an accurate snapshot of the current state of your relationships with people who are not yet Christians. They will help you avoid putting too much or too little content of the gospel into those relationships. But they will also provoke you to realising where the weaknesses are in your relationship. What are the inhibitors that prevent you being more open about your faith with your friend? And what can you do about them? This takes us to the next part of our strategy.

Developing your networks

This third part of our strategy for friendship evangelism helps us build on the ground we have taken so far. There's no premium in identifying networks and evaluating them if we are not prepared to develop them. Development acknowledges that there is nothing wrong with driving a ten-ton gospel message into a relationship, providing we have a ten-ton relational bridge! This is the part of the strategy that demands not only assessment, but also proactive deeds. Development starts to take us from where we are to where we might be. It therefore demands faith and action. Again, here are two tools to help you in developing (i.e. widening/strengthening/deepening) your networks.

The goal sheet

First the proactive setting of goals. Christians or not, we live our lives on a daily basis by the setting, keeping or breaking of goals. You can't help but do so. Every task accomplished, shopping list made, budget drawn up and adhered to, every diary engagement kept, tank of petrol bought, house cleaned, child picked up from school. All these require goals to be set and met or missed. We live our lives through the conscious and/or subconscious setting, accomplishing or missing of goals.

Then why, oh why, when it comes to the deliberate setting of goals related to our faith, do so many Christians shy away from this area? Perhaps it is because we feel that goals somehow remove our dependence upon the Holy Spirit. If that is your problem, then simply call goals 'faith targets'! Because that is surely what they are. Perhaps we feel that when it comes to evangelism, or any other 'spiritual' activity, God Himself does not set goals. But God has clear goals and targets for evangelism; He is unwilling for any to perish. That is a goal. Maybe we have an unbiblical fatalistic theology that God will get it all done anyway. Or perhaps we are averse to goals because to set a goal is a threatening thing to do. A goal set means that our target can be checked. Did we hit it, or did we miss it? Or possibly for you goals speak too much of management training courses, as though somehow truth revealed there was not truth from God. Whereas Scripture is clear; all truth comes from God. Goals can be threatening.

I sometimes think that many of us would prefer to live our Christian lives in retrospect; we see where we end up, and then we draw our target around that! But one thing is for sure; if we aim at nothing, that is exactly what we will hit. The truth is that God sets goals, God is a Strategist, goals have a remarkable propensity for releasing faith and energy, and they provide a realistic method of assessing, monitoring, evaluating, encouraging and adjusting how we are doing and where we are getting to.

S.M.A.R.T. goals

But if we're going to set goals, they need to be S.M.A.R.T. goals. If you are not used to setting goals (or faith targets), a common mistake to fall into is to mistake a goal for a purpose. Purposes tend to be psychologically useful, but are generally vague. They express desire and motivation, but carry no hint of process. However, a goal is:

- Specific – It is detailed and precise.
- Measurable – A true goal is capable of being measured and assessed in quality and quantity.
- Achievable – Setting impossible goals is a recipe for disappointment, despair and disillusionment. Real goals are at least 75 per cent achievable, thus giving a sense of movement and satisfaction, but also allowing enough room to spur us on, and for God to do what we cannot do once we have done what we can do!
- Relevant – Real goals make sure that they are realistically aligned to the point of arrival as well as departure. In other words, they always keep an eye on what we are seeking to achieve, and do not confuse the *method* of achieving them with the *desired result*. If your goal is not relevant, you will end up bogged down with the methods and forgetting the ultimate aim. Many churches do this. They set off seeking to reach a defined people group, but end up wallowing in a plethora of maintenance projects instead of missionary endeavours.
- Time-related – Time is only one of the elements by which goals may be measured. But all goals should contain some element of time-related criteria. This prompts us to a realistic assessment and possible adjustments as opposed to a never-ending attempt to 'get there in the end'.

So with these hints in goal-setting in mind, look at the goal sheet in Figure 7.5. As you can see, for the sake of anonymity, I have filled this in with a fictitious, but entirely realistic

NAME	PRESENT SITUATION	GOAL	ADVANTAGES	DISADVANTAGES	ACTION
Fred	Work colleague Meet Mon–Fri Casual acquaintance	Invite to introductory *Alpha* Supper by 1 Sept by mid-August	Enquiring mind, sociable, same lunch hour, likes squash	Currently only casual acquaintance; too big a leap to invite to *Alpha*; I'm bad at squash	Pray for a God opportunity to talk further; invite to lunch (pay for it!) by end of May; ask if he would like to play squash and help me with my game; book in weekly squash game and/or lunch starting June; invite to *Alpha* Supper mid-August

FIGURE 7.5 – GOAL SHEET

scenario. This gives an idea how best to use the goal sheet. When you write your own, check your 'Goal' column against the S.M.A.R.T. criteria. Fill in your 'Advantages' column *as they relate to your goal* and your 'Disadvantages' column *as they relate to your goal and your advantages.* If you juggle these three things correctly you should end up with a very specific 'Action' column which you can go away and do. This is an intensely practical tool.

One last thing about goals. Goals are *not* absolutes. Absolutes are absolutes. For example, there are certain absolutes about the nature of God. God is love. Jesus Christ is His Son. Christ died for us and rose from the dead. These are absolutes. It is from these absolutes that we derive our values. Values are not absolutes. Absolutes are absolutes. Values *derive* from absolutes. So if one of the absolutes attributable to God is that God is love, then our value is that we must love Him, be loved by Him and love others. These are values. If it is an absolute that Christ is risen from the dead, then our value must be to get to know Him in intimacy, for He is alive.

Then from absolutes and values come our purposes. A purpose would be to know Christ in greater intimacy, but a goal would be to fast one day a week for 12 months and read Scripture from CWR's *Cover to Cover Through the Bible in a Year* over the same time, in order to know Jesus better. That is a goal. So our purpose is derived from our values, our goals from our purposes, and our plans derive from our goals. Our plan in this case would be to write into our diary one day's fasting, to choose whether we are fasting food, TV, sex(!) etc, and write that in. To purchase one of CWR's *Cover to Cover* volumes, and to programme the reading of that in on a daily basis. These derivatives and this process can also be represented diagrammatically, as shown in Figure 7.6.

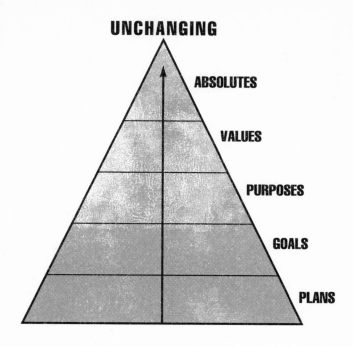

FIGURE 7.6 – FROM ABSOLUTES TO PLANS

As you can see in Figure 7.6, absolutes don't change but, as you work your way down the process, change potential increases. When it comes to goal-setting, none of them is set in concrete! They can and they do change. But it's more likely that our method/plan of how to get to the goal will change *first*. An example would be the paralytic brought to Jesus by his friends (Mark 2:1–12). I have no doubt when they set out that day to reach Jesus they had no intention of boring a hole through someone's roof! Their sole *goal* was to get their friend to the feet of Jesus, for they had heard that He could heal. When they got to the house they couldn't get into the house because of the surrounding crowds. Did they change their goal? No, they didn't. Did they change their *plan/method* of achieving their goal? Yes, they did! Instead of going through the crowd and the door to Jesus, they went up onto the flat roof and bored their way down to Him. Unorthodox, maybe. But effective, certainly! Goal-setting and strategy are so important that we'll come back to them at the end of this book in Chapter 11.

The Engel's Scale revisited

The second tool takes us back to Chapter 2, where we looked at the nature of evangelism and the paradigm shift, and touched on process evangelism as illustrated by Engel's Scale (Fig. 2.2, page 59). I have found this to be a very practical developmental tool when it comes to progressing my friendships with not-yet-Christians. Here's how it works for me. I imagine where I think they are currently at in their relationship to Jesus along the Engel's Scale. Do they fall somewhere between point 0 to point 4, where the emphasis is on befriending, servanthood evangelism, ways in which I can help them with the good works of the gospel? This is where most friendships start.

Or have we moved on beyond that, such that they now fall between 4 and 7, so that while we continue to sow rather than reap, they are probably going to be receptive to gradually increasing gospel content? If not, then I need to pray, build and work towards that goal. If so, and the last time we had supper I simply mentioned how God had recently answered some prayers, and they made a positive, if slightly incredulous response, then maybe *next* time I move them from point 5 to point 6 by offering to pray *for* them (rather than *with* them, which might move them on again to point 7). Get the idea? And if they have had lots of content, but no opportunity to respond to that personally, then maybe I should be working and praying towards a point from 7 to 10, when we might not be sowing, but rather reaping. Perhaps that will involve miraculous intervention and wonders, or an invitation to some kind of reaping event? The Engel's Scale can be a really good visual aid towards not only picturing where your friends are currently at (evaluation) but also what the next steps might be (development).

Fill in the blanks

As you'll see from the groupwork coming up, again we'll make this intensely practical through application. None of these tools and methods in and of themselves can see someone come to faith in Christ. That is a relational thing. It's never so simple as 'if I do A, B and C then the natural result will be D.' It never was for Jesus. It won't be for us. On the other hand, if there are proven tools available, we would be foolish not to make the best use of them. So *please* let me urge you to take the following groupwork seriously, before we move on in the next chapter to the final two parts of our five-part strategy for friendship evangelism.

GROUPWORK

1. Individually fill out Figure 7.1 as explained in this chapter (page 188)
2. Share these names with your group, select two names each, and spend a minimum of ten minutes praying for them. Pray for their *felt* needs *and* for their *ultimate* need of salvation.
3. Individually use the same two names to fill in the Evaluating Relationships Triangle (Fig. 7.3 on page 197)

and the Profiling Friendships Chart (Fig. 7.4 on page 199), as outlined in this chapter.

4. Share and discuss your evaluation with your group.

5. Individually fill out the Goal Sheet (Fig. 7.5 on page 203) and put names onto the Engel's Scale (Fig. 2.2 on page 59), using the same two names throughout.

6. Share and discuss your goals for developing these relationships with your group.

7. In keeping with the time frames in your goals, monitor and evaluate the effectiveness of these goals with your group for further prayer and adjustment on a minimum monthly basis.

Chapter 8

AND THERE'S MORE ...

The next part of our five-point strategy for friendship evangelism is totally and utterly vital to its success. It will keep us focussed on the reality that we can save no one. That unless God intervenes, it doesn't matter how many strategies and methods we develop, nothing will happen, for apart from God we can do nothing (John 15:5), but with God all things are possible, and nothing is impossible (Luke 1:37). This latter is a particularly encouraging verse as it has a double meaning; as usually read, it means that with God everything is possible. But it also means, that with God it is *impossible* for *nothing* to happen! Think about the double meaning, and have a look at the verse again.

When it comes to evangelism there really is no point talking to people about God, until first of all you have talked to God about people. Scripture is clear that prayer is two-way communication with God; both talking and listening. Prayer is also a lifestyle. It's about developing a state of continuous awareness of God; what used to be called 'practising the presence of God'. Prayer is not reserved for those moments when we draw aside on our own and storm heaven with our requests. It *is* that, but it is also the prayer evoked by 1,001 simple moments during the day. The sight of a scudding cloud across a spring sky. The expression on your neighbour's face. The sound of an ambulance siren passing by. Letting incidents like these turn our thoughts God-ward is all a part of prayer. Otherwise the apostle Paul must have been lying when he said that he prayed 'constantly' (1 Thess. 1:3; 2:13; 5:17; Rom. 1:9; 2 Tim. 1:3), because we know that he also planted churches, raised the dead, advised elders, proclaimed the gospel, made tents and so on.

So prayer is both those special moments *and* a lifestyle of prayer. It can be individual and corporate, something which is unique to the Christian faith. And we have a God who delights in the prayers of the saints (Prov. 15:8; Rev. 5:8). But if ever there was a kind of prayer which rose like incense straight into the nostrils of God, a category of prayer with its own 'fast track' path, a package of prayer marked 'Special Delivery', then it would be prayers for the lost. Given that the salvation of humankind is at the top of God's list of priorities, you had better believe that God pays particular attention to the prayers of His saints on behalf of the lost. For ultimately all the trials and tribulations of the saints, real though they are, are cosmetic. For we know what our destiny is. But for the lost it's an issue of life and death.

There is a wonderful example of how eager God is to answer such prayers and how effective He is at it in Acts 1:8, where the disciples are commanded to wait in Jerusalem until they receive the Holy Spirit power (Greek *dunamis* – English 'dynamite'), in order that they might become witnesses in Jerusalem. By the time we reach Acts 5:28, we discover that in what has been a short period of time they have effectively already 'filled Jerusalem with … teaching' about Jesus.

Doesn't this intrigue and perhaps irritate you? How did they manage to reach a city in such a short period of time? The only indication that we get of any activity that those disciples undertook, which could operate outside of the sphere of the saints and be a method of reaching the lost, is found in Acts 2:42. Here, amidst all the other things that they began to practise as early church, is their outward focus: prayer! What do you imagine they were praying for? They were praying for the lost of their city. That's how they got to Acts 5:28 from Acts 1:8; via Acts 2:42! Prayer for the early church was as much about evangelism as about anything else.

Nowadays we tend to have prayer strategies for all kinds of things – for our day, our week, our budget, our career, for our health and our families and so on. But the question which most troubles me is: Do we have a prayer strategy for the lost? And is it the kind of strategy that will help us keep on praying? With persistence and intelligence? I don't know about you, but without a cohesive strategy, a sense of progress and process, I find that praying for my not-yet-Christian friends can become bland, repetitive, religious, ritualistic and somewhat boring (I suspect as much to God as to me!). How many times and for how long can I continue to meaningfully pray, 'Dear God, please save Roger'? And with what variations? 'Dear God, *please* save Roger. Dear God, please *save* Roger. Dear God, Roger – please save him'! It's pretty limited stuff, isn't it? So what follows are a few suggestions, which I've 'field-tested' to help keep us on track in our prayers for the lost. Try them out. Don't try them all at once, but rather take time to explore different ones, until you've eventually tried them all.

PRAYING FOR YOUR NETWORKS (OR STRATEGIC PRAYER)

Hold onto your hats! I'm going to give you a whistle-stop tour of 14 stations to stop at on route to praying for our not-yet-Christian friends. Here goes.

1. Pray for boldness (2 Tim. 1:7)

Isn't it interesting that when Jesus remarks on how ready the fields are for harvest (a reference to salvation reaping going right back into the Old Testament) that the difficulty He highlights isn't to do with the harvest itself (the unsaved) but rather to do with the harvesters (God's workers, i.e. us)? So at the end of Matthew 9 Jesus commands the disciples to pray for workers to go into the harvest fields. And then, with wonderful irony, at the beginning of Matthew 10 Jesus (I imagine gleefully!) informs His disciples that God has heard their prayers (cheers all round!) and that He has answered them (even louder cheers!) and that the answer to their prayers is … them! (panic-stricken glances all round, I imagine!). Real prayer gets you *more* involved in the answer, not *less* involved. In Matthew 10 the disciples are sent out with instructions to reach the lost in teams of two. So the first practical tip when it comes to praying for the lost, is that we start off by praying for ourselves! We are the primary means that God is likely to use to reach our not-yet-Christian friends. I don't know about you, but I massively lack boldness and courage when it comes to putting my faith on the line and opening my mouth for Jesus, and I am an evangelist! So a good place to start is to ask God to give you His Holy Spirit of boldness. That He would give us the words to speak when we need to speak them (Matt. 10:19–20).

2. Pray for wisdom (James 1:5)

Ever feel that you lack wisdom when it comes to witnessing? So do I! Wisdom to know when to speak. When to shut up.

Wisdom to know what to say and what not to say. Wisdom to answer difficult questions. Wisdom to portray moral integrity without prudish superiority. The list seems endless. But the promise of God is clear. If we lack wisdom, we should ask for it in faith and God will give it.

3. Pray about what to pray about

Sometimes I think that we get things the wrong way round; we pray as though it all depends on us, and we behave as though it all depends on God (i.e. we do nothing). Surely it's really the other way round; we pray as though it all depends on God (for it surely does) and we behave as though it all depends on us (ie we do something). It's quite likely that God has His own agenda concerning what we should be praying for when it comes to reaching the lost. So it might be a good idea for us every now and then to ask God what to pray about! I've found it's much easier and more effective to join in with what the Holy Spirit is doing when it comes to praying, rather than try to generate my own prayer agenda. Sometimes God will inform our heads about the prayer process, sometimes He will inform our hearts, which is when we pray with our spirits rather than our minds (1 Cor. 14:14). Under these circumstances the gift of tongues is vital when it comes to praying for the lost.

4. Making the most of the opportunities (Col. 4:5)

We'll come back to this in more detail in Chapter 9 where we look at the story of the woman at the well (John 4). For now perhaps just note that it's always worth asking God to help you recognise when the opportunities occur, as well as giving you boldness to take them! Perhaps you need to pray for opportunities to meet the unsaved and to befriend them? Or maybe you need to pray for developing opportunities in existing relationships? Wherever you are at in your relationships with the unsaved, one thing is sure; God will want to move you on. It's a great prayer habit to develop, approaching each day, proactively, in faith, looking for and taking opportunities which God will surely give us to reach the lost. It takes a bit of energy and faith, but the rewards are remarkable both for the lost (most importantly) and for you (less importantly!).

5. Pray people along the scale

You remember looking in the previous chapter and in Chapter 2 at the concept of the Engel's Scale? Well, I not only find it useful to visualise where my friends are at along that scale, in order to develop and deepen my relationships with them, I *also* use the Engel's Scale as a useful spur to faith and prayer as with the eye of faith I 'see' them move along a stage through the power of intercession. Try it and see if it works for you!

6. Redemptive gifting

This is a great area to pray into on behalf of the unsaved! It's based on the idea that each of us was made in the image of God, that each of us is utterly unique, and we are all created and designed to have a meaningful relationship primarily with God, and with other people. Therefore each of us is potentially utterly and uniquely gifted naturally by the Father, supernaturally by the Holy Spirit and ministry-gifted by Jesus. When you become a Christian these three areas of gifting begin to come to life. So when we are praying for people who are not yet Christians, we can ask God to show us what their redemptive gifting might be. And we can begin to pray into it, that they might begin to inherit it in their journey towards faith. And what's even more exciting, as you build a sufficiently strong relationship you can actually talk to them about it as well! You should see the impact knowing that God has a specific purpose and destiny for your unsaved friend can have upon them!

In case you think that this sounds a bit wacky, I suggest that many of you have probably already experienced it. Ever looked at some of your unsaved friends and found yourself thinking, 'If only you got saved you'd make a fantastic ...'? Fill in the blank for yourself, but I'll guarantee that among your unconverted friends you've spotted perhaps a potential evangelist (currently in sales). Or a pastor (a carer perhaps). Or Bible teacher of the future (with a passion for truth). Or perhaps a gift of hospitality, maybe driven in the unsaved by insecurity, but just waiting to be redeemed. Praying for the redemptive gifting of unsaved people is such a positive way to pray. It's about praying for a blessing for their (as yet) unrealised future and destiny.

7. Felt needs

We looked in the previous chapter at how Jesus gave attention to people's felt needs, and how Maslow prioritised them. We can get in on this by praying for insight into people's felt needs, and then praying into those felt needs. I've sometimes found it necessary to pray that God will open the eyes of my unsaved friends so that *they* recognise their felt needs! Taking this one step further it's even necessary on occasions to ask God to bring our friends to just the right 'pastoral moment' when they will be receptive to the gospel. We'll look at this in more detail later in this chapter under the heading 'Working Your Networks', but for now it's enough just to recognise that there are certain times in our lives when we are more inclined to be open to the gospel and to respond to God than at other times. It's not as though we are asking God to create nasty moments in our lives, but rather that in prayer we will co-operate actively with Him (Rom. 8:28) to see Him 'in all things ... for the good'. This principle can be extended through prayer into the lives of not-yet-Christian friends.

8. Binding and loosing. (Matt. 12:29; 16:19)

Jesus is clear in these two verses about our need to bind down negative influences in the lives of others, and about our authority to do so. The first verse is specifically to do with deliverance, and that is something that we would be ill advised to embark upon in the life of an unbeliever, if they are not then immediately prepared to surrender their lives to the infilling work of the Holy Spirit. Otherwise they will end up in a worse state than they started. But what we *do* have authority to pray for is to bind down or severely restrict the influence of enemy activity in the lives of the unsaved. Not at this stage to remove him and his activity from their lives, for to do so without their will being in line with our prayers would be both ineffective and dangerous for them. But rather to restrict his influence. The principle then is that where you bind the negative, you loose the positive. So in practical terms, if one of our unsaved friends is consistently afflicted with fear, then we have the authority to restrict or bind that fear down in their lives, and to loose the opposite of fear, which Scripture makes clear to be love (1 John 4:18). Similarly we can bind down deception and release truth, or confusion and release peace (John 8:44–47; 1 Cor. 14:33). And so we bind down the negative and loose the positive, thus making more space in the lives of our unsaved friends for the Holy Spirit to move in with conviction of sin and fruits of repentance.

9. 'You do not have ...' (James 4:2)

Our next prayer pointer is a plea for specific requests. For years and years as a young lad I would pray a nightly prayer that God would 'bless Aunty Mary'. Truth is, I wouldn't know if God had blessed Aunty Mary if I fell over it, because my request was too general and vague. General and vague prayers tend to get general and vague answers! And to provoke general and vague faith! But God encourages us to pray specific prayers so that He can say 'Yes' and 'Amen' to them (2 Cor. 1:20). Praying for your friend to get a job, or be reconciled to her husband, or to meet another Christian at work is better than asking God to simply 'bless' them.

What's more, there are three key stages to praying specifically for your not-yet-Christian friend. First, you pray *for* them and they *don't* know about it. Then as you build the relationship sufficiently, you tell them that you are praying *for* them, so now you are praying for them specifically and they *do* know. And third, and most excitingly, you reach the place of relationship where you can actually pray *with* them before they are saved. This is great! It will deepen your friendship. It will certainly build faith, because God longs to answer prayers like these. And it will test your religiosity! Do you pray long-winded prayers to build your own faith up? Or can you use short and simple prayers? Do you use jargon and the 'language of Zion'? Or will you pray in everyday language? Do you have to have your eyes closed when you pray? Or can you pray with your friend while you walk down the street? Or at his desk? Praying doesn't just deal with the problem, it changes the person. So praying for and with the lost increases the faith capacity in our own lives, much like changing the fuse in a plug from a 5 amp to a 13 amp!

10. Finding favour (Acts 2:4–7)

The biblical injunction is that we should be at peace with all people in as much as it depends upon us (Rom. 12:18). So we should be praying that we, like the early church, find favour with the unsaved. Not for our benefit. But for theirs. So we begin to find favour for friendships. Favour to serve. To give. Favour when we offer to pray for or with our friends. Favour when we make specific invitations to the appropriate kind of events (more on this in Chapter 11). If I am going to invite my neighbours to my cell's next *Alpha* course, I don't just want to go round and invite them; I want to do so after praying that I'll find favour with my invitation, and a positive response.

11. Mementoes

There's an intriguing film about a guy with acute memory loss, whose only way of keeping track of who he is and what he is doing is to write himself mementoes on his mirror, or even on his body. I think we could do with some of that when it comes to praying for the lost! So the next port of call in our prayer journey is to advocate some system of reminders, whatever works for you, that jogs your memory to pray for the lost. For some it will be a prayer list kept in their Bibles, because they go there every day. For others it will be a knot in their handkerchief. Or a prayer list halfway down the door (at eye level) inside the loo!

I use three main methods of prayer reminders. First, there is my diary. The nature of what I do means that I virtually have to live out of my diary, and I refer to it without fail every day. So when I'm targeting specific requests for my unsaved friends, I will normally jot them in against a date or time in my diary to remind me. If someone looks at my diary, I don't want the only way that they can tell I'm a Christian to be the plethora of 'spiritual' meetings I go to! I would be happier to see prayer for the lost reflected there than simply a stack of Christian meetings! The second memory aid I use is photographs. In my study at home at the top of the house there are not only photographs of Christian missionaries I use as reminders for prayer, but also of the unsaved family of some of our closest friends. Another batch of photographs downstairs under a fridge magnet in the kitchen also helps! The third thing I do is to ink in a coloured dot in the centre of my watch glass with a felt-tip pen. Each time I do this it's for a specific prayer for a specific unsaved friend. It is remarkable if you do something out of the ordinary like this how much you notice how very often you glance at your watch in the course of a day! If you then link prayer to this you have a powerful and frequent reminder to pray for the lost.

12. Fasting (Matt. 6:16)

There's no such thing as a spiritual short cut, but this is the closest to it that I know of! This reference makes it clear that Jesus expected His disciples to fast. So He says, 'When', not 'If'. In the Old Testament, fasting tended to be restricted to fasts from food for sin or mourning, or preparatory to celebration. There was only one day (the Passover) when fasting was commanded in the Old Testament. But by Jesus' day the Pharisees had declared that every Thursday should be a fast. Jesus widens out the principle of fasting and, together with prayer, seems to link it to intimacy with God and increased authority (Mark 9:29 NIV footnote).

Clearly fasting is not for God's benefit, but for ours. It's not an attempt to spiritually twist God's arm! It's rather us demonstrating to ourselves and to God (not to others) that we're in control of our appetites and not they of us. It's also a means of focus, of creating time and space for prayer, and serves as a practical reminder (see Point 11) to seek and depend upon God. I can see no reason why every Christian shouldn't fast one day every other week as a minimum. We can be creative about what we fast. It need not just be food, particularly if there is some medical reason why that would be inadvisable. Married Christians can also fast sex if they agree to together (1 Cor. 7:5), while unmarried Christians will already be fasting sex! At various times I have fasted alcohol, chocolate, tea, coffee and television, as well as food. I know a church leader who fasted for an unsaved guy on the fringe of his church who was about to go into hospital with severe leg pain. This pain was so severe that the guy couldn't sit down and cross his legs, so the church leader decided to fast leg-crossing! Every time he went to cross his legs (a very common occurrence for most men) the church leader would stop himself, and pray for the salvation of his friend! We can be as creative as we like when it comes to fasting.

13. Church rhythm

For the Christian, prayer is not only an individualistic thing but can also involve the corporate, so an essential part of the prayer process is praying with others for the lost. When was the last time your church held a prayer meeting specifically for the unsaved? Or called a half-night of prayer, or prayed 24–7 for a week, where prayers for the lost were going up to God? Does the rhythm of your cell each time it meets include praying for named unsaved people? If it doesn't, it should! How about prayer triplets? Even if we only met once a month with two other people to pray for the lost that would probably be an increase for most of us.

14. 'The power of God for salvation' (Rom. 1:16)

Last, but not least, I encourage you to pray specifically, persistently and passionately for your unsaved friends to be converted! I know that sounds obvious, but the strength of friendship evangelism (process, trust, relationship, consistency, etc) can also be its weakness (protraction, loss of focus, settling for influencing rather than salvation, etc). We don't want to get so taken up with the process, with the journeying, that we forget about the destination, about where we want them to arrive. We can't make them arrive, but we can pray that they will. Jesus didn't call us to be 'influencers of men' but rather 'fishers of men' (Matt. 4:19). So pray for the salvation of your friends and, when you've prayed for it, pray some more!

There you are – 14 pointers to an effective prayer strategy for the lost. Now to the fifth and final part of our five-point strategy for friendship evangelism. So far we've looked at: 'Identify Your Networks', 'Evaluate Your Networks', 'Develop Your Networks' and 'Praying for Your Networks'. We will close this chapter with my top ten tips (PG's Tips!).

WORKING YOUR NETWORKS

There follows an eclectic collection of final thoughts gathered together from the nooks and crannies of my own experience in friendship evangelism, offered to you in the hope that it proves of practical use. As with the prayer strategy, I encourage you to explore and experiment with all of these, but probably to home in on three or four tips at a time and give them a good try. At the end of the day you've got to find what works best for you and your unsaved friends.

1. *Set aside regular time for your not-yet-Christian friends.* You can do this formally by booking it into your diary in the guise of dinner parties, visits to the gym, etc. And you can do it informally by building little bits of space and time ('cat-flaps' of opportunity!) around the course of your everyday life. Instead of speeding from one thing to the next, you develop little 'oases' of unplanned time. This way your day and your attitude becomes more interruptible.

   My failure to do this was highlighted ironically one Sunday morning when, late and irritated as usual by the task of trying to gather the family together to get out to the Sunday meeting, we flung ourselves into the car with merely a cursory nod at our next-door neighbours, who were outside tending their front garden. As I drove away I imagined, to my embarrassment, what a conversation at that moment with my neighbour might have gone like.

   'Sorry, Barry, can't stop! Got to dash! Off to a church meeting, so I can worship the God that you don't know. So I can learn how important it is to spend time with people who haven't found Jesus!'

   You see what I mean, don't you?! For some of us this first point is about spending time that we already have with those who are unsaved. But for some of us it is about *making* time that we currently *don't* have in our busy diaries, but we *should* have.

2. *Always look for the practical area of service.* This way your life becomes a demonstration, which demands an explanation. *Be* good news, don't just *have* good news. You'll be able to particularly apply this in areas of your gifting, belongings and your finances. Remember that generosity (buying that round down the pub, giving that lift in the car, lending that brand-new lawn mower, etc) is a kingdom value.

3. *Expose* your faith, don't *impose* it on people. The key here is simply to relax. Don't get into the habit of having one set of language and conversational topics for your Christian friends, and another set for your not-yet-Christian friends. This is a short cut to Christian schizophrenia! I'm as likely to talk to my next-door neighbours or my colleagues in the Magistrates Court about my homegroup meeting, or about what God has done in or through me this week, as I am to talk to my cell about it. I am equally likely to expose my *unsaved* friends to other of my *saved* friends. This is an absolute key. You must be prepared to introduce your not-yet-Christian friends to your Christian friends, otherwise you'll fall into the trap of thinking that because they are *your* friends, their salvation depends upon *you*. But, you may have taken them as far as you possibly can on their journey. It may need another of your Christian friends to stimulate their interest, or highlight their needs, in a way that you can't. Yes, they are your friends, but remember, we're in this witnessing thing together.

Moreover, I will often deliberately adopt an attitude of treating my unsaved friends as though they were saved! The latest census results indicate that 72 per cent of the people in this country wish to identify themselves as Christians. Rather than make a point about how much they aren't Christians, I prefer to behave towards them as though they were. In this way you *include* them until *they exclude* themselves. There might come a point in your conversation about God's provision where they look uncomfortable and back off and begin to exclude themselves. That's fine. All you need to do is simply stop, back off, and then come at it again a little later from a different angle!

4. *Identify key opportunities, and involve yourself in them.* We touched on this in the prayer strategy, where we looked at praying people to the right 'pastoral moments'. There *are* times when people are more open to the gospel than at others. Some of these times are very positive, some are times of great pain and stress. Here's a list of what research tells us are the times when people are potentially most open to the gospel.

- Marriage
- Divorce
- Separation
- Reconciliation
- Pregnancy
- Arrival of a new family member
- Starting or leaving school
- Sibling leaves home
- Changing school
- Changing residence
- Personal injury or illness
- Family health
- Death of spouse/partner/family member/friend
- Change in working conditions
- Being made redundant
- Foreclosure on mortgage
- Increase or decrease in work responsibilities
- Retirement
- Custodial sentence
- Revision of personal habits
- Outstanding personal achievement
- Financial change for the better or worse

5. *Looking out for your neighbours.* Remember, you worked together with God to end up living where you currently live.

So opportunities to be a good neighbour should be seized. How about throwing open house parties for the neighbours at any and every opportunity? These could include house-warming, Christmas and New Year, birthdays, etc. Coffee mornings work really well in some neighbourhoods. Taking the initiative to set up a local Neighbourhood Watch Scheme will give you the excuse to visit every neighbour in your road and invite them to regular meetings! Operating a key-holding service for your neighbours and watching out for their property when they are away are further ways of developing relationships. So too is keeping an eye out in your street.

When we spotted the police at the house of some of our near neighbours, it prompted us to drop a card through the door, asking for no details, but offering any help if appropriate. This in turn led to our neighbours coming round, and we got into quite an emotional conversation concerning God's great love for them at what was a very difficult time in their lives.

But it is not always as dramatic as that. Watching out for banners advertising birthday or anniversary celebrations can be a prompt to you buying a bottle of wine or a bunch of flowers, and popping them round. A funeral cortege leaving from a neighbour's home, or a visiting ambulance or doctor's car, can all produce what is often a very welcome opportunity for compassion, comfort and support to be expressed to your neighbour, in Christ's name.

6. *Honouring your family.* As we noted in the section on identifying your networks, it's unlikely that all of your family will be saved. But all of your family can be honoured. Helping around the house says a lot, more powerfully, about how Jesus has changed your life, than any number of mini-sermons on John 3:16! So too does proactively taking time

and trouble with birthdays, with Christmas, with social visits, with invitations to meals, with regular phone calls and so on. God is into family. God wants your family. Let's make sure as part of that family that we open as wide a door to Him as possible.

7. *Jesus and your workplace.* I have met Christians who in their lunch hour hive off to their car and sit in the car park having their quiet time! Who refuse to join their colleagues in the local pub, because there is alcohol there (Well, there would be, wouldn't there?), or because it's smoky! Who don't go into the canteen because the atmosphere can sometimes turn a little turquoise with the humour. But a Christian should be at the heart of any social time. Should be the first to buy in a round. And should be the most willing in their attitude toward work, their integrity with timing and resources, their honesty in relationships, their serving of their colleagues and employers (Eph. 5:5–9; Col. 3:22–4:1). Refuse to live in boxes! God is at work at your workplace.

8. *Community connectedness. Do* make sure that you are involved in the life and expression of your local community. *Do* join in with the things that you like doing and do them with the unsaved. But this principle is wider than the merely social. We need to aim beyond social action towards social transformation. More than washing cars for free, more towards long-term, sustainable social involvement. Connectedness with community might involve you in foster care. Or being on the PTA or governing body of your local school; you don't have to have children to get involved. How about helping to plan the local carnival? Or running the local residents association, or standing as a local councillor, or magistrate? Connectedness with community not only gives you access to build an increasing circle of unsaved

friends, it also is about taking spiritual territory and possessing the land. More of this in Chapter 10.

9. *Believe in yourself!* As Christians we have much to give away. Never sell yourself short. Don't apologise for your faith, or indeed for church, which is the body of Christ even though it's full of imperfections. There is no such thing as a boring testimony! Every story of salvation is about God's unique dealing with unique individuals. You have your own. Believe in it. Be prepared to give away some of your riches. The world knows little of wisdom. Of compassion. Of community. It knows little of restored relationships. Of the healing power of forgiveness. You have much to give away, if you will only believe in and share the wisdom which God has given you. Give away godly advice and counsel where requested. Bend a listening ear to a world desperate to be listened to.

10. *Contextualise.* Remember that you are not alone in all this. If you are in the right church, then your church life should be bent around facilitating your witnessing. If it isn't, move to where it is! My final tip is to fit your witnessing into the right church context. What is the rhythm of evangelistic opportunities in your church life? What will be the right event at the right time to invite your unsaved friends to? If the strategy is there already, then identify the appropriate access points. What is the sense of progression? If you have invited a friend to a church social event, what is the next step? And when? And if the strategy *isn't* there, what can you do to serve the church by bringing it into being? Chapter 11 will help further.

Well, there is plenty there to keep us going! There is a lost world to save. You and I both have lost friends who need to find Jesus. Jesus wants them, and He deserves them. So the only question is, will I get on with it? And will you?

GROUPWORK

1. Choose and adopt three points from the prayer strategy and practise them for a minimum of one month.
2. Do the same thing with three of the top ten tips.
3. Share these six points with your group and pray for one another.
4. Build in a time frame of feedback and accountability with the group for these six action points.

Chapter 9

PERSONAL WITNESSING, JESUS STYLE

The pointers and principles that we cover in this chapter can all be used in the context of friendship evangelism. However, they can also be used with casual acquaintances and conversations, and don't rely on longevity of established friendship for their efficacy. They are gleaned from an examination of how Jesus handles Himself in John 4:1–42, although it can be seen that Jesus follows similar pointers and principles in other places (for example, in John 8). If this approach to personal witnessing works for Jesus (and it did!) then it can also work for us, since He is in all things our example. That they *do* work I can state, because I've tried them. And so can you! Could I encourage you then to break off from reading this book, and to read through John 4:1–42, and then get back to me? What I would like to do is pick out just a few of the lessons that we can learn from this passage.

'GOD APPOINTMENTS'

Verse 4 tells us that Jesus *had* to go through Samaria. The problem is that the Bible has got it wrong! Now, before your hands twitch and you reach to pick up stones to metaphorically stone this author, let me explain what I mean! Of course the Bible hasn't got it wrong. But geographically Jesus *didn't* have to go through Samaria. In fact, under normal circumstances, Jesus would have gone around Samaria, and not through it. Most Jews would have made a detour of approximately 17 miles simply to avoid going through Samaria. This was the extent of the enmity between Jews and Samaritans. If the Bible is right, and Jesus *had* to go through Samaria, it must have been for some reason other then mere geography. That reason is because Jesus was en route to a 'God appointment'.

God is very into these when it comes to the gospel. Remember Philip and the Ethiopian eunuch, resulting in the gospel reaching the continent of Africa? It's not I think that Jesus woke up that morning with a word of knowledge and a prophetic picture of a woman by a well! It's not as though He was compelled like some mind-controlled zombie to go to Samaria no matter what.

I suspect that this 'God appointment' worked for Jesus just like it works for you and me. We have a sense of what is right and wrong. We have an inkling that God may want us to speak to someone. We are in the middle of a conversation with a neighbour over a garden fence when an opportunity arises, and we feel a sense of quickening or urgency that God would have us say something. But we don't *have* to. *Having* a 'God appointment' is not the same as keeping a 'God appointment'.

After all, this 'God appointment' booked by His Father wasn't terribly 'convenient', geographically speaking, although it was to be very important and productive. Jesus was weary. Not just tired. Weary. It was very hot out in the open at noon.

And He was alone, not surrounded by friends. But it was God's timing nonetheless to present an opportunity for witnessing.

If you want to witness but don't know how to, start by booking a 'God appointment'. As you drift off to sleep tonight, in the glorious state between waking and sleeping, ask God to get His great, big heavenly diary out! 'God, give me an appointment tomorrow where I can share something of You in a natural way with someone, something that will stretch me, but that I can cope with.' I guarantee you that He will book the appointment. Every time I have asked Him, He has given them to me. Most recently I went to a service for the legal profession at Portsmouth Cathedral. The night before I went I specifically asked God for an opportunity to talk to one of my colleagues about the implications of faith. In fact, if I'm honest, that's *why* I went in the first place. And sure enough at the end of the service, my wife and I ended up in an interesting chat about the nature of church, relationship versus religion, with the wife of one of the JPs that I trained with.

I'M OBLIGED

So having responded to the prompting of the Holy Spirit and taking His 'God appointment', how does Jesus move things forward? In verse 7 Jesus asks the woman for a drink. Now, this is the Son of God. Had He wished for it, legions of angels would have sprung to His aid. Celestial chalices could have poured from heaven! Artesian wells could have sprung up in the desert! But what does Jesus do? He asks for help. Put simply, He places Himself under obligation to the woman at the well. *He* asks *her* for help, before He gives help to her.

It's obvious, isn't it? We get the most easily irritated when people who we don't know try to give us things that we don't know that we want, and answer questions that we aren't asking! Many of us find it easier and feel safer to be in a position of strength than of weakness, to be a strong giver and a weak receiver. This was never better demonstrated than when I was doing street work and trying to draw a crowd by the offer of free money! Standing halfway up a step-ladder, I would announce that we were giving away £1 coins, and that anyone who wanted one should come and take one from me. Now, people would stop. They would stare. They would watch and listen closely. But *would* they come and take the free money? No, they wouldn't! Indeed, the only people who ever did, perhaps significantly, were young people.

You have to receive the kingdom of God like a little child (Mark 10:15). In our suspicious, materialistic society, 'There's no such thing as a free lunch.' But one of the ways around this is in humility to place ourselves *under obligation* to the people we are seeking to reach. That is how Jesus behaves with the woman at the well. He asks her for a drink of water. Something that she can do for Him, before He offers life to her. If you put yourself under obligation to the person you are witnessing to, you have earned the right, by receiving, to give back to them. If I want to tell my neighbour about Jesus, I will first of all allow my neighbour to tell me about football, which is something he is passionate about. That way it's more likely he'll listen to something that I'm passionate about. In essence, you are helping people feel better about both giving and receiving. You are all the more likely to be able to 'scratch people where they itch'.

CROSSING BARRIERS

Another interesting point here. In verse 9 the woman is amazed that Jesus has spoken to her at all! This is because to do so requires Jesus to cross several barriers. He crosses a gender barrier because she is a woman. And Eastern men don't speak to women outside the house. He has crossed a religious barrier because He, a Jew, is talking with a Samaritan. The Samaritans were a mixed race, resulting from the intermarrying of the Israelites left after the fall of Samaria with people from other nations who introduced idol worship into the Jewish religion. Only a little while after this recorded incident (around about John 8), a marauding band of Samaritans threw a bag of chicken offal over the wall into the Temple precincts, thus making it ritually unclean! There was no love lost between the Jews and the Samaritans. That's why Jesus' parable of the 'Good Samaritan' packed such a punch. A modern-day equivalent would be a story about the 'Good Paedophile', or the 'Good Drug Pusher'. The two statements seem mutually exclusive. It just doesn't equate.

Jesus has also crossed a cultural barrier. Male teachers (rabbis) never had female disciples. Indeed, the rabbis taught, 'Better to be born dead than to be born a woman' and 'Better to teach the Scriptures to a dog than to a woman'. This was an incredibly chauvinist and sexist society and culture. Part of Jesus' actions (here with the woman at the well, in having other female disciples, in first appearing post-resurrection to women whose word normally would not even be allowed in a court of law, etc) is to redeem this fallenness.

So what's our lesson? Well, we too need to break down the social, cultural, religious, geographical and gender barriers that tend to push us towards certain kinds of people. You know what I mean. British reserve means that if you smile at someone on the Tube in London, and you're male and they're female, then you're trying to flirt with them. If they're male too then it means that you're probably gay! It's the same reserve that stops you talking with your neighbour. If you are in Year 10 at school it stops you talking with those in Year 8. If you are a bank clerk, you might conceivably talk to another bank clerk, but the same reserve would stop you talking with the manager or the window cleaner of the bank. We need to cross these false barriers of prejudice, ignorance and fear, just as Jesus did here.

PROMPTING QUESTIONS

Note next in verse 10 that, once Jesus has got the woman into conversation, He doesn't then hammer her with the whole counsel of God, from Genesis to Malachi in one go! Instead, He drops into the conversation an interesting comment, a provoking and stimulating remark that almost demands further response from the woman. First, He alludes rather mysteriously to Himself. But He does so in the form of an enigmatic offer. She can be the recipient of 'living water'.

Our problem is that this is a well-worn story. Because of our grasp of Scripture we've realised that water is one of about 17 symbols used in the Old and New Testament for the Holy Spirit. Or perhaps because we're familiar with the story and have read on a bit, we've realised that this 'living water' is synonymous with eternal life. We have lost the impact of this interchange, through familiarity. But you gain some sense of it again by looking at the woman's response. Let me paraphrase her first response. Basically she says, 'What are you going to get the water with? You haven't got a bucket!' Clearly she hasn't understood the deep significance of 'living water'.

Perhaps this enigmatic method doesn't work, then? Jesus has to have another go. And so He does, this time making it more explicit that He is talking about eternal life. Now the woman's response seems more promising; 'Give me this water' she begins. I don't know about you, but at this point I am about ready to cry 'Hallelujah, she's seen it!' But not so! She *hasn't* seen it! For she goes on to say that she likes the sound of this water, because it would save her a trip to the well!

Has Jesus failed in His communication attempts? Is this woman really thick? Not at all. Jesus has been successful in engaging the woman in conversation. In drawing her out of herself (she was possibly quite ashamed of being seen in public, which is probably why she came to the well at the height of the noonday sun in the first place). He has succeeded in getting her to ask questions, which is a hallmark of successful personal witnessing. Our starting place in any 'God appointment' doesn't need to convey the whole plan of salvation instantly. Far better if it leads on to further conversation as it does here in John's Gospel.

The Communist cells that were planted all over the United States of America at the height of the Cold War operated on a similar principle. They preached commitment to the Communist cause to their members, and then sent them out onto the streets to speak out and propagate the message of Communism with their neighbours. Of course, being ill-trained, they met all kinds of problems, and so at their next cell meeting they would be given more teaching on techniques, and then sent out again. And so on, progressively. It's a simple principle of giving enough to leave people wanting/needing more. And it certainly grabs the attention.

Jesus talking to a woman at a well in the heat of the day is probably the equivalent of my meeting you in Sainsbury's, where I catch you pondering one of life's difficult questions. Should you buy Sainsbury's baked beans (which are cheaper, but are like little bullets) or Heinz baked beans (which are more expensive, but have a lovely rich sauce)? If I sidled up to you at this point and said, 'If you knew who was talking to you right now, you would have asked me, and I would have given you a can of living baked beans!' I think that your reaction would also have been one of bewilderment, misunderstanding and intrigue! We need to learn to pepper our conversation (or perhaps salt is a more biblical analogy!) with allusions to talking to God, hearing from God, answered prayer, God's provision, freedom from guilt, forgiveness, reconciliation and so on. Slightly offbeat comments (not odd for the sake of being odd) carefully dropped into the conversation will provoke a reaction that can be an 'in' for your witnessing.

TAPPING IN TO HOLY SPIRIT POWER

Once the conversation has got going, it doesn't stay general, does it? Jesus doesn't allow the conversation to stay vague or impersonal. Suddenly, apparently cutting across the flow of the conversation, He asks the woman to bring her husband. Now, where did that come from? I imagine the woman was asking the same question! Jesus is here tapping into Holy Spirit power. There are a number of reasons why this is an essential part of our personal witnessing. First, we need the Holy Spirit's power to be evident in our own lives so that we become living demonstrations of the gospel. We never want to get into a situation of 'do as I say, not do as I do'. That's because this is hypocrisy. It's the fruit of the Holy Spirit in our lives (have a look at Gal. 5:22–23) that make for an attractive modelling of the gospel and close the credibility gap between what we believe and how we live.

Second, and as we have already seen in the section on prayer, we need Holy Spirit power when it comes to boldness in witnessing (Acts 1:8; 2 Tim. 1:7; Matt. 10:19; Luke 24:48–49). Third, we need the gifts of the Holy Spirit for effective personal witnessing. It's a poor salesman who has no samples! When we're witnessing we need to ask for and operate specific Holy Spirit gifts, particularly perhaps gifts of wisdom, knowledge, prophecy, healing and discernment; they save so much time in witnessing and revealing the heart of God to people. The context of Holy Spirit gifts in the New Testament is usually evangelism. Jesus here operates a specific gift of the Holy Spirit: the gift of knowledge. Look at the result for the woman. She dashes back to her friends and begs them to meet a Man who told her everything she ever did! This isn't the case, but this is how it felt to her. She suddenly realised that there is indeed a God in Heaven who thoroughly knows her *and* loves her. And that she has just met His Son.

It's worth pointing out that the gifts of the Holy Spirit worked for Jesus in the same way that they work for us. Jesus didn't know this about the woman because He knew everything; it is clear that He *didn't* know everything (Matt. 24:36), but that He, like us, needed to reach out for Holy Spirit gifts on the basis of obedience, faith and risk. I reckon this is why we have two ears and only one mouth! We should listen twice as much as we speak, and we should listen to God with one ear, and the person with the other!

We also need to tap into Holy Spirit power for the conviction of sin. By verse 16 the Holy Spirit is homing in on a point of specific conviction. Providing it's the Holy Spirit convicting a person of sin, and not me or you being self-righteous or condemning, we mustn't shy away in our personal witnessing from the issue of specific sin. It's not good to metaphorically pat someone on the head when they start to get uncomfortable under the conviction of specific sin, in effect saying, 'Well, well, never mind, don't feel too bad, we're none of us perfect, it will all pan out OK!' There *is* a need to be direct, as Jesus is, and to be straight with people. Much of postmodern society has removed behavioural and experiential boundaries, and is wallowing in a sea of doubt and anomie, mistakenly believing that there is no longer any meta-narrative, and yet is instinctively looking for parameters and values. If a postmodern society is denying people these things, we as God's people mustn't. It's no good denying what the Holy Spirit is doing through the work of conviction in someone's life. It is, after all, one of His jobs (John 16:8). And so in verse 16 Jesus is able to put His finger right on the 'sore spot' of sin in this woman's life, in a way that He couldn't possibly have known humanly, by tapping in to Holy Spirit power. And what happens when you initially touch a 'sore spot'? There is a reaction. Read on ...

FISHING FOR RED HERRINGS

I can't read verse 19 without imagining the woman going red and stuttering her way through the sentence. 'Ah, yes! Well, er, I can see that you're ... er ... a prophet. Yes! A prophet, that's it! Now, some people say this, and some people say that, blah, blah, blah. Er, what do you think?' It's classic. As the Holy Spirit convicts, so we wriggle. Metaphorically speaking, the woman is hauling in a red herring to get heresy off the hook!

Given the religious culture of her day, her question is a relevant one. One of the sources of contention between the

Jews and the Samaritans was that the Samaritans had set up an alternative worship centre on top of a mountain in Samaria. The Jews, on the other hand, maintained that God must be worshipped in the Temple in Jerusalem. You and I, however, are unlikely to be asked this question over a pint down the pub, or a game of squash at the gym! In our postmodern society the most frequently asked questions about God will be similar to these:

- Surely the route doesn't matter, as all roads lead to God?
- Isn't it OK as long as it works for you?
- What's so special or unique about Jesus?
- Isn't it all just in the mind, a kind of mental crutch?
- If God is both all good and all powerful, how about suffering?

Ever heard one or more of those? I'm sure you have. We must be prepared for, and even be encouraged by, such red herrings. There are only a limited number of them, and they come up time and again. In one sense there are no definitive answers to these questions, otherwise they would have ceased to be the hoary old chestnuts that so many of them are. But it is incumbent upon us to have done our homework when it comes to these questions. You might remember that I encouraged you to have a look at this and to check your attitude when we focussed on 1 Peter 3:13–16 in Chapter 3. You might want to go back and have a look at the subject of apologetics, and the recommended reading listed there.

CATCHING RED HERRINGS

Verses 22–24 do give us some pointers and principles in how to answer questions like these. First, Jesus doesn't say, 'Now look here, you stupid woman, that's quite beside the point, so let's get down to where the truth really hurts, shall we?'! No, very gently but firmly, Jesus answers her question and then He applies the important principle of 'refocussing'. In other words, Jesus gets the woman off the red herring ('*Where* do we worship?') and back to the personal issues of relational faith (to paraphrase and summarise His words in verses 22–24, 'It's not *where* you worship, it's *Who* you worship; God is a Daddy'). So, as in 1 Peter 3:13–16, attitude and gentle firmness are the keys here.

REFOCUSSING ON JESUS

So, just as Jesus did, we take the question, we answer it gently, but we refocus the question back onto the real issues. What *is* the answer that we want to leave the questioner with? What *is* the answer to every question ultimately? The answer is Jesus. The best way to refocus that I've come up with is to keep your thoughts focussed on Jesus *in the first place*. As you get into a witnessing situation, train your mind to think 'Jesus … Jesus … Jesus …'. In this way the conversation won't shift from a personal application of Jesus into a kind of woolly pseudo-intellectual sea where red herrings abound! It's easily demonstrable that our minds are capable of this kind of focussing/refocussing.

Just recently our very old cooker gave up the ghost, rolled over and died! Its grill hadn't worked since we moved ten years ago, and more recently the oven refused to cook anything unless it was on Gas Mark 9 for several hours! Then it simply expired. So we did some research on replacement cookers, and came up with what worked for us in terms of features and finance. And then a strange thing happened! We suddenly began to see the very cooker we wanted to buy all over the place! We'd go into someone's home, and there it was! We'd be talking to someone in the school playground, and they would have one! Then we'd see the same model advertised as a promotional feature in a magazine! Of course, the oven wasn't really everywhere. The sales hadn't dramatically suddenly increased. It was simply that my mind was ticking over 'Rangemaster … Rangemaster … Rangemaster', and so I noticed them more. And so too with Jesus. When you're witnessing, keep Jesus in the front of your mind, and then avoiding red herrings, gently but firmly, won't be so difficult. Refocussing the issue onto Him will come more naturally.

DEMONSTRATION AND PROCLAMATION

The last point to emphasise from John 4 comes in verse 26. At the end of the day, our lifestyle must demonstrate the gospel, including the power of God through gifts, signs and wonders. People need to see as well as hear about the gospel. The world is weary of words only. In the words of a song from the Broadway musical *My Fair Lady* – 'Don't give me words, show me!' A words-only gospel is not the true gospel, which throughout the New Testament comes to people in power with deeds, signs and wonders (1 Thess. 1:5; Rom. 15:19). That's another reason why we should be asking God for greater gifts and more power – so that we can show as well as tell the gospel of Jesus Christ. The Old Testament prophets demonstrated God's Word (Isa. 20; Jer. 13; 19; Ezek. 4; 5;

Hosea 1; 2) and so did Jesus (John 1:14; Acts 1:1). He demonstrates the power of the gospel here through the use of a word of knowledge, but He also links that to a clear proclamation.

John's Gospel is partly about seven great signs and demonstrations of the kingdom, and seven great proclamations of Jesus as the gospel, the great 'I ams'. Seven times Jesus makes this statement (e.g. *I am* the resurrection and the life; *I am* the way, the truth and the life, etc). And each time the proclamation is linked to some dramatic demonstration. These great 'I am' statements are echoed in John 4:26.

If it's untrue that Jesus is the Son of God, then what He states in verse 26 is blasphemy, because the phrase 'I (who speak to you) am (he)' actually embodies the name that Yahweh had given to Himself in Exodus 3:14: 'I am who I am'. The phrase that Jesus uses, in the Greek *ego aeme* is the equivalent of the Hebrew name 'Yahweh' (later translated from the Latin as 'Jehovah'). This is the name for God Himself. The name 'Yahweh' derives from the Hebrew verb *hayah*, which means 'to be'. So in a way that the woman would have understood, Jesus is in effect stating that He is on a par with God Himself. He is stating that Yahweh is speaking to her! This same claim is most clearly stated in John 8:58: 'Before Abraham was born, *I am*.' The same statement causes the crowd to react in horror, as they try to stone Jesus. And the point for us? That at some stage in our witnessing there has to be some clear proclamation of who Jesus is, what His claims are upon us, and what our response to those claims should be. Otherwise people will end up simply thinking that we are terribly nice people, or perhaps even Mormons or Jehovah's Witnesses!

So ... some very practical pointers and principles that Jesus used in His witnessing. We should use them too. In the closing pages of this chapter there are two more brief topics I would like us to look at.

TELL US A STORY!

The constant cry of my two children since they were very young indeed has been, at any and every opportunity, and particularly when we are on long walks in the countryside, that I should tell them a story. I have to say that as a family we all delight in such opportunities and my wife keeps consistently encouraging me to write some of the adventures that I tell the children down in book form, believing there to be a ready market for such tales! I have yet to do this, but watch this space ...

When it comes to witnessing we have a very powerful and personal story indeed to tell. No one else's story will be the same as yours. No one can take it from you, or deny its validity. It is both biblical and practical to communicate and to learn by the example of others. Paul constantly exhorts his hearers and readers to remember the things that are past. And he exhorts them to follow him as an example, as he follows Christ (1 Thess. 1:6–7; 2:14; 1 Cor. 4:6; 11:1). Remember what I said earlier? There is no such thing as a boring testimony to the work and grace of God.

When I was growing up as a young Christian we often talked about people giving their 'testimony'. That's now a rather archaic phrase, and I prefer to think of it in terms of people telling their 'stories'. The passage we've just looked at in John 4 clearly demonstrates the remarkable power of personal stories of encounters with Jesus. The woman at the well goes back to her village to tell her neighbours and friends about Jesus. As a result of this, many believe her. Some, however, do not, but are sufficiently provoked to go and find Jesus for themselves and they in turn then believe. What you have in the closing parts of the chapter is nothing less than the description of a mini-revival hitting the village of Sychar. Like any other aspect of personal witnessing, a little investment and effort now has the potential of reaping remarkable dividends in the lives of the lost later. You might find the following structure helpful when it comes to formulating your own story.

1. *Your story consists of three parts.* The first part describes 'how you were', without Christ, pre-conversion. It should give enough information to stimulate and evoke understanding and empathy. But it shouldn't give too much so as to glorify sin. Strenuously avoid imbalance in this area. The second part of your story relates to 'this happened'. This middle part of your story needs to make clear how Christ encountered you, what that felt like, and what you did about it. It should be longer and more detailed than the first part of your story. A good thing to check is whether in this middle section you have actually explained what a person needs to do in order to receive Christ. Ideally you should have done so. Then the third part of your story, taking up the most space in terms of time and detail, should deal with the 'I am now'. In this section you should usefully dwell on the difference that following Christ has made, the sense of freedom and forgiveness, dreams, development and destiny, the way your life *has* changed, and *is* changing. The relative proportions of these three stages and the way that the last stage is open-ended (that is, continuing), can best be represented pictorially as shown in Figure 9.1.

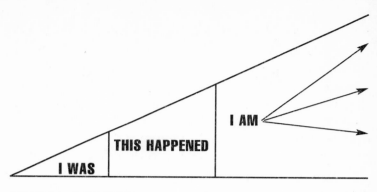

FIGURE 9.1 – YOUR STORY

2. *Your story needs to be a current one.* God still talks and acts in our lives. So our story shouldn't merely be historical, but also contemporary. The best stories finish with the excitement and encouragement of what God has done for us this week. Living in answered prayer is an exciting place to be. If you aren't, it's probably because you are not praying enough, specifically enough, risking enough.

3. *Integrity.* Your story must be honest. This is not least because Jesus is truth (John 14:6) and Satan is the father of lies (John 8:44). God blesses and responds to truthfulness and hates a liar (and Satan stimulates deceit). So at all costs avoid the 'I was saved from a life of sin and iniquity, of drugs, danger, deprivation, sex and rock and roll, and was gloriously converted at the age of three!' More seriously, I have known Christians slightly exaggerate their story in order to make a better impression of the work of God and grace in their lives. *Don't do it!* I had a friend who, when involved in personal witnessing, consistently explained that at university he had been on the edge of alcoholism until God saved him. Only latterly did he respond to the

conviction of the Holy Spirit and come back to me and others to confess that he had exaggerated this, and had simply indulged rather too freely in the student bar! God doesn't need it. Nor will He use it. It's certainly true that there may be occasions in the telling of your story that you will find yourself giving different emphases to better fit the people to whom you are speaking, but they must always carry the ring of truth and integrity with them. Don't manipulate or prevaricate.

AN ILLUSTRATION

The force of these three principles was clearly demonstrated to me some years ago when we were running a major mission in the East End of London. We had been in schools all week and the climatic event was to be a concert in the local town hall in Leyton, London E10. We'd trained up Christians on the basics of leading someone to faith in Christ, youth groups had been pre-prepared to receive new converts and when the night came several hundred young people turned up. It was a lively evening, with a real battle on for the hearts, minds and lives of the young people present.

One of the Christian volunteers who had come along was Dorothy, a little old lady who worked for us as administrator in our office base. Recently widowed, she'd offered her services to us to help her to connect with people, get out of the house and to better serve God. This was a lady with a strong Christian inheritance and a real integrity. Originally from a Brethren background, she had actively explored the fullness of the Holy Spirit and His gifts, and wanted to be at our evangelistic schools' concert in order to serve and see young people come to faith in Christ. But she was *very* nervous. She'd asked me what she could do, how she could help? Her nervousness lay in the fact that she was (then) in her sixties. She had grey hair. She was hard of hearing. She was recently widowed. She lived in Chingford, London E4, a much 'posher' area than Leyton, London E10. Her concern was that she would have nothing in common, would not be able to relate to the young people. What should she do? I gently encouraged Dorothy to put her faith in action and her trust in God, and to see what He would do.

I can't tell you then what a privilege it was as the first people started to stream into the counselling room having made a response to Christ, to see Dorothy immediately hook up with the very first respondent! And guess what? The first person into that room in response to Christ was a spinster in her sixties, grey hair, hard of hearing, but living in Leyton. What a perfect way God has of matching and blending our stories to the people who need to hear them! *That's* why we daren't tamper with them. Why they need to be current. Why there needs to be enough that people can relate to, but more of what God has done, and what He is doing. Dorothy and Olive got on like a house on fire and for the rest of their time in the London Borough of Waltham Forest, until Olive died and Dorothy moved, they remained firm friends, and indeed Olive joined Dorothy in helping us with our administration! And that's not a one-off story. I could go on for pages and pages telling how God uses the power of personal stories to see others come to faith in Him. If it's worked for them and for me, it will certainly work for you.

RECEIVING CHRIST

The final topic in this chapter on personal witnessing deals with how to lead someone to Christ. There's really no point in spending all this time looking at the process if we never bother to look at how you turn the corner into the final road, which takes you to your ultimate destination! That would be like having directions and a map, but no final address!

A friend of mine recently booked himself and his wife into a small country hotel via his laptop at an airport terminal. It was only once they were en route, and then bereft of access to the Internet, that my friend realised to his horror that he had a set of directions which appeared to peter out in the middle of the countryside, and no final address. Not even the name of the hotel with him. Needless to say it didn't produce one of the most blissful moments of marital harmony!

So as we conclude this chapter, how *do* you lead someone to Christ? Well, first of all being born again (John 3:5), like being born the first time, is a natural process and not a mechanical one. There is no equation that works in each and every circumstance. Some conversion births, like natural births, need to be aided – with careful apologetics, or with healing from emotional trauma. Some conversion births, like natural birth, may require a degree of 'surgery' – when there is a need for spiritual separation from demonic influence. But however straightforward or messy, each and every process of conversion involves at least four things:

1. Faith (John 3:16)
2. Conviction of sin (John 16:8–11)
3. Repentance from sin (Acts 2:37–41)
4. Rebirth (2 Cor. 5:17)

I finish this chapter with an intensely practical application, providing we can agree together that there is nothing mechanical or formulaic about being born again? There follow four steps, with appropriate Bible verses (which I would encourage you to read and memorise), which if taken together and owned in the heart and not just the head, *will* result in new birth. But remember, no formulae ...

Step 1 Admit (**Rom. 3:23; 6:23**)

No one is converted without a willing admission of their sinful state and their need of forgiveness through Christ.

Step 2 Believe (**1 Pet. 3:18**)

No one is converted without believing (remember in the Hebrew that means faith in action, not merely a mental assent) in the efficacy of Christ's sacrifice on the cross, and His subsequent resurrection. This is the only way for sins to be forgiven, and for fullness to come.

Step 3 Commit (**Mark 8:34**)

In the light of the two previous steps, and to save them from being mental assent only, an individual must then commit themselves wholeheartedly, whole-mindedly and whole-bodily to the love of God and to following Christ.

Step 4 Receive (**Luke 11:13; John 1:12**)

New birth, new creation, inheritance into the family of God, assurance of salvation and relationship with Christ – all these are there to be explained, appropriated and enjoyed by the new Christian. More than this, the fullness of God's Holy Spirit is available to empower the new believer, and these steps should lead swiftly and biblically to immersion in water as a believer (Acts 2:37–41).

Admit, Believe, Commit, Receive! A-B-C-R! It even rhymes if you say it. That'll help you to memorise it!

I do hope these three chapters have been helpful and very practical. Taken together they should move us forward in the most effective form of evangelism that there is: person-to-person, friendship-based, personal witnessing.

GROUPWORK

1. Over the next month, form the life habit of asking God each night for 'God appointments' to help your witnessing the following day.
2. In your group, pray for one another to be filled with the Holy Spirit and to receive spiritual gifts.
3. Begin to practise spiritual gifts in the group environment, and commit to practising them in an evangelistic context, with group feedback and monitoring.
4. Discuss what might be answers to some of the most common 'red herring' questions asked by people in a postmodern society. Try to answer them using personal experience, a visual aid or story (for better communication) and, where appropriate, a Bible verse(s).
5. Discuss and then write out the salient features of your personal story. In pairs in your group, swap personal stories, paying particular attention when listening to the eradication of Christian jargon or technical terms.
6. Memorise the Admit-Believe-Commit-Receive process and the attendant Bible verses.

Chapter 10

WHOSE TURF?

War is a terrible thing. And it exacts a terrible price. Upon people. But also upon places. In human terms the cost is obvious. And in materialistic terms, where the economy is shot to pieces, buildings and monuments blown apart, culture and artistic heritage ravaged and raped, perhaps it's equally obvious. But spiritually warfare also exacts its toll. In Scripture there are a number of issues which can pollute the land itself. These include sexual immorality, occult pagan idol worship, broken covenants and the shedding of blood.

VIMY RIDGE

This has never been more dramatically illustrated to me than during the first visit I paid to Vimy Ridge. I was camping and travelling through France with a friend from university during a long summer vacation back in the 1970s. One afternoon we decided to visit one of the many war memorials that are scattered around France, the battlefield of Europe. The war memorial at Vimy Ridge is approached by a long dusty avenue cut between fields once drenched with the blood of tens of thousands of fighting troops during World War I. The ridge was deemed strategically important as the highest ground for miles around, and now erected on it is a towering white stone monument to the lost of the war. As we approached the monument we could see that its surface was not entirely smooth, but seemed to be covered in hundreds of metres of wavy lines. As we got closer these formed themselves into the names of thousands of people who died there. The fields around the monument were gouged and ripped into vast craters, tears and trenches, albeit grassed over. There were still barbed wire-protected woods full of undiscovered and unexploded bombs and shells, and places where thousands of troops simply 'disappeared' into the muddy morass of those hellish battles. Few birds flew and no birds sang.

Going back, as I did twenty-five years later, the same is still true. Warfare, violence and shed blood has in a very material and spiritual way polluted and scarred the earth. There are even places where you can still view the frontline Allied troops trenches, separated from the German trenches by a matter of mere metres. This place is truly about the clash of two opposing factions, of two encroaching kingdoms.

And that is also the nature of spiritual warfare. Spiritual warfare can best be defined as the clashing of two opposing, expansionist kingdoms. In the Old Testament, the word most commonly used for 'kingdom' (Hebrew – *malkuth*) usually referred to a geographical entity, whereas by the New Testament the word 'kingdom' (Greek – *basilea*) used in relation to the kingdom of God places more of an emphasis on the rule and reign of Christ in His kingly authority, wherever that is demonstrated in and through the lives of His people. We touched on this in Chapter 1.

Although many professing deists (believers in an unknown god) live their lives as though there are *three* options (a kingdom and force for good, a kingdom and force for bad, and their own personal little kingdom!) and much Eastern mysticism (and occult practices) maintain that there is only *one* all-embracing kingdom (a force for both good and ill – Ying and Yang, with material creation an illusion – *maya*) still the biblical and experiential reality is simple. There are *two*, but *only* two kingdoms. One is the kingdom of God and His dear Son Jesus, a kingdom of light and life. The other, the kingdom of Satan, is a kingdom of darkness and death. Both of these kingdoms are expansionist in that they are seeking to take ground, first and foremost, in your life and mine and second, in the lives and therefore the territory of those around us. When two such radically opposed expansionist kingdoms both seek to take the same territory, a clash is inevitable, and that is the nature of spiritual warfare. It's also therefore logically why spiritual warfare and evangelism will and must always go hand in hand. I'm grateful for the influence of my friend, Martin Scott, in some of what follows.

A MATERIALISTIC WORLD-VIEW

But the previous statements have been strongly refuted by those whose world-view precludes the possibility of any spiritual experience. Granted, such a materialistic or humanistic world-view is in great decline. The British Humanism Society is in terminal decline, and by and large the rationalistic, modernistic world-view has given way to a postmodern culture, wherein spirituality is more easily embraced, if less easily defined. Nonetheless it's worth noting that in a materialistic world-view the spiritual realm doesn't exist; the only reality is that which can be seen, touched, tasted, felt, smelled or heard by the rationalistic senses and these things together combine to form the material realm. This can perhaps helpfully be represented as shown in Figure 10.1

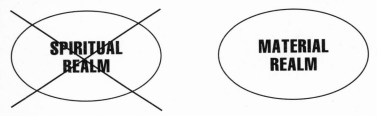

FIGURE 10.1 – A MATERIALISTIC WORLD-VIEW

A SPIRITUAL WORLD-VIEW

This is an increasingly common perspective born from the bankruptcy of rationalism, consumerism, science and technology. The growth of this world-view is also due in no small part to the encroachment of Eastern mystical philosophies and/or cultic and/or occult practices. This is a reverse of the previous world-view. Adherence to this position maintains that the spiritual realm is the only realm of reality and meaning, and that the material realm is in fact an illusion, the *maya* of Eastern religion. This world-view can be denoted as shown in Figure 10.2.

FIGURE 10.2 – A SPIRITUAL WORLD-VIEW

A CHRISTIAN THEORETICAL WORLD-VIEW

I suspect that this is the predominant world-view of most Western Christians. It proceeds from an uneasy tension; an acknowledgment of the reality of the spiritual realm, with all too frequent lack of understanding and experience (at worst a denial) of its implications for the material realm. Nor is this position reserved for those of a non-charismatic theological bent. I know many 'card-carrying charismatics' who seem to have adopted a minimalist approach when it comes to the practical implications of the spiritual realm, who as charismatics have privatised their faith to speaking in tongues or a perverted prosperity gospel, and who are convinced that their ultimate destiny lies in some separate and other spiritual existence with an ethereal space reserved for them in heaven! This apparently Christian but entirely theoretical world-view does at least acknowledge the existence and reality of both the spiritual and material realm, but tends to keep them separate, with the spiritual accessible to the material predominantly through the portal of death! Thus angels and demons exist, but to all intents and purposes, only in theory. This perspective can be illustrated as in Figure 10.3.

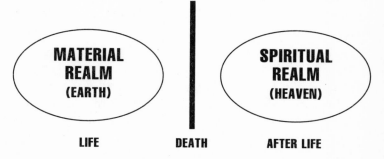

FIGURE 10.3 – A CHRISTIAN THEORETICAL WORLD-VIEW

A BIBLICAL WORLD-VIEW

Unless we adopt a biblical world-view we will be unable to pray as Jesus Himself commanded us to. In Matthew 6:10 He exhorts us to petition God that His 'kingdom come ... on earth as it is in heaven'. As we have seen, this kingdom of God is already at hand and here, but not yet in fullness, although its fullness is promised (Luke 10:9; 17:21; Matt. 6:10, 33). Clearly then there is some integration between the spiritual realm of the kingdom of God and the material realm in which we live and breathe, not forgetting that according to Scripture we live and breathe and have our existence in God as well! So in this more biblical world-view the spiritual realm is real, the material realm is real, but the two of them intersect and interpose one upon the other. What is effected in the spiritual has its effects in the material, and vice versa (see Figure 10.4).

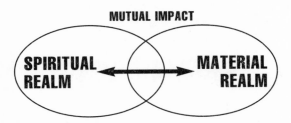

FIGURE 10.4 – A BIBLICAL WORLD-VIEW

A good illustration of this biblical world-view is when Moses raises his hands in obedience to God. In this symbolic demonstration of surrender and of receiving, the action affects not only the spiritual realm but also the material realm, because when Moses has his hands up, Joshua wins, and when he puts his hands down, Joshua loses. So much so that eventually Moses' hands are held aloft by members of his team (see Exod. 17:10–13).

A New Testament example occurs in Revelation 12 where angelic warfare is being waged, but the parallel and deciding factor is that it's the saints of God who overcome the enemy on the earth. And so whatever we bind in heaven shall have been bound on earth, and whatever we loose on earth shall have been loosed in heaven (see Matt. 16:19). With this in mind then, our aim in spiritual warfare as Christian witnesses is to bring heaven to earth through the church into the world; this is a 'down-and-out' approach! It is diametrically opposed to a more traditional and more unbiblical viewpoint, which maintains that our role is rather to bring people out of this world into the church and thus off to heaven (which in contrast is an 'in-and-up' approach!).

WHERE DO I STAND?

If the world-view I have described above as biblical is the correct one, it raises very real and practical implications. Not least, who does the world belong to? Who is in charge? Is it the case that everything that happens is foreknown by God, and even predestined by Him? Or is it that, in a fallen world, warfare theology is the only kind of theology which makes sense? I rather think so. Put simply, God will win the war, but we do lose some battles. The casualties are real, but they are neither designed nor desired by God to happen.

We have to maintain four biblical perspectives in tension. The first is simple; this is God's world because He created it. This is clear throughout Scripture, from its very beginning to its very end. God created everything (Gen. 1:1), 'and it was good' (Gen. 1:9), and by the time He had finished His creation, He crowned it with humanity, which was not merely good but 'very good' (Gen. 1:31).

But that is not the whole picture. For the Bible also goes on to say that this world is Satan's world, not because he created it, but because he corrupted it. Satan is himself a created being, and in his limitations can only take that which God has created, and corrupt it. Thus God creates beauty, and Satan corrupts it to vanity. God creates sex, and Satan corrupts it to lust. God creates appetite, and Satan corrupts it to greed. And so the Old and New Testaments refer to Satan as the god or prince of this world (Gen. 3; 2 Cor. 4:4; Eph. 6:12; John 12:31; 16:11; 1 John 5:19).

Yet these two perspectives are in themselves incomplete. For although the battle is on, it is not an 'either/or' battle. This is not a two-horse race! The clash of the kingdoms is not like some vast cosmic see-saw, with on some occasions God in the ascendancy, and on others Satan, as though they were equally matched, balancing on the fulcrum of time. Rather there is a third biblical perspective which must be held in tension. For the Bible teaches that this is God's world because He created it, Satan's world because he corrupted it, but ultimately Jesus' world because He conquered it. So although Satan may be referred to as the god of this world, there is only one *God* of this world! Satan may be called the prince of this world, but he is not nor ever can be the king of this world. In defeating Satan, sin, sickness and suffering, Jesus bought back what we had given away into enemy hands. Remember that vivid military picture we looked at previously (Col. 2:15) where Jesus is described exactly as the returning conquering hero displaying a beaten enemy to the Godhead? And so Jesus Christ (fully human) wins fully through for humanity, so that we too can become more fully human.

Christ's climatic confrontation with Satan in Luke 4 (later confirmed and affirmed at the cross) is a direct reversal of Genesis 3. For in Genesis 3 Satan goes onto God's territory (the Garden of Eden) with the insinuating question, 'Did God say?' Humanity succumbs to temptation to disobedience, and eats forbidden fruit, in order that they might 'be like God'. See how Luke 4 countermands this. For now Jesus goes onto Satan's territory (the wilderness) and there makes the repeated authoritative statement, 'God said.' In obedience He abstains from eating, and does not grasp equality with God, even though He is God. The first Adam disobeys God to get his own way; the second Adam obeys God to get His way. But there's more!

For the fourth and final biblical perspective which gives us the most rounded answer to the questions, 'Whose world is it anyway? Where do I stand?' is that – as well as being God's world because He created it, Satan's world because he corrupted it, Jesus' world because He conquered it – it is also your world because you are commissioned to it. Having being raised with Christ we now stand in a place of authority to rule and reign with Him, sharers in His victory and partakers in His spoils, commissioned by God (Matt. 28:16–20) as His church to outwork His kingdom rule on the earth. Have a look at the incredible descriptions of this, our position in Christ, in the first two chapters of Ephesians.

To revert to the military illustration with which I started this chapter, in terms of spiritual warfare and evangelism we now live in the equivalent of that odd time-span in World War II between D-Day and V-Day. In World War II, the Normandy beach landings were the bridgehead which was to liberate Europe, and see the final defeat of Hitler's Third Reich as a foregone conclusion; it truly was Decision-Day. But the fighting didn't finish at D-Day. Skirmishes continued. Battles were lost and won on both sides. People were killed. Injustice and oppression continued. It wasn't until Victory-Day took place that the war was over and the world was at peace.

So too for us. Our D-Day took place when Christ defeated our enemy in the wilderness (Luke 4) and at the cross. Victory is assured, but not fully delivered, until the equivalent of our V-Day; the second coming of Christ. And in the interim, in evangelistic terms, you and I are God's Mop-Up Squad! We liberate as many captives as we can to the gospel. We bring healing to as many casualties as possible. We continue to do as much damage as possible to the enemy. But we await the victorious and final return of our Commander-in-Chief and the restoration of peace, justice and freedom. Can you see the connection to Chapter 4 and the military terms used there to describe this glorious gospel?

This battle then is no longer between God and Satan, but rather between Satan and us. It's a battle that involves us as individuals. But behind every individual you'll find a system (be it a world-view, an organisation, a political party, a club, a cult, a nation state, etc). And behind every system you'll find values that underpin, affirm and maintain that system. Only look a little more closely and a little more deeply, and behind those values you'll find principalities and powers. It's a moot point as to whether they latch on to such values and systems, thus affecting individuals, or whether in some way they are even generated by the amalgam of individuals, systems and values. Certainly these principalities and powers are ordered, with indications of hierarchy. In Ephesians 6:10–12 the very specific (and indeed geographical and military) terms which are used in the Greek indicate something of this order. We read of a hierarchical pyramid of control in the kingdom of darkness which consists of rulers (*arche*), authorities (*exousias*), powers of this dark world (*kosmokratoros*) and evil spiritual forces in the heavenly realms (*atmos*). Not only is there order, but there are schemes (Eph. 6:11; 2 Cor. 2:11) and clearly this enemy realm is organised (Matt. 12:22–28).

LET BATTLE COMMENCE

What does all this mean for us in a book on evangelism? Well, as we've noted before, right beliefs are more likely to lead to right thoughts which are more likely to lead to right attitudes, which in turn are more likely to lead to right actions. And if we act right, we will come out right! That's why I have taken the time, albeit very briefly, to outline my understanding of the Bible's teaching on spiritual warfare, for it inevitably relates to evangelism. I would like to end this chapter with four practical observations that will help us to appropriate Christ's victory, not only for us, but for the lost.

BATTLE DRILL

Before ever we look to identify strongholds 'out there' we should first look to identify them 'in here'. For most strongholds are strongholds of the mind (2 Cor. 10:4–5) and the enemy would far rather get his strongholds in us than around us. So spiritual warfare starts with us, not with others. Warfare first in us, rather than through us. We need God at work on *our* strongholds, before we move on in haste with much shouting (and sometimes not a little projection!) to search for strongholds in our cell, our church, our town, our nation or the nations!

A stronghold is any mind-set in us that raises itself up in opposition against the Word and will of God, and in so doing removes any sense of hope and faith that life could ever be other. Theoretically a stronghold could be almost anything, but common ones include sexual immorality, materialism, coveting and abusing power, idolatry and unforgiveness. It is beyond the scope of this book to outline further strongholds, or to go in any detail into ways of obtaining freedom, but the personal spiritual disciplines of submitting our lives to others, of praise and worship, of memorising and meditating on Scripture, of accountability, of servanthood, of prayer and fasting and deliverance, are all vital components of our battle drill.

SPIRITUAL MAPPING

If we are engaged in spiritual warfare (and, like it or lump it, we are!) then it's important that we know and understand the terrain. Where, why and how is the enemy strong? What are his lines of communication? In which areas might he seek to lay an ambush? Or a full frontal assault? In any given specific terrain, what weapons is he likely to use? We have two main weapons, both of them biblical, at our disposal here. The first is that we understand our terrain by *research*. Jesus was not averse to this method of understanding enemy strategy. You see Him employing it in Mark 5:30, and again in Mark 9:21, where He elicits information by asking the relevant questions; He engages in research. You should do no less for the area which God has given to you, and given you to.

This was borne strongly in upon me when we planted a church in Bognor Regis in 1986. One part of our strategy in gaining presence in the town was to engage in street work once a month on a Saturday in the pedestrianised section of London Road. We had been doing this for some time when a pattern began to emerge. At one end of London Road we could have remarkable success in drawing large crowds, engaging people in meaningful and positive conversations and even on one occasion seeing demonic manifestations, physical healings, and someone saved (as well as a confrontation with a witch!) all in the same afternoon there! But every time we moved our pitch a matter of a mere couple of hundred metres to the other end of London Road we encountered oppression, negative atmosphere, difficulty with worship, ebbing faith levels, small or non-existent audiences, few if any conversations and little progress.

It took me a while to realise it and think of what we might do, but eventually I commissioned a member of our evangelism team to do some research for us on Bognor Regis in general and London Road in particular. Paul came back to us with some remarkable facts, which I believe had affected (infected?) this part of our patch. At the 'difficult' end of London Road there had once been seven different churches. You can make out the outline of some of these buildings above the shops to this day. One of these buildings had been a Seaman's Mission, on which a compulsory purchase order had been served by the local council. In their anger and bitterness (and perhaps arising out of the often superstitious nature of sailors) the seamen had cursed the other churches in Bognor Regis for refusing to come to their aid. The curse was that nothing spiritual would ever succeed in Bognor Regis, and within a few years of this happening all of the other churches in that end of London Road had closed down. Obvious, once you know, eh? But it took *research* to find it out. So when we planted a church in Portsmouth in 1992, you can bet that one of the first things we did was do our homework and our research!

It's not difficult to do. You could do worse than starting off looking at the political wards, at census survey results for your area. At the information contained in the electoral roll. Your local council will have very detailed demographic breakdowns concerning matters such as population levels and trends, male/female ratios, age brackets, unemployment statistics, house tenure details and so on. Almost certainly your town's history will have been written about. Trips to the local library, historical society and council offices are all good starting points. But if you want to go further with this (and I think you should!) then I can do no better than recommending John Dawson's excellent book, *Taking Our Cities for God* and Ed Silvoso's book, *That None Should Perish*.

The second weapon in our armoury when it comes to spiritual mapping is *revelation*. This *as well as* research. Jesus also employed this method. In John 4:16 you don't find Him asking questions; instead He makes a direct statement based, one can only assume, on a revelation from the Holy Spirit. So a part of spiritual mapping must consist of listening to the Holy Spirit when it comes to your territory. The spiritual gifts of prophecy, word of knowledge, and discernment or distinguishing of spirits are keys here.

When we were about to church-plant in Portsmouth in 1992, before ever we got across to the city, God began to speak to us prophetically about some of the things we would find here. This included a strong warning about a demonic principality based around island insularity. Subsequently moving here and establishing a church in the city has proved this to be the case. On a major mission in Byfleet some years ago, God spoke to the team and church intercessors about spiritual pollution and corruption connected to the river which runs through Byfleet. That which should symbolise life was bringing death to the area. We didn't fully understand this until, on a prayer walk along the river we came across very clear evidence (I needn't go into details) of ritualistic occult practice. No amount of research would have brought this to light; this came through revelation.

ENGAGING THE ENEMY

Here is another practical implication of spiritual warfare. In Scripture, spiritual warfare is about close-quarters combat, not long-distance, inter-continental ballistic missile prayer offensives! Not least because real prayer gets you more involved and not less involved, as the disciples discovered in Matthew 9, when Jesus urged them to pray for workers to go into the harvest, which was ripe. By the beginning of Matthew 10, as we have already seen, they become the answers to their own prayers! In Ephesians 6, where we have a clear description of the armour of God, the word used for 'armour' is *panoplia*, which refers to equipment used for hand-to-hand combat. So connectedness/closeness is a key to spiritual warfare.

When in the Old Testament God wanted to give land to the Hebrew nation as they came out of Egypt, that gift went in three stages: first it was promised (to Moses), but then it had to be possessed (by Joshua – Josh. 3:7–8), before it could finally be purified (Josh. 5). This is all about connectedness. In part, this is how as the body of Christ we grow up to fill out all the spheres of creation mentioned in Ephesians and that we looked at in Chapter 1 (mind-sets, marriage, family, relationships, workplace, etc). You have to connect with a place to do this effectively.

Could this be a part of what's going on in the rather strange story found in Mark 5:1–20? Again I'm indebted to my friend Martin Scott for some of this thinking, and again would strongly recommend you read his excellent book,

Sowing Seeds for Revival (published by Sovereign World). There are at least four odd responses in this story. The first is found in verse 10 where Legion begs Jesus not to send the demons out of the area. I'd expect Jesus *not* to listen to this entreaty and to remove the demons completely. But He doesn't. Why is this? Because the demons had a certain amount of 'legal' right to be on that particular turf. This legal right would have been given to them by the people of the area, in the same way that it was people who gave Satan legal territory to corrupt creation. At the beginning of the book of Job, when God summons Satan into His presence and asks where he has been, Satan replies that he has been striding up and down about the earth, and this is a technical and legal term meaning, 'I have been on my own property'. So perhaps what we are dealing with in this story is a principality and a power over a territorial region.

The second odd response in the story comes two verses later when the demons beg Jesus to send them into the pigs. I'd expect Jesus to ignore this request. But He doesn't ignore it, and He does comply with it! Why is this? Because in this cultural and geographical context, the pigs represent the world system and materialism of the area, which was a Gentile region, where investment into porcine livestock would be viewed by Jews literally as 'filthy lucre'. Certainly the action of the demonised pigs goes some way to demonstrating the limitations of the system and the destructiveness of the demons, to anyone who has eyes to see and ears to hear, and certainly to Legion.

The third odd response in the story is found in verse 17, where the people plead with Jesus to leave the region. I'd expect Jesus do the opposite, to stay around the scene of such a dramatic demonstration of the imminence of the kingdom of God. But He doesn't. Instead He does as the people request and leaves! Why is this? Because the spiritual principle is that you reap what you sow (Gal. 6:7) and you get what you go for. God's high premium on free will (given to us because He has free will and we are made in His image), means that He will never force a favourable response from people, and will give them the consequences of their choice, be it a right or a wrong choice, positive or negative consequences.

The fourth and final odd response in the story is in the next verse. Legion, now dressed and in 'his right mind' (a phrase which literally means 'to have been adopted by', in this case, by Jesus), begs to be allowed to go with Jesus. I'd have expected Jesus to say, 'Certainly, come with me!' But He doesn't. He tells the man to stay. Why is this? The key is connectedness. The man is directed instead to go to his family and 'tell them' (the verb used is a specific missiological/evangelistic one) what the Lord (Jesus) has done. The man is obedient. He affects ten whole cities in doing this, the response is favourable, and consequently we find that, the next time Jesus revisits the area, He is met with acceptance rather than rejection. Obedience to the Word of God, being on the turf, persistence in purveying truth, connectedness with the people, ownership of the turf, purifying the turf, all of these are demonstrated in this remarkable story of Legion, and are keys to spiritual warfare and effective evangelism.

COMMUNICATING WITH COMMAND

This is the last of the four practical implications for spiritual warfare and evangelism. We've looked at battle drill, spiritual mapping and connectedness. Please understand that I have covered these in a very specific order, which is the order I would encourage you to embark upon. It's not that you complete the first stage (battle drill) before you move onto the second (spiritual mapping). But I would suggest that you should make significant headway in the first stage, so you start it before you move onto the second stage, and so on. But don't wait for God to demolish all your personal strongholds before ever you look at spiritual mapping, otherwise you'll never get off first base. And don't wait to connect with your community until you've finished every last contour of your spiritual mapping, because there's always more to learn by research and revelation. And so it goes. But eradication of personal strongholds, spiritual mapping, and connectedness with turf *must* lead to activity in *prayer*.

Spiritual warfare is about prayer, which leads to action. This kind of prayer (and fasting usually goes alongside it) is best done corporately rather than individually. It should involve your cell or house group. It certainly should involve your whole church. Even better, it should involve inter-church prayer. Again I refer you to the books by Dawson, Silvoso and Scott. Enough here to say that your prayer strategy for spiritual warfare and evangelism shouldn't only consist of praying for named individuals, but also into the history and geography of your area, and against the negative, predominant spiritual forces over your turf, as revealed by research or revelation. You should be waging effective warfare against rulers, authorities, powers, and spiritual forces in heavenly realms (Eph. 6:10–12). As a cell, church and churches in your area, you should be considering prayer strategies like Silvoso's *Lighthouses of Prayer*. Or 24–7's Prayer Room Strategies (have a look at a useful website: www.24-7prayer.com), church-based half-nights or whole nights of prayer and fasting with prayer boards, requests, photographs, maps and so on. All should be a healthy part of our spiritual rhythm.

Our church has conducted a number of '40-day stands', where church members agree together to fast in a chosen area (food, alcohol, chocolate, TV, etc) for 40 days, while aligning ourselves with and meditating on specific scriptures pertinent to what we are asking God to change and shift. But in all of this remember that prayer is pragmatic. It's never a case of pray *or* act. Prayer provoked by spiritual warfare should have tangible results in taking turf. And in evangelistic terms that means we should be looking for new birth, for conversion growth.

ASK GOD

I am aware that some of the things I've briefly outlined in this chapter are contentious. That some would have other theological perspectives concerning things like territorial spirits, or even the very concept of spiritual warfare as waged by Christians. All I can ask as we close this chapter is that you don't take issue with me, but take these matters up with God and with His Word and with His Spirit. See what He would say. And what He would have you do. For much may rest upon this.

GROUPWORK

1. Individually identify and write down your own personal strongholds.
2. Craft and then pray a prayer of renunciation and closure on these.
3. Share this prayer and the strongholds with your group, consequently ripping up the paper on which you wrote them, and as a group perhaps have a celebration bonfire of the pieces!

4. Identify and map your area using research.

5. Identify and prayer-walk your area seeking revelation.

6. Identify the connectedness that you currently have, or want to have, in your area. Include within this connections God may have given you with other Christians not in your church, and pray for them.

7. As a group, plan and commit to a 12-month cycle of prayer and fasting into issues raised in 4, 5 and 6 above. Review this cycle monthly.

Chapter 11

STRATEGIC EVANGELISM

When we come to the subject of strategy the dangers of anthropomorphism are obvious, but the fact is that we have strategies because *God* Himself is a strategist, and not vice versa. When humanity first fell away from God there is a clear indication of the redemption strategy of God in Jesus (Gen. 3:15). The unfolding covenant throughout the Old Testament, God's strategy for Noah – the ark – for Abraham, Joseph, for Israel, all of these litter the pages of the Old Testament, which is the backdrop strategy, the dictionary and the commentary for the New Covenant – God *is* a strategist.

JESUS THE STRATEGIST

Jesus Himself came at a strategic time and place, of God's choice and initiative; it could have been otherwise. But He came when the scene had been set (Old Testament, angels, wise men, John the Baptist); He came when the Roman road systems, common language, weights and measures, and government systems facilitated the quickest and easiest means of communication. He came to a people under Roman rule to best demonstrate how to deal with injustice, racism and oppression (Matt. 5). He had a strategy for training and developing His disciples (pupils observe and question teacher, teacher observes and questions pupils, pupils go out in pairs without teacher, teacher takes feedback from pupils) and also a strategy for evangelism (Matt. 28:16–20; Acts 1:8).

STRATEGY IN THE EARLY CHURCH

While there are no blueprints for how to do church in the New Testament, there are clear indications of evangelistic strategy. Such strategy is both God-initiated (Philip and the Ethiopian official in Acts 8) and church-initiated (the apostolic appointing of deacons in Acts 6).

The great church-planting apostle to the Gentiles, Paul himself, stated part of his strategies in Romans 15:17–21, where he advocates evangelism done on virgin territory, by a saturation method, over a defined area (Jerusalem to Southern Albania). This he accomplished by the strategic planting of resource churches with a capacity and heart to replant other churches. These were usually placed at strategic points of commerce, transport and occult activity. Paul's missionary journeys, so confusing with their proliferation of red lines on the maps at the back of many Bibles, do actually confirm Paul's strategy of getting the gospel to the Gentiles (Acts 13–15). His orderly progress with Barnabas through Cyprus from Salamis in the north to Paphos in the south (Acts 13:4–6) indicates attention to strategy, as does his method of getting the gospel from Ephesus to Asia in Acts 19:8–10.

God is a strategist. Jesus is a strategist. The church of Jesus is to be strategic.

GOALS AND EVANGELISM

Strategies are biblical because God uses strategies to get His will done. Strategies require the setting of goals, and goals are vital to radical evangelism. God has a goal for evangelism (Matt. 24:14, 2 Pet. 3:9). In Matthew 9:35 Jesus seems to have had a clear goal, which Josephus defines in his histories as an attempt to reach approximately 15,000 people in 204 villages. If Jesus had goals to accomplish strategies, so should we. God is looking for active, positive, faith-filled participation (Matt. 11:12). Examples of goals in Scripture do away with the notion that goals and strategies are somehow 'unspiritual'. Goals and strategies don't determine where or how the wind of the Holy Spirit blows, but they do help us to reset our sails. They do carry quite a high threat level, however, because specifying a strategy and a goal means that failure will probably be both assessable and obvious, should it occur. It's easy to insist that we've hit our target if we draw it after we've fired; if we aim at nothing that is exactly what we'll hit!

But pre-stated strategies and goals stop this kind of nonsense, and save us from super-spiritualising failure ('It must have been God's will; He's trying to teach us something; it's very difficult in this area; this is just a wilderness experience/dry patch/valley experience', etc!). Failure can either be a doorway to maturity or a trapdoor to obscurity, but super-spiritualising failure will definitely mean that it's the latter, because there will be no lessons learned, no adjustments made, and no need for perseverance. Goals and strategies can be threatening and difficult to write, but the advantages are many.

1. Goals and strategies release *motivation* into individuals and churches. Church growth expert Peter Wagner says, 'if you get some goals that people believe are achievable

273

and are worth achieving, people will lay down their lives for them.'

2. Goals and strategies release *energy*. Wagner again says, 'Some power is released through setting positive goals that otherwise remains dormant ... it is a biblical principle that God seems to honour.'

3. Goals and strategies take the emphasis off present problems and puts it onto future *possibilities*.

4. Goals and strategies establish a proper *sense of limit to our call* – establishing right limits rather than false barriers (Rom. 12:3).

5. Goals facilitate *prayer* (James 4:2–3).

6. Goals lead to *growth*. Yonggi Cho said, 'The number one requirement for having real church growth is to set goals.'

It's worth remembering in all of this that goals need to be S.M.A.R.T. goals, as we saw in Chapter 7.

If a goal is too big (and therefore produces lassitude or fear) then it needs to be sub-divided into primary and secondary goal sets. (How do you eat an elephant? A bite at a time!) Goals learn from the past but are not limited by it, getting us to do today what will affect tomorrow.

Goals really should be clear, uncomplicated, easily communicated, fitting well into our strategies, focussing existing resources, while high-lighting the need for further future resources, and therefore leading to development, training, more prayer, more evangelism! After all, the more people we have in our churches, the more resources we have! Goals should have an historical perspective – that's to say, they should have a short-, medium- and long-term range, and also have an inbuilt method of evaluation and assessment, through feedback, in order to determine whether we're on target. You might find it helpful to consistently ask the following questions when determining strategies and goals:

1. How *important* is the strategy and goal? (What am I investing in? Can I afford the investment? Will I afford the investment? What will happen if I don't do it?)
2. How *urgent* is the goal? (Refers more to the stress level and time demands.)
3. Am I working from long- to medium-, and medium- to short-term goals, and therefore not just responding to need and to the immediate?
4. Can I forecast where we'll be in five years', ten years', 20 years' time, without change? What goals and strategies are necessary to get us to where we want to be, as opposed to where we'll be without change?
5. How often must various tasks be done to accomplish the goals and to fulfil the strategies, and can someone else do them better/quicker?
6. By looking at my strategies, can I prioritise my goals? This means that I learn to *leave* that which is low in urgency and importance, *delegate* that which is low in importance but high in urgency, *plan* that which is low in urgency but high in importance and *do* that which is high in urgency and importance.

GROWING A STRATEGY FOR EVANGELISM: COMMITMENT

Strategic evangelism demands commitment from two sources. First of all there must be a very real commitment from the leadership of the church, thus avoiding the frustration of 'growth bottleneck'. The core leadership team (and biblically it should be a team, not a one-person ministry), should reflect a variety of gifting (Eph. 4:11–13) and must own the vision. The wider leadership team (e.g. cell leaders, youth group leaders, nurture group leaders, praise and worship team leaders, administrators, etc), must in turn communicate that vision to the church. It won't do for one leader or one small group of core leaders to own the vision without the wider leadership team both owning the vision and communicating that vision to the church. Remember, servant leadership doesn't simply set out a grand corporate vision and expect loyalty and 'buy in' from the 'plebs'! Servant leadership's vision is to identify, develop and release the vision of the many.

Second, church members must in turn be submitted to one another and to their leadership, so if that leadership isn't committed to growth (an unbiblical position), then church members cannot be submitted to those leaders, which will necessitate either a change of leadership, or a change of church. As we saw from Chapter 3, it's the *whole* church that is to be involved in evangelism. All disciples are 'goers' so, in the context of evangelism, the question is not '*Should* I go?' but rather 'Why *shouldn't* I go?' Thus church members and all church leaders alike need to be committed to a growth vision. What will this commitment entail?

Commitment to Communication

There is always a danger that what the core team (plurality of leadership) spend days praying and strategising over is then communicated to the wider leadership team in one two-hour session, and to the rest of the church in a five-minute cell-group notice. Leaders would do well in such circumstances not to express surprise that the whole church doesn't seem to have caught the vision! Any strategy for growth must incorporate multiple methods of communicating that vision.

Communication must be *creative* (e.g. weekends of prayer

and fasting, audio-visual aid presentations with PowerPoint, motivational preaching, training sessions, teaching sessions, cell- or house-group notices, church-meeting notices, church web page and news letter, personal letters, phone calls, feedback forums, round table discussions, members' meetings, etc).

And such communication must also be *repetitive*. In Korea Yonggi Cho estimates that it takes an individual six hearings of the gospel before an intelligent response is made. In the UK the number is seven times. So perhaps we shouldn't be surprised that communication about the spreading of that gospel *also* takes time and must be repetitive. Juan Carlos Ortiz (author of the classic book *Discipleship*) maintained that he would preach on one subject repetitively until his church were doing/living what he preached on. John Wimber (Christian evangelist who had a healing ministry) had the same experience of a year's preaching on healing before anyone in his church actually was healed!

A strategy for evangelism will include alterations to the preaching/teaching timetable, to the cell-group or house-group study plan of the local church, not only until the vision can be written down by every church member in a two-minute exercise in any such forum, but also until the vision has been *owned* by all church members and not just understood by them. This is the ideal. Communication is vital. Because of the nature of church we'll never get all of the church going in any one direction at any one time, but certainly we should be aiming for a minimum of 75 per cent of our church's membership.

Commitment to Change

Many churches have become institutions of religion rather than conveyors of life. Organisations rather than organisms. Their methods of worship are designed to bring comfort and security to the worshipper instead of pleasure to God. Their traditions and ceremonies speak of a God who is remote and irrelevant, their vestments speak of authority and institutionalism. Even when the wind of the Holy Spirit of change blows, all too quickly church can settle back into repetitive chorus singing, with some charismatic churches simply switching a 'tongue' sandwich for a 'hymn' sandwich!

Yet in the kingdom of God constant change is here to stay. Only God is Holy. Only His character doesn't change. His methods certainly do. A mark of maturity is the ability not only to change, but to embrace positive change positively, and also to cope with negative change.

Evangelism has the capacity to make church evaluate everything it does from an outsider mentality, assessing how 'seeker-sensitive' we are and how effective our 'seeker-targeting' actually is. A commitment to evangelism is a commitment to change. The make-up of our *leadership teams* may change. Our *meetings* will change to be more meaningful, and perhaps our style of public communication also. The way that *praise and worship* times are led/explained may also need adjustment. The *structures* of our church may be too unwieldy or parochial. The make-up of our *house-group or cell-group leadership* may change. The nature of our *youth work* and its direction may change, as may *church diaries*, adding guest meetings here, dropping in-house church celebrations for evangelistic cabarets there, freeing one cell-group evening per month for friendship evangelism, running monthly prayer walks in the town centre and so on.

The *priorities on our agendas* will also shift – from leisure to warfare, from maintenance to mission, from roof repairs to funding an evangelistic schools team. Make no mistake, those we share our lives with will give priority to whatever *we* give priority too. Especially if we're leaders. And the *church name* itself may need to change.

We may need to move away from an overt allegiance to denominationalism, wherever that has promoted lack of understanding, or even misunderstanding. Denominationalism (as opposed to denominations) is often divisive and promotes disunity, which is detrimental to the evangelising of your territory. Many New Churches call themselves 'Christian Fellowships', yet the word 'fellowship' smacks of introversion and exclusivity, and is rather sect-like. Perhaps a better phrase would be something like 'Community Church', both of which words say something about who we are and are something that the average person on the street, who's not yet a Christian, can understand. Appending a place name to the front of Community Church (e.g. Little Wapping-on-the-Marsh Community Church) may not be the most helpful, as the vision of the local church may expand beyond the local town, particularly as church planting gets underway. Such a name would therefore then be limiting, and a more neutral name might be more appropriate.

GROWING A STRATEGY FOR EVANGELISM: DEVELOPMENT

After commitment (to growth, to communication and to change) comes the need for development. There are three levels on which a church must be developed to produce growth and healthy evangelism, so that the church becomes evangelistic, rather than merely doing evangelistic events. These are:

1. The whole church – See Jesus' relationship with the 70 in Luke 10, with the 120 and with the 500.
2. The 'able keenies'(!) – See Jesus and the 12 in Luke 9.

3. The anointed individuals – See Jesus and the three in
   Mark 9:2, and Jesus and the one in John 21:22.

These three groupings will determine the content and the
style of the developmental approach in order to secure strategic
evangelism.

Whole church

Development of the whole church should include *motivation
and envisioning* (Prov. 29:18), and *teaching*, which establishes a
biblical base, thus increasing head knowledge and understanding (Hosea 4:6), and also *training*, which is the application
of theory to practice. In effect this is a discipleship model.

From my perspective this should involve a minimum of six,
monthly, joint cell- or house-group training sessions with
homework set after each one-and-half-hour session. Indeed this
book arose out of one such series of sessions, delivered over a
12-month period, at a rhythm of one meeting per month, plus
meetings with the key leadership teams of a large church in
Basingstoke. These training sessions should be centred around
the kind of topics covered by the chapter headings in this book.
Really they ought to follow from one to three motivational
preaching sessions on evangelism to the whole church.

Please note that this isn't simply a matter of going through
the material in this book, which is actually best suited to small
groups, as indicated by the groupwork at the end of each
chapter. Rather, the local church evangelist must be involved or
in their absence an evangelist must be drawn in from the
church's network of individual friendships and apostolic
relationships. This is essential, since the evangelist will always
spot other evangelists in the church (those 10 per cent referred
to earlier), even when they are still in the embryonic 'rough

diamond' state. The evangelist will tend *not* to have people blindness, which can lock church leadership into seeing only their people's past problems and pastoral failings (due to familiarity), rather than seeing their potential in God. It's also essential to involve the evangelist in their role of 'equipping the saints' (Eph. 4:11–13), as much of the call and commission to evangelism is about what is 'caught' as well as what is 'taught'.

'Able keenies'

Once *whole* church development along the lines outlined above has taken place, it will give access and opportunity to the evangelist to spot evangelistic potential, and for the leaders then to recruit that potential by invitation, perhaps onto an evangelism team. But no evangelism team should be allowed to 'do' the evangelism on behalf of the rest of the church! Rather, the nature and role of an evangelism team should be to stimulate good practice and evaluation of evangelism across the *whole body*. So the evangelism team could perhaps be spread across cell groups in positions of leadership, on the wider leadership team, into the youth leadership team, praise and worship teams and so on. Such 'able keenies' should next benefit from more specific teaching/training (eg on particular areas of evangelism, working into different congregations, working as part of leadership and other teams etc), which are relevant to the church's strategy.

There may also be a need for teaching and training to be pitched at specific methods of doing evangelism, in order to promote good practice. Such methods might include: training on prayer strategies, door-to-door work, street work, schools work, youth club work, pub evangelism, questionnaire work, detached youth work, events evangelism, guest meetings, prophetic evangelism, healing meetings, planning events.

Anointed individuals

It's from the group of 'able keenies' that the anointed individuals will appear, and the need for sending trainees from the church onto specific training projects (which essentially ought to be church-based) may then arise. It's for this reason that a significant portion of my time is spent training and developing people in the areas of their character, understanding and skills, in the context of mission. I run Pioneer's DNA Discipleship Year Out Course. For details of this course write to the Pioneer DNA address at the back of the book. It may very well be for you!

Certainly, as a minimum, such anointed individuals need to be discipled and allowed to 'shadow' evangelists within the life of the local church, and if possible outside of it as well. In turn their development will be essential to the development of a strategy for evangelism in the life of your church. Indeed, because you're reading this book, we may even be talking about *you*!

GROWING A STRATEGY FOR EVANGELISM: INTERNAL ACTION

After commitment and development comes action. This will need to be both internal to the church and external to the community. As a *minimum*, internal action should include the following.

1. *Leadership* – It's likely that the local church leadership team will need to be wider, along the lines of Ephesians 4:11–13. Ideally local church evangelists will be brought alongside of or onto the core leadership team of the church (elders, oversight, deaconate, PCC, whatever) and also distributed across the wider leadership team (house- or cell-group leaders, youth work leaders, praise and worship team leaders,

administration, etc) where their heart, thinking, strategies and perspectives can be both harnessed and released. As we saw in Chapter 1, many local church leadership teams are still pastoral in orientation and maintenance-minded, and this *must* be changed.

Where the local church seems not to have such an anointed evangelist then relational *links*, which are *apostolic* (i.e. more than friendship/advice, but rather recognising apostolic function, fathering, moral and doctrinal input, leadership appointment and church-planting oversight) must bring in such a ministry at this strategic and leadership level, until it can reproduce itself within the church and the church's leadership. It isn't always necessary to have an evangelist on the core leadership team, nor as 'bottom-line' or as 'first among equals' of such a team, although many times that will be appropriate. Sometimes that kind of responsibility and function will lock the evangelist up into practical and pastoral detail that may blunt their gifting. Where such lock-up occurs it will not only be unhelpful to the evangelist, but it will also be unhelpful to the local church. Levels of frustration will be high! But it's *vital* that the evangelist has *access* to core leadership and wider leadership teams, in order to help develop evangelistic strategy.

2. *Meetings* – Meetings and meeting venues may also need internal action to make them more accessible to not-yet-Christians. The centrality and suitability of the premises, where you have them, are important – a Baptist church in a town in the south of England recently had the only unlisted cinema in that town demolished in order to make way for their new church building. This despite much protest from local residents, making entry to that new church building for most of those residents both unlikely and unwanted! Social

accessibility is more important than décor. I know of several inner-city church plants that meet in local pubs. Neutrality of premises, rather than any kind of ecclesiastical building, is a factor in favour of evangelism. It's worth remembering that for the first 300 or so years of the early church's life, it didn't own buildings at all. It met in the open, in the synagogues or from house to house.

Where buildings *are* involved it's important, in growing an evangelistic strategy, to be aware of the capacity of the building. Church growth studies indicate that when 80 per cent of the capacity is reached a 'comfort factor' creeps in, inhibiting further growth. So 60 per cent of capacity is about right; much smaller and the 'insignificance factor' kicks in, making the group feel smaller than it is, as though they are 'rattling around' on the premises. Most churches in the UK are now between 60 and 120 in size and churches grow quickest between 100 and 150. So further internal action, involving meetings and meeting venues that will encourage growth, *might* be the apostolic formation of multiple, community-relating congregational plants. These plants might together form one church with shared resources and many congregations. Or they might be (or become) individual and autonomous congregations relating to particular towns or parts of towns, with a *relational* connection together. In this model each time an already-established congregation reaches the figure of between 120 and 150, it looks to plant. The only exception to this would then be when there is one 'mother church' that is planting several times and whose base therefore probably needs to be more like 200- to 400-strong.

Church planting is of course a subject in itself, but it's a key part of an effective evangelistic strategy. A good number to start a church plant with at a congregational level is about 30, headed by a core leadership team representing different ministries. Sometimes it's appropriate for such a team to be headed by a 'breakthrough' person who has a clear understanding of church and the kingdom of God, a ready conceptual grasp of practical theology, who can draw people around themselves through their leadership gifting, and is anointed of God to make things happen with a clear evangelistic edge, although not necessarily an evangelist themselves. But an equally valid and alternative model would be the planting of church through the development of an individual cell rather than a congregation. This model places more emphasis on body ministry and empowering the saints, and has the advantage of not requiring such things as premises, worship team and public address systems, but rather can operate with small numbers (an optimum of between 8 and 12 people) from someone's home.

Whatever the model, our 'public' meetings must be just that. They must have a clear sense of purpose. They should consist of growth-favourable numbers. Ideally they should be seeker-sensitive, with explained worship and gifts of the Holy Spirit, gospel content threaded throughout, an opportunity for response to the gospel, and the avoidance of 'in jokes'. Visitors should be welcomed with applause, free publicity about the church and invitations to social meals, and so on. No one part of the meeting should take too long (including the talk!) and there should be a sensitive approach to prayer groups, communion and collections. Consistency of meeting times and places is also helpful in getting profile and visitors.

3. *Structures* Other structures, apart from the leadership and meeting structures, might also need internal action. For example, is the youth group, if it exists, only catering for

Christian youth? Are there nurture groups in place, and *Alpha* or 'just looking' groups being utilised? Is there/should there be church membership? How does a new convert become part of the membership, if it exists? Are church definitions and expectations spelt out in the current structure somewhere? Are cell/house groups too introverted? Do we have a welcome team? Do we need a visitation team? Should our cell/house groups be defined through relationships? Or through adopting a geographical area? Any evangelism strategy must put into place the means of church-based discipling, to make followers out of converts. A responsible church must strategise and structure for growth *before* receiving it. I've seen churches that fail to do this lose 70 per cent of their converts. And I have seen churches that then put such structure for growth and discipleship in place *keep* 70 per cent of their converts! Which would you rather?

4. *Prayer* A church's prayer structures are a further internal adjustment that should be affected by growing a strategy for evangelism. Multiple means of evangelism-related prayer must be found in the life of the church. For example, each house or cell group can spend 15 minutes at the start of each of its weekly meetings praying in triplets for three named not-yet-Christian friends. Such a small group could then go on bi-monthly prayer walks and drives around its geographical area, while the church gathered could organise prayer marches or vigils into strategic centres. Corporate prayer walking the boundaries of the area together that God has given to your church, pulling together prayer concerts (using video, PowerPoint, photographs, maps, prayer boards) and half-nights and weekends of prayer and fasting are all possibilities.

The evangelists and/or evangelism team can feed regular

prayer information into the life of the church prayer meeting. Prayer in groups and all together can be prioritised in the church's main meetings. Telephone prayer chains, prayer letters and schools of intercessors are other ways of raising prayer profile, linked specifically to evangelism, across the whole church. If the whole church is to be talking to people about God, then the whole church should be talking to God about people.

5. *Finance* Jesus said it! 'Where your treasure is, there your heart will be also' (Matt. 6:21). The reverse is also true. We tend to put our money where our heart is! Evangelism will cost in terms of time, faith, energy and money. Any evangelistic strategy will demand financial resources for one or more of the following: the booking of venues, the use of publicity, generous funding of guest evangelists, evangelistic musicians, drama teams, provision of food and drink at cabarets, lights, public address systems, provision of suitable literature (e.g. *Alpha* course work, Bibles), administrative back-up (follow-up forms, computer database, stationery, phone and fax). A hard look at a church's budget will often indicate the extent to which it takes evangelism seriously, or not.

My suggestion would be that any local church should be looking to budget 45 per cent of its gross income on evangelism, 45 per cent on maintenance, and 10 per cent to be given away outside the local church situation, and not necessarily to Christian causes. How about to the poor of your church's area, for example? The release of 'full-time' personnel should reflect that same balance, giving equal priority to putting evangelists out 'full-time' as to putting out pastors, teachers and administrators.

GROWING A STRATEGY FOR EVANGELISM: EXTERNAL ACTION

This book thus far has placed a deliberate emphasis on accessing communities through friendship evangelism (Chapters 6, 7 and 8), on personal witnessing (Chapter 9), and on the research and revelation necessary in waging effective spiritual warfare (Chapter 10). In this final chapter I just want to make sure that we're not hearing an 'either/or' approach. And so we finish with seven (a good biblical number!) suggestions for external action, which will help you and your church strategically to engage in your community. These are to be built *on top* of friendship evangelism, personal witnessing and spiritual warfare, not *instead of* them.

1. *Events evangelism* Evangelistic events are that part of a strategy for evangelism which is designed to service the friendship evangelism already going on among (all) church members. Perhaps these members (of the whole church, or of the individual house or cell groups) could be polled as to what type of event they would like to invite their not-yet-Christian friends to. An evangelistic rock concert might attract a people group made up of teenagers, but might do little for middle-aged doctors, solicitors and accountants. The best evangelistic strategy is to develop a range of evangelistic events of different styles.

   This alone is insufficient for an events strategy, however. In addition to this range of *style*, the event should differ in the *amount of gospel content*, ranging from purely social to a full-blown gospel presentation with appeal. Thus an evangelistic event in January, which is a rock concert, might have very little gospel content, but by December the evangelistic event might be a rock concert with gospel preaching and appeal.

The sliding scale of content can work over the course of one year or much longer.

Another important factor in assessing the scale of content is the nature and hardness of the area. I know a council estate that responds very quickly to neighbourly based coffee mornings, while another very middle-class area responds better to charitable events. Thinking this way will help you to estimate whether you're looking at a short-, medium- or long-term approach. Some areas may take five years to crack evangelistically. Some only one year.

Yet another strategic approach with events would be more of a 'peak and trough' approach. Instead of spreading the gospel content across a certain time period (like a year, or five years) it's possible to alternate high gospel content with low from one evangelistic event to another. This is because there will always be some people ready to be reaped into the kingdom. It's also worth bearing in mind that some events will have their 'seasons of success' – I've known some churches use evangelistic cabarets very successfully, but then find their fruitfulness declining, necessitating a switch towards, for example, play schemes and family fun days, or towards *Alpha* courses. Change and creativity are hallmarks of events evangelism. As is the key concept that each people group, and probably each geographical area, will require a different set of sliding-scale evangelistic events.

2. *Seasonal evangelism* Any attempt at an effective evangelistic strategy would do well to take into account the fact that events can often be linked to key times of the year in the life of any local community. I would suggest that any strategy for growth needs to take account of at least seven such times and to work a year's evangelistic programme accordingly.

Starting at the top of the year in January, New Year provides a good opportunity for events like a disco, a ball or a plethora of New Year's parties in people's homes. Next, Valentine's Day might prompt a Valentine's Ball or barn dance. It depends upon the nature of your area. Easter is a good time for guest and healing meetings. Summer time lends itself very well indeed to detached youth work, to a Midsummer's Day Ball, family fun days, treasure hunts or play schemes. Halloween might suggest an alternative buffet or a saints and sinners fancy dress party. Bonfire night is a good opportunity for a bonfire with fireworks, food and games, and Christmas, of course, lends itself well to pantomimes, guest meetings, street work with free mince pies, door-to-door carol singing with gospel presentation and so on.

The above outline of seasonal evangelism would probably hold true for just about any area in the UK. But it's very likely your local community will have its own local seasonal opportunities. In addition, if you are rural, you might well be able to add in some kind of harvest thanksgiving. Or there may be local festivals or carnivals to get involved with on a regular basis. Certainly there are many other imaginative events that can be added to such a framework, and that can be run across the whole church or by cell/house groups. These might include pub trivia, beer and skittles, Pimms and pancakes, coffee and gateaux, cheese and wine, games marathon evening, make-up evening, coffee morning, beach barbecue, drinks and nibbles. Or how about issue-related events such as debt advice, parenting courses or stress management?

The key thing with seasonal and events evangelism is to make sure that the whole church knows exactly what the event will be, and how it will be pitched so that they can determine two things. First, who to bring to which event.

And second, what is the next event to bring people to that has the potential for increasing the depth of relational/social involvement and also increasing gospel content? Church members *must* know how to progress their friendship evangelism contacts. The best way to visualise this is shown in Figure 11.1.

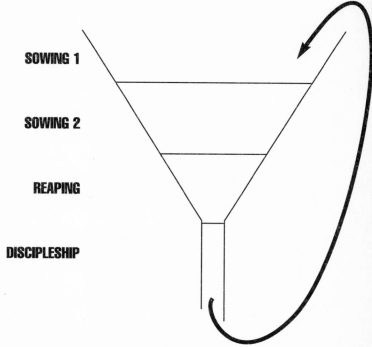

FIGURE 11.1 – FRIENDSHIP EVANGELISM CONTACTS

- Sowing 1 events typically attract many people but are low in content. Therefore they include things like family fun days, pub quizzes, play schemes, etc.

- Sowing 2 events are those we take people to who've had a successful experience of Sowing 1 events. Sowing 2 events are typically more relationally based, attracting fewer numbers but with higher content. They therefore include things like wine and wisdom testimony evenings, dinner parties, *Alpha* courses, etc.
- Reaping events are necessarily part of the process of friendship evangelism, and often involve even fewer people but with much greater content, and an opportunity for people to make some sort of response to the gospel. This might be an appeal for salvation. Or to sign up for a discipleship course. Or become a member of a cell/house group. Reaping events are typically: guest meetings, healing meetings, *Alpha* weekends, etc.
- Discipleship events should be a mix of one-to-one and small-group work, or effective incorporation into a cell/house group for the express purpose of turning converts into disciples! They also need to spell out definitions and expectations of church and church life. Certainly they should cover issues like prayer, Bible reading, Holy Spirit, baptism, etc.

It's worth noting from Figure 11.1 that the end of this process, which is discipleship, should then loop back into the top of the funnel, since experience indicates that it is relatively new converts and disciples who have the greatest number of not-yet-Christian friendship networks.

3. *Pioneering evangelism: visitation programmes* Given that friendship evangelism does fail in respect of saturation evangelism (we will never know everyone in an area!), a growth strategy must also incorporate a high level of cold-contact evangelism. Points of contact other than friendship must be found so that the principle of multiple contacting

can work alongside saturation evangelism. This means that 'little Johnny' is seen in his cub group, his sister at her school, both of them and their mother on the streets, and their father through door-to-door contacting; the whole family is then at a family fun day event, and one or more of them are subsequently saved at a church guest meeting or through an *Alpha* course. This isn't a theoretical illustration; it's an actual case study.

So as *part* of a comprehensive approach, an evangelistic strategy should include a comprehensive door-to-door visitation programme, where the aim is to accrue information, to build relationships and friendships across the doorsteps as quickly as possible, and to find valid responses for return visits and to see people saved. Such a visitation programme also makes a significant statement in terms of spiritual principalities and powers (spiritual warfare), and raises the profile of the local church. If people in the UK do tend to respond to the gospel on the seventh time of hearing, then our door-to-door strategy should include a revisiting tactic. This might run along the following lines:

Visit 1. Community survey

Visit 2. Results report

Visit 3. Invitation to events designed to alleviate felt
        community needs discovered through Visits 1 and 2.

Visit 4. Attitudes survey on beliefs

Visit 5. Results report

Visit 6. Offers of prayer/social action (a church in Wigan,
        having targeted a specific area, pushed prayer
        request cards through the doors, collected them,
        prayed over them, and then revisited and noted a
        10 per cent response from the door-to-door work).

Visit 7. On-going leaflet/invitation visit

Creative use of a marketing and publicity strategy along-side this visitation sequence might incorporate into this strategy a 'progressive' leaflet drop (three small handouts, which get progressively clearer in the message), for example between visits 3 and 4.

Any such scheme must have a good database; who's been visited by whom, and with what results? What literature was given, if any? What impressions/words of knowledge were received? Who was out? Who wants further literature/contact/return visits? This database should be constantly monitored by the door-to-door team, and 'hot' contacts worked upon, invited to meetings, prayed over, etc.

Perhaps the best way of carrying out this visitation is to have it spearheaded by a team of trained church members (the 'able keenies'), and supplemented by all cell-/house-group members around the area of that group, which ideally has geographically as well as relationally constituted membership, through 'waves of evangelism'. This means that members of each cell/house group could go out on the doors in pairs approximately two evenings a week for two weeks, every four months. Light evenings lend themselves to survey and questionnaire work, darker evenings to leaflet drops. Each 'wave of evangelism' can carry its own pre-action training, as outlined earlier.

On average the take-up from door-to-door work is only 1 per cent. With a good prayer, warfare and events strategy linked in, I have seen that rise to 17 per cent! We seem to have been put off this in recent years by a mixture of bad experience and apathy. Perhaps it's time to test the climate and see what has shifted? And to ask ourselves the question why one of the fastest-growing churches worldwide (the Church of the Latter Day Saints of Jesus Christ; the

Mormons) still advocates visitation programmes?!

4. *Street work* – this is another means of maximising pioneering or cold-contact evangelism and of giving profile to local church. A strategy for street work should include questionnaire work (e.g. outside a shopping parade, by a railway station), presentation street work (drama, busking, preaching, testimonies, etc, in a shopping mall or precinct), and detached youth work (outside the local youth club, pub, video shop, takeaway, park, amusement arcade, etc), and can involve working bus or bank queues with a free shoe-shining service or sampling different kinds of cola, etc.

   Imagination, creativity and fun are the hallmarks of good street work, which is best done by a trained team of church members (those 'able keenies' again!) *with* other church members as 'rent-a-crowd'! Again, this approach has gone out of fashion lately, but I do feel it's due a comeback, given the spiritual climate shift which I feel has taken place in the last ten years in the UK. If every cell/house group has an evangelist as well as a pastor in leadership, plus some form of evangelism team representative, as suggested earlier, then it shouldn't be too difficult to encourage other members of that cell group to join in on the street work from time to time. One Saturday per month would be a good target for regular street work into one defined area, with more during special events like play scheme weeks, etc.

5. *Focussed teams* By combining whole-church evangelism with focussed teams, the best of both worlds is achieved in a strategy for growth; mass mobilisation and people power, plus expert breakthrough personnel. These focussed teams can be targeted at specific people groups, and should at least cover youth (the optimum age for salvation in the UK was for many years 14 years and 9 months, but has recently shifted up

to 18 years), through detached youth work, schools' work, existing youth clubs in the church and outside it. Additional focus teams could include a visitation team aimed specifically at door-to-door work. A streetwork team could be covering presentation and questionnaire street work. A 'teddy bear' team can cover welcomes at guest meetings. Social action teams can cover community involvement and the local political scene. Depending on your area, another example might be a prison visitation scheme.

If people power isn't available across all of these groups, then perhaps the development of one evangelism team to target these areas would be vital. Such an evangelism team should be recruited by personal invitation from the leadership, with clearly defined expectations and criteria (for example, one evening per week on the doors, one Saturday per month on the streets and regular input into guest meetings, cell/house-group strategy formation, church prayer meetings). It will need a leader (an evangelist) and deputy leader (also an evangelist) and should determine its own training course, bringing in specialists as necessary for focussed training on such topics as street work, door-to-door work, running evangelistic events, signs and wonders in evangelism, spiritual warfare, voice projection etc as necessary.

Such a team will also need either its own administrative gifting or access to the church's administration base (for example, for follow-up, venue booking, publicity purposes, budgeting) and should ideally have its own praise and worship leader and drama co-ordinator. The numbers in such an evangelism team should approximate to 10 per cent of the membership of the church, in order for that team to be healthy and sufficiently representative of the life of that local church. Setting up such a team or teams is part of an evangelistic strategy. I repeat, however, *the role of such a team is not to 'do' all the evangelism, but rather to stimulate it effectively across the whole church.*

6. *'Kick-starts'* These may from time to time be an important part of an evangelistic strategy. They would take the form of major missions, church-planting thrusts and initiatives, bringing in evangelistic teams from extra-local evangelistic initiatives (e.g. a Pioneer DNA team, a YWAM team; details at the end of the book). These can give a really powerful, fast and dynamic impetus to local-church evangelism, particularly when that church is involved in church planting.

7. *Assessment and persistence* These are my final suggestions for growing a strategy for growth. Every part of the strategy outlined above needs to be assessed and to have clear goals by which success and failure can be measured; each must have its own clear criteria and parameters – commitment levels, leadership and whole church involvement, communication and vision, flexibility for change, development and training, research and revelation, internal and external action.

Assessment accesses adjustment. When failure occurs (some parts of the strategy *will* work better than others, some parts won't apparently work at all), there is then the opportunity for such adjustment. Assessment balanced by persistence will help answer such questions as: When do we move on to the doors on a new street or estate? When do we change from evangelistic concerts to cabarets? How often do we run an *Alpha* course? Do we run an *Alpha* course as a cell or as a whole church? How soon can we expect to see a convert from our street work? How many converts have become church members three, six or 12 months after conversion?'

So we finish this strategy with a list of questions, which might help you, your church and any church leadership team towards growing a strategy for growth. I suggest that you use them as a kind of check list. If we only learn to ask the right questions, then hopefully we are on the right route to finding the right answers!

1. What is your area?
2. What is the social make-up of your area?
3. What is the geographical distribution of your area?
4. What is the social make-up of the church?
5. What is the geographical distribution of the church?
6. What is the age distribution of the church?
7. What are the social needs of the area?
8. What contact do church members have with not-yet-Christians? (Is this encouraged or discouraged? How?)
9. What evangelism is going on at present in the church?
10. What are the resources available for evangelism? (Money? People? Are they enough?)
11. What skills do church members need to acquire in order to be more effective in evangelism? How can they be provided with these skills?
12. Do we have any individuals in the church with specific evangelistic skills, whom we need to encourage and recognise?
13. What are other churches in the area doing in evangelism?
14. How is the church perceived in the area? Can this be changed?
15. Are there individuals in the church with key roles in the community who can be supported (e.g. doctors, teachers, local councillors, youth workers, social workers)?
16. What type of event would the church members like to

invite their friends/neighbours/workmates/family along to?

17. How does the church follow up new Christians? Does it work?

18. Does the church have a fringe which can be evangelised?

19. How would church meetings be perceived by a newcomer? Would they be welcome? Would they understand what was going on? Would they find out how to get further involved? Would they be invited back afterwards and to what?

20. How do people find out about our church? Would they be able to get to one of our meetings if they wanted to? Are our meetings in the best place? What about access for the disabled?

21. Do we have any church literature? Profile in the local press? A website? Are these any good?

22. Are there opportunities in local schools/youth groups? Do we have any people who can be encouraged to reach their friends?

23. Should we be considering church planting?

24. Are there any dominant spiritual holds on the area or the people in the area, which need to be specifically resisted and prayed against?

25. Is there anyone from outside the area that we should consider bringing in to assist us with our strategy/ planning/training/doing?

26. Should we be considering sending certain individuals on evangelism training (e.g. Pioneer's DNA)?

27. Should we be restructuring our meetings or leadership to encourage evangelism?

28. Where is the life of God currently expressed in the church?

29. What aspects of this book can I embrace, first personally, second corporately?
30. *What does God have to say?*

Any evangelistic strategy must be made to work at *each of the four levels of church life.* These four levels are necessary to help your church growth, so your commitment/development/action/assessment must affect and be effective at the level of:

- Single person – individual church member
- Cell – the cell or house group, plus the specialist focussed teams (e.g. evangelism team)
- Congregation – God's incarnational means of culturally contextualising the gospel community into the world's community, healthily between eight and 12 in number (for a cell plant), 30 (for a new church plant) and 150-strong for a church, with an optimum of around 130, the exception being a reproducing 'mother church' whose membership needs to be around 200 to 400.
- Celebration – joining congregations of a sufficient size together to affect a whole city and to spread resources across congregations; initiating projects too big for any one congregation, but ensuring the links are through relationship and vision; unity and evangelism go hand in hand.

Finally, I have found a helpful tool in the analysis and development of a church based evangelistic strategy to be a mission audit. There are a number of these around, and certainly contacting the Evangelical Alliance or Churches Working Together would be a way of becoming aware of some of the resources available in this field. My one word of caution would be that you do not embrace a purely administrative or bureaucratic exercise. Therefore the best mission audits are those put together and delivered by working evangelists. The audit that I do is an involved and in-depth process, which takes from between three and six months, and subsequently produces a list of recommendations covering an 18- to 24-month period. Again, details can be found under the resources list at the back of this book.

GROUPWORK

1. Write down, then share and discuss your personal goals in evangelism.
2. Discuss what are the challenges and benefits of a commitment to growth and change.
3. How is your church currently communicating its evangelistic strategy? How can this be improved?
4. As a group, identify your training needs in evangelism.
5. How could you make your church meetings more 'seeker-sensitive'?
6. What church structures would need to be changed or created for effective evangelistic strategy?
7. How can your group encourage more prayer for the lost, first in your group, second across the church?
8. How much of your church's budget currently goes on evangelism? Should this be increased and if so how?
9. As a group plan your own evangelistic strategy. Which of the following would you include/leave out?
   - Events evangelism
   - Seasonal evangelism
   - Visitation programmes
   - Streetwork
   - Focussed teams
   - 'Kick-starts'

FINAL WORDS

I so hope that you have found this book helpful. I didn't write it so that you wouldn't read it! But neither did I write it so that you would *only* read it. This book contains many of my passions. It's my hope that I have communicated some of them to you. Certainly friends that I have shown the book to in draft form have said that they can 'hear me' as they read it. At least I suppose that's better than reading it and hearing someone else! In the writing my hope and my prayer is that you and I would not 'merely listen to the word', but rather would 'do what it says' (James 1:22). And the book was written not simply to help you individually, but also corporately.

So take it and use it. Take it, use it and share it. Get it into the hands of your cell group, of your house group, of your leadership team. Engage also with the resources that the book suggests. The groupwork at the end of each chapter isn't there to fill pages. Let it stimulate prayer, discussion, argument if need be. But above all let it promote action. If I could reach off the page into your hearts, minds and actions, I would. But I can't, so instead I'll close, as Paul did when he concluded his letter to the church at Colossae in AD 62, by quoting his words:

Devote yourselves to prayer, being watchful and thankful.
And pray for us, too, that God may open a door for our message, so that we may proclaim the mystery of Christ ...
Pray that I may proclaim it clearly, as I should.
Be wise in the way you act towards outsiders;
make the most of every opportunity.
Let your conversation be always full of grace, seasoned with salt, so that you may know how to answer everyone.

Colossians 4:2–6

Resources

A number of books and initiatives have been mentioned throughout these chapters. These are summarised here.

William A. Beckham, *Second Reformation: Reshaping the Church for the 21st Century*, Touch Publications, September 1995

Antony Campolo, *A Reasonable Faith: The Case for Christianity in a Secular World*, Paternoster Press, October 2001

Philip Greenslade, *Cover to Cover God's Story*, CWR, 2001

John Dawson, *Taking Our Cities for God: How to Break Spiritual Strongholds*, Charisma House, October 2001

John Finney, *Finding Faith Today: How Does It Happen?*, Bible Society, 1992

Roger Forster and Paul Marsten, *Reason, Science and Faith*, Monarch Publications, April 1999

Stephen Gaukroger, *It Makes Sense*, Scripture Union, September 1996

Nicky Gumbel, *Alpha* course material,

Nicky Gumbel, *Questions of Life*, Kingsway, 1993

Ishmael, *Angels with Dirty Faces*, Kingsway Communications, 1989

Josh McDowell, *Evidence that Demands a Verdict*, Campus Crusade for Christ, 1972

Josh McDowell, *More Evidence that Demands a Verdict*, Campus Crusade for Christ, 1975

Josh McDowell, *More Than a Carpenter*, Kingsway Communications, March 2001

Ralph Neighbour, *Where do we go from here?*, Tower Publishing, 1990

Martin Scott, *Sowing Seeds for Revival*, Sovereign World, April 2002

Ed Silvoso, *That None Should Perish: How to Reach Your City for Christ Through Prayer Evangelism*, Regal Books, February 1997

Jim Thwaites, *Renegotiating the Church Contract: The Death and Life of the 21st Century Church*, Paternoster Press, May 2002

Jim Thwaites and David Oliver, *Church Beyond the Congregation*, STL, June 1998

Jim Thwaites and David Oliver, *Church That Works*, Word 2001

www.24-7prayer.com

Revd Roger Whitehead, Churches Working Together Group for Evangelisation, The Manse, High Street, Harrold, Bedford MK43 7BJ

Evangelical Alliance, Whitefield House, 186 Kennington Park Road, London SE11 4BT

The Pioneer Network of Churches' Discipleship and Training Scheme in the context of mission: Pioneer DNA, PO Box 58, Chichester PO19 8UD; Mobile: 07905 625195; Tel: 01243 531898 option 3; Fax: 01243 531959; Email: pioneer.dna@virgin.net; Website: www.dna-uk.org

Pete Gilbert may be contacted for evangelism teaching, evangelism training and evangelism doing, as well as for Church Mission Audits at the Pioneer address.

National Distributors

UK: (and countries not listed below)
CWR, Waverley Abbey House, Waverley Lane, Farnham, Surrey GU9 8EP.
Tel: (01252) 784710 Outside UK (44) 1252 784710

AUSTRALIA: CMC Australasia, PO Box 519, Belmont, Victoria 3216.
Tel: (03) 5241 3288

CANADA: Cook Communications Ministries, PO Box 98, 55 Woodslee Avenue, Paris,
Ontario. Tel: 1800 263 2664

GHANA: Challenge Enterprises of Ghana, PO Box 5723, Accra.
Tel: (021) 222437/223249 Fax: (021) 226227

HONG KONG: Cross Communications Ltd, 1/F, 562A Nathan Road, Kowloon.
Tel: 2780 1188 Fax: 2770 6229

INDIA: Crystal Communications, 10-3-18/4/1, East Marredpally, Secunderabad – 500 026.
Tel/Fax: (040) 7732801

KENYA: Keswick Books and Gifts Ltd, PO Box 10242, Nairobi.
Tel: (02) 331692/226047 Fax: (02) 728557

MALAYSIA: Salvation Book Centre (M) Sdn Bhd, 23 Jalan SS 2/64,
47300 Petaling Jaya, Selangor.
Tel: (03) 78766411/78766797 Fax: (03) 78757066/78756360

NEW ZEALAND: CMC Australasia, PO Box 36015, Lower Hutt.
Tel: 0800 449 408 Fax: 0800 449 049

NIGERIA: FBFM, Helen Baugh House, 96 St Finbarr's College Road, Akoka, Lagos.
Tel: (01) 7747429/4700218/825775/827264

PHILIPPINES: OMF Literature Inc, 776 Boni Avenue, Mandaluyong City.
Tel: (02) 531 2183 Fax: (02) 531 1960

REPUBLIC OF IRELAND: Scripture Union, 40 Talbot Street, Dublin 1.
Tel: (01) 8363764

SINGAPORE: Armour Publishing Pte Ltd, Block 203A Henderson Road,
11–06 Henderson Industrial Park, Singapore 159546.
Tel: 6 276 9976 Fax: 6 276 7564

SOUTH AFRICA: Struik Christian Books, 80 MacKenzie Street, PO Box 1144,
Cape Town 8000. Tel: (021) 462 4360 Fax: (021) 461 3612

SRI LANKA: Christombu Books, 27 Hospital Street, Colombo 1.
Tel: (01) 433142/328909

TANZANIA: CLC Christian Book Centre, PO Box 1384, Mkwepu Street, Dar es Salaam.
Tel/Fax (022) 2119439

USA: Cook Communications Ministries, PO Box 98, 55 Woodslee Avenue, Paris,
Ontario, Canada. Tel: 1800 263 2664

ZIMBABWE: Word of Life Books, Shop 4, Memorial Building,
35 S Machel Avenue, Harare. Tel: (04) 781305 Fax: (04) 774739

For email addresses, visit the CWR website: www.cwr.org.uk

CWR is a registered charity – number 294387

Trusted
All Over the World

Daily Devotionals

Books and Videos

Day and Residential Courses

Counselling Training

Biblical Study Courses

Regional Seminars

Ministry to Women

CWR have been providing training and resources for Christians since the 1960s. From our headquarters at Waverley Abbey House we have been serving God's people with a vision to help apply God's Word to everyday life and relationships. The daily devotional *Every Day with Jesus* is read by over three-quarters of a million people in more than 150 countries, and our unique courses in biblical studies and pastoral care are respected all over the world.

For a free brochure about our seminars and courses or a catalogue of CWR resources please contact us at the following address:

CWR,
Waverley Abbey House,
Waverley Lane,
Farnham,
Surrey GU9 8EP
UK

Telephone: 01252 784700
Email: mail@cwr.org.uk
Website: www.cwr.org.uk

CWR CRUSADE FOR WORLD REVIVAL *Applying God's Word to everyday life and relationships*

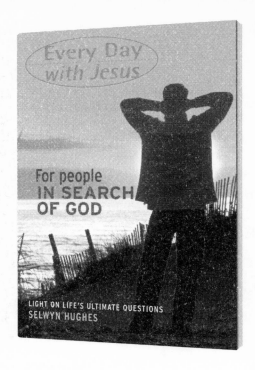

EVERY DAY WITH JESUS FOR PEOPLE IN SEARCH OF GOD

This is a great tool for friendship evangelism, because when it comes to those hard, demanding questions people want clear, thoughtful answers. Here Selwyn Hughes offers an intelligent and helpful perspective on those big issues, including:

What is life all about?
Who is God and what is He like?
Why does God allow suffering?

Is there life after death?
How can we know God?

72 page booklet ISBN: 1-85345-226-2

£1.99

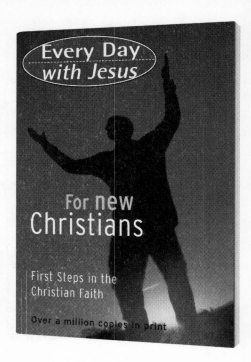

EVERY DAY WITH JESUS FOR NEW CHRISTIANS

A powerful and relevant guide for people new to the Christian faith or for people who need the basics presented to them clearly and dynamically. A favourite with churches across all denominations.

64 page booklet ISBN: 1-85345-133-9

£1.99

Foreword by Dr Larry Crabb

SELWYN HUGHES

CHRIST EMPOWERED LIVING

Life-changing teaching that has transformed multitudes

NEW EDITION!

Christ Empowered Living is Selwyn Hughes' dynamic core teaching in one easy to digest volume.

It will transform your life with essential principles of Christian living and develop you to your full spiritual potential. You will discover biblical insights that will revolutionise your approach to the way you live and help to renew your mind.
This new edition improves readability and gives larger margins for notes.

Softback, 312 pages ISBN: 1-85345-201-7

£7.99